50

D0889056

дд·10/70

logbook
for
Grace

TIME Reading Program
Special Edition

TIME INCORPORATED • NEW YORK

ROBERT CUSHMAN MURPHY

logbook
for
Grace

whaling brig *Daisy*
1912-1913

with a new introduction by George Gaylord Simpson

TIME LIFE BOOKS

EDITOR *Norman P. Ross*
EXECUTIVE EDITOR *Maitland A. Edey*
TEXT DIRECTOR *Jerry Korn*
ART DIRECTOR *Edward A. Hamilton*
CHIEF OF RESEARCH *Beatrice T. Dobie*

EDITOR, TIME READING PROGRAM *Max Gissen*
RESEARCHER *Joan Chambers*
DESIGNER *Ladislav Svatos*

PUBLISHER *Rhett Austell*
GENERAL MANAGER *Joseph C. Hazen Jr.*

TIME MAGAZINE
EDITOR *Roy Alexander*
MANAGING EDITOR *Otto Fuerbringer*
PUBLISHER *Bernhard M. Auer*

COVER DESIGN *Sita Gomez de Kanelba*

contents

ROBERT CUSHMAN
MURPHY

editors' preface

Logbook for Grace is one of those rare books that are published to the applause and admiration of the critics and then unaccountably sink out of sight. Published in 1947, it received lavish praise from reviewers everywhere. "A book to set on the shelf beside *Moby Dick* and *Two Years before the Mast*," said one review; another called it a book to "live forever in the solid and lasting literature of a civilization." Yet by 1950 the book was out of print and apparently forgotten by the public and publisher alike. It deserves a far better fate. *Logbook* is the fascinating chronicle, in diary form, of a voyage of one of the last Yankee whaleships in the twilight days of sail. More than that, it is an adventure story, a travelogue, a naturalist's notebook and a charming love story all rolled into one—written, it must be added, by a man whose profession is not writing, although he has written scientific works.

Robert Cushman Murphy is a naturalist—one of the world's great authorities on birds. In the course of six decades of tireless devotion to nature, he has achieved an eminence that is substantiated by half a dozen medals, numerous academic honors, nine books and more than 500 articles. His monumental work, *Oceanic Birds of South America,* is the classic in its field. He has been associated with the American Museum of Natural History in New York for 44 years and was the first curator of oceanic birds in any museum anywhere. He is now a retired but still tireless research associate.

But young Bob Murphy was fresh out of college when, in July of 1912, he sailed from the West Indies aboard the half-brig *Daisy.* He was bound for South Georgia Island on the edge of Antarctica, only a few hundred miles from the end of the world, armed with a commission from the American Museum to study and bring back specimens of the birds and other animals of the South Atlantic.

More to the point, he was leaving behind his young bride Grace, married to him only four and a half months before. Urging him to make the voyage for the sake of his career, Grace had moved their wedding date forward. The *Daisy* would be out of touch with civilization for at least a year. Murphy resolved that in addition to making the scientific notes his job required, he would keep a log for Grace that told her everything he did and how he felt about it. From the raw material of that loving report—which ran to 400,000 words—*Logbook for Grace* was later distilled.

During the voyage, and when he was not studying birds, Murphy found himself absorbed in the ways of whaling and whalers. The old vessel *Daisy* was itself an intriguing part of this story—a colorful postscript to the past. Seventy-five years before, great fleets of Yankee whalers had sailed from the whaling ports of Nantucket, Buzzards Bay and Long Island; whale oil had kept the wheels of the nation turning and its lamps burning. In 1846 there were 736 Yankee whaleships roaming the sea. But when *Daisy* set out on her voyage she was a lonely remnant of a disappearing fleet. The number of sperm whales had been sharply reduced; petroleum and electricity had largely replaced whale oil, and steam and steel had almost driven the windjammer off the seas.

Murphy was fully aware of his role as a commentator on a dying era, and in a straightforward reportorial way he sets down its customs and superstitions, its techniques and tools, its faults and fancies with a clarity and accuracy that have been matched by few books on the subject. Perhaps comparisons between *Logbook* and *Moby Dick* were inevitable, for Murphy, though harboring no literary illusions, showed the keen mind for detail which helped make Herman Melville's chronicle a report on a way of life as well as a great novel. And Murphy, like Melville, could pull his oar with the best of a whaleboat crew. A lean, 25-year-old six-footer, he had a youthful zest for what was, after all, a great adventure.

"This has been the most exciting day of my life," he begins the entry for October 10, 1912. There follows what must surely be one of the finest whaling accounts of its kind ever written: for nine hours, Murphy's whaleboat is dragged back and forth in a "Nantucket sleighride" across the Atlantic by a "forty barrel whale." To say that Murphy had no literary pretensions is not to say he could not spin a good yarn or capture the mood and drama of a scene that caught his fancy. "If there is any modern counterpart of an uncouth revel around a witches' brew," he writes in describing the blubber-boiling operation, "it is the scene of the trypots at night. . . . The *Daisy*, with topsails aback, rolled gently in the quiet swell. . . . The flickering glare showed the hulk of the whale alongside and the flash of bloody wavelets beyond. On deck . . . the fiery chimneys of the tryworks in full blast cast enough illumination to reveal the great blankets of

blubber and the greasy, toiling figures scurrying about
amid the shouting of orders, the creak of tackles and the
clank of chains."

Unlike earlier, contemporary chroniclers of the whaling
era, Murphy was writing from the perspective of another age.
It may come as a shock to find him talking of trying to use
the telephone and, within a page, telling of *Daisy's* anchor
being hauled up by hand to the hoarse sounds of a capstan
chantey. Yet, while he was no old salt himself, Murphy well
knew that in living with men who went about whaling the
way their grandfathers had done it—in living, almost literally,
cheek by jowl with the past—he was having a rare experience. This perspective makes Murphy's account anything
but remote or quaint: it is all relevant to the modern reader;
it comes alive as no dated account now could.

Logbook would be a classic if it were only about whaling. But Murphy has caught the whole breadth of his varied
interests between its covers. A ship at sea is in the middle of
nature's own laboratory, and as a naturalist Murphy had his
eyes open and mind working every minute. Wind, wave and
water; birds, bugs, butterflies, whales, dolphins and fish—
even fish inside other fish—are noticed and described with
scientific insight. Moreover, because Murphy was writing for
his bride, the scientist in him is always edited by the man.
His very precise descriptions of birds and animals are always colored with personal interest and affection. Objec-
tive observations and subjective reactions are intermixed.
For example, he writes of walking over the wintry waste of
South Georgia Island and coming suddenly upon a pond of
icy snow water:

*"With a tingling of my spine, I perceived that the bottom was
strewn, layer upon layer, with the bodies of gentoo penguins that
had outlived the perils of the sea to accomplish the rare feat among
wild animals of dying a natural death. By hundreds, possibly by*

thousands, they lay all over the bed of the cold tarn, flippers out-stretched and breasts reflecting blurred gleams of white. Safe at last from sea leopards in the ocean . . . they took their endless rest; for decades, perhaps for centuries, the slumberers would undergo no change in their frigid tomb."

Murphy's temperament made him keenly aware both of nature's drama and its drolleries. He ends one delightful entry, which describes a visit to a penguin colony, with this observation:

"Today a cock bird laid a pebble at my feet, a compliment properly followed by ceremonial bowing and, I hope, by mutual sentiments of high esteem."

Above all, *Logbook* reflects the profound schooling which this voyage afforded a fledgling scientist-at-sea. In *Moby Dick*, Herman Melville's Ishmael avers that "A whale ship was my Yale College and my Harvard." For Murphy, educated at Brown University, the whaleship *Daisy* was a unique graduate school which offered him as intimate a study of marine zoology as a young naturalist ever had. As George Gaylord Simpson points out in his new introduction to this special edition, the voyage had a significant effect on Murphy's future career. His interest in seabirds and marine animals, kindled then, has never flagged. Casks full of specimens which he brought home from the South Atlantic after that trip filled display cases at the American Museum for many years. Murphy's sea leopard and king penguins are still to be seen there. His report on the shocking overkill of whales and sea elephants at South Georgia had much to do with the later strengthening of international whaling and sealing laws.

On the basis of his studies in the South Atlantic, Murphy was later able to expand greatly what was known about seabirds—and to correct a widely held misconception. By studying and watching, he proved that these birds were not the aimless migrants scientists had thought them to be.

Rather, he showed, they lived according to patterns just as distinct and orderly as those of any land birds. In the words of the citation accompanying one of his honorary medals: "By following the sea birds to their haunts he has deepened our knowledge of the world of waters."

The versatility of the career which began on the *Daisy* recalls words Murphy himself wrote in tribute to his old mentor Dr. Frederic A. Lucas, former head of the American Museum. He called Lucas a man "unafraid to contemplate the whole scope of natural science and capable of becoming familiar with a surprisingly large part of it." During his studies on South Georgia Island in 1913, Murphy named a glacier in the barren Bay of Isles for Dr. Lucas. Now, in a sense, history has come full circle. In recognition of his own contributions to science there are two mountains named after Murphy—one in Antarctica, the other on South Georgia Island itself, overlooking the very harbor where he made his first acquaintance with the penguins.

Throughout the year on *Daisy*, Murphy diligently penned his notes and his log in that frigid clime—at the prolific rate of 1,000 words a day come cold or high water. After the voyage, he was caught up in new work—among other things, leading 13 world-girdling scientific expeditions. Although he did not get around to publishing the log for 35 years, the quality of *Logbook* suggests that, inadvertently, Murphy had found the perfect formula for writing a book: do something exciting and significant when young and enthusiastic, and write copiously about it. Then, when time and experience have put things in perspective, forge the account into a book, tempering the pages with all the whimsy and lighthearted exuberance that bubble up through the sea of original notes.

Not much is left of the old *Daisy* now. The whaler itself sank while serving as a cargo ship in World War I, as Murphy tells us in his preface to *Logbook*. One of *Daisy*'s whaleboats rests in a whaling museum in Cold Spring Harbor, New York, and a few mementos were preserved by the Murphys on the walls of their home. The last surviving member of its crew, the cooper Correia, died in 1955. Everyone else is gone. But in his preface, Murphy noted proudly that his own grandchildren numbered more than a whaleboat's crew. His great-grandchildren could now fill a second whaleboat in their own right.

One thing Murphy does not tell in his preface is how the book came to be written in the first place. A publishing house, interested in his scientific work, asked him to try his hand at something more personal. Murphy demurred, pleading lack of time. However, he said, he had kept a daily log during a whaling voyage he had made nearly 35 years before; would the publishers care to see that? The publishers winced, but it was too late to back down. They agreed to read a few sections. That was enough. Apathy turned to enthusiasm, and after sorting out his original notes and letters, Murphy delivered the finished manuscript. Surely a happy accident.

—THE EDITORS OF TIME

introduction

George Gaylord Simpson, Agassiz Professor of Vertebrate Paleontology at the Museum of Comparative Zoology, Harvard University, is a former curator of fossil mammals and chairman of the department of paleontology and geology at the American Museum of Natural History. He has written widely in the field of natural history; his books include *Attending Marvels,* a personal account of a scientific expedition he led into the desolate reaches of Patagonia.

Most boys are potential naturalists. Unless confined to the depths of the slums, they like to roam about fields, hills and waters. There they observe and quite often collect minerals, plants, insects and other animals. For most of them this activity soon becomes only a memory or, at best, an avocation—but for a few it develops into a true vocation. The precise direction of this vocation is frequently decided by their first major expedition. "Fields" become *the* field, the professional designation for the open spaces of living nature, out beyond the confines of office and laboratory.

So it was for Charles Darwin, the most distinguished example of the fixing of a vocation in the field. An amateur interest in nature overran his half-hearted attempts to study medicine and theology. His great, decisive field trip was the voyage of H.M.S. *Beagle,* on which he served as volunteer naturalist. After that five-year expedition around the world, Darwin made no further excursions into the field, although characteristically he found much of nature to observe in his own backyard at Down. It was the *Beagle* that determined his vocation, making him a professional (although always unpaid) naturalist.

During his long expedition, Darwin kept voluminous records, and a narrative journal was published soon after his return. It is still in print in various editions, generally under the title of *The Voyage of the Beagle,* and is still one of the best accounts of travel and scientific exploration ever written.

To be a Darwin has been given only to Darwin, but not the least of his contributions to history is that his example has inspired so many other incipient naturalists. Thus when Robert Cushman Murphy entered on his decisive first major expedition at age 25 he consciously took Darwin as his model. He determined that the voyage of the whaler *Daisy* should be to him, as far as possible, what the voyage of the surveying ship *Beagle* had been to Darwin. He undertook to observe all the phenomena of nature that came into view and only regretted (as indeed had Darwin) that he was not equally prepared in all branches of the natural sciences. He kept voluminous notes, both technical and personal, and also wrote (again as did Darwin) detailed letters about his adventures. In Murphy's case the letters were principally to the bride whom he had left behind after a few months of marriage.

Whether from modesty or from more pressing involvement in the requirements of an institutional career, Murphy did not emulate Darwin in prompt publication of the narrative of his early expedition. Not until 33 years after he left the brig *Daisy* at Barbados did Murphy compile an account of the voyage from his personal journal, his technical notebooks, his letters to his wife, and his still vivid memories. The book is thus a product of the author's maturity, written after he had become a scientist of recognized eminence. Nevertheless he has managed to retain much of the freshness and impact of that voyage of his youth. Although we know as we read that the author had already become an important figure in science, we can recapture many of the qualities of the young man that were to make him so.

Murphy's interests and career were always to bear the stamp of the *Daisy*, as they still do. The immediate possibilities were circumscribed by the fact that the voyage was strictly a commercial one, intended to profit by obtaining oil from whales and seals. Scientific observations had always to be opportunistic, occurring as they did within a decidedly nonscientific context. As will appear from the narrative, even such specific assistance as the master of the *Daisy* had obliged himself to give was not freely forthcoming. Observations by the budding scientist were perforce limited; he had to concentrate on the marine mammals that were the objects of the *Daisy*'s commercial attentions and on the oceanic birds that were the other conspicuous inhabitants of the seas and islands visited.

As a narrative, the chief interest of this *Logbook* for most readers will probably lie in its accounts of whaling and sealing. It is surprising to find that an author still decidedly active today took part in a whaling voyage that could have occurred with no change a century ago and with little change several centuries earlier. The *Daisy* was strictly a sailing vessel, technically a hermaphrodite brig. Her cetacean prey was taken by hand harpoons from whaleboats. Oil was rendered from blubber on deck, and all parts of the animals except their oil were simply cast away. However, as became apparent when the *Daisy* encountered faster company at South Georgia, she was already a decided anachronism in 1912. For better or for worse, modern whaling methods were already in use: pursuit by steamers, attack by harpoon guns, utilization of the whole animal by both shore and floating factories.

The *Daisy* was not, indeed, a survivor from the great days of sailing whalers. She had been built 40 years before as a merchant ship and had been converted for whaling only in 1907. And while she was an ideal ship for adventure, she was far from being ideal either for whaling or for scientific work.

But because the *Daisy* was an anachronism, Murphy's *Logbook* shows us the whaling of long ago through modern eyes. It had its daring, even sporting, aspects that could not fail to appeal to an active young man, but on the whole it was a nasty business. It was butchery, to the point of extinction, of beautiful, inoffensive animals. It had aspects of almost incredible brutality, especially when it involved the slaying of seals of both sexes and all ages. It is all the more surprising, therefore, that Murphy found humanity and decency among the men who committed such deeds. (Modern whaling is less brutal only to the extent that it is more businesslike and that some effort is made to permit survival of the species pursued.)

When the *Daisy* visited South Georgia, the fur seals, which had once abounded there, were already gone. Elephant seals, sought for their blubber alone, were in imminent danger even though regulations (ignored by the *Daisy*'s skipper) confined hunting to adult males. Murphy's observations and the specimens of elephant seals he brought back contributed much to man's knowledge of those fascinating animals. His dismay at their slaughter led to a lifelong concern with the conservation of marine mammals. The situation is still far from perfect, but thanks largely to such interested naturalists as Murphy most species seem to be safe for the time being. Fur seals and elephant seals are not so widely distributed as formerly but are in no immediate danger of extinction. Other species, such as the sea otter, which were at the point of extinction, seem to be making a moderate comeback.

The youthful Murphy had an admirable desire to know all things. He was, however, clear-sighted enough to realize that in the 20th Century breadth of scope entails some shallowness of grasp. Even the generalist, if successful, must have an anchor in the depth of some specialty. When Murphy set out on the *Daisy* the nature of his specialty was not yet entirely clear. As with Darwin, again, it was engendered by the voyage. The *Logbook* abounds in remarks on gulls, frigate birds, Mother Carey's chickens, penguins (most particularly) and other birds of the open ocean, its islands and its adjoining shores. Such creatures as these were to become the central theme of Murphy's vocation. The work begun on the *Daisy* was continued through other voyages into tropical and southern latitudes. The principal result, based on both his own expeditions and those of others, was what may fairly be called the masterpiece among Murphy's many works: his two volumes on the *Oceanic Birds of South America*, published in 1936. It is one of those rare scientific monographs that also have literary quality, and that can be read for pleasure by scientist and by reasonably sophisticated nonscientist alike.

As the title makes clear, this *Logbook*, constructed in considerable part from letters to a recent bride, was offered in 1947 in book form to the same woman, then the author's wife of many years. The book contains numerous references to this personal relationship; they add a suitably romantic touch to a voyage already fascinating beyond the reach of fiction.

—GEORGE GAYLORD SIMPSON

author's preface

Toward the end of the year 1911, six months after I had received my bachelor's degree from Brown, my friend Dr. Frederic A. Lucas, then Director of the American Museum of Natural History, spoke to me about an opportunity of voyaging to the edge of the Antarctic in a New Bedford whaling and sealing vessel. The suggestion provoked an evening of lively discussion which related, however, to other naturalist-candidates. I was planning to be married in June, 1912, and my own eligibility for such a cruise never entered my head.

The conversation was routinely reported by letter to Miss Grace Emeline Barstow, "of the State of Rhode Island and Providence Plantations." With characteristic forthrightness, she awakened me by a telegram delivered in the middle of the next night. The message urged me to hold the seafaring option pending further consideration, and to hasten the latter by catching the first train to Providence. Her subsequent argument was that the projected voyage would serve as the best possible launching of my career, and that we would be married immediately so as to have several months together before my departure.

I was persuaded without undue difficulty, but she alone had the audacity to invite a conventional and aghast family to prepare for her early wedding with a youth who would thereafter disappear for a year or longer!

Nevertheless, everything worked out in just that way. We were married on February 17, 1912, and on May 25 we departed by steamer for the Lesser Antilles in company with Captain B. D. Cleveland, master of the brig *Daisy*, and his wife. Following a memorable stay at Barbados, where the whaler had made port after a year's cruise under command of another captain, we all boarded the *Daisy* and voyaged to Dominica. On July 1, the matron and the bride left us, taking passage on the steamship *Guayana* from Dominica to New York. That point marks the opening of my log.

Most Americans knew little, and thought less, of wars at the time I shipped on the *Daisy*. No torpedoes or bombs were a source of worry, but there was little solace as regards means of communication. Radio was merely something we had begun to hear about, air mail hardly that. Going to sea as I did meant leaving the world.

I found plenty of occupation, as all may learn who have patience to read on. Foremost among my jobs was writing the records of day-to-day experience in the logbook I kept for my courageous wife and also in a separate set of scientific notebooks. My model for the latter was the journal of the youthful Darwin of the *Beagle*, for which I felt, and still feel, an unbounded admiration. Average daily jottings exceeded a thousand words, so I returned to New York, after an absence of precisely a year, with about 400,000 words of notes.

The substance of many of these entries has long since been published in 67 different articles and in a two-volume book entitled *Oceanic Birds of South America* (1936). But nothing of the human aspect of the long voyage—of how 34 men lived together, cooped up in a sailing craft of 383 tons net—has ever been told. My relations with the master of the *Daisy*, to whom the American Museum agreed to pay a flat sum in return for specified assistance given me on the voyage, are an instance of what I mean. They required a certain exercise of tact, because Captain Cleveland was a man of parts and of both strong and outspoken prejudices. A minor example concerned his views on the relative inferiority of New Yorkers and most other humans to the residents or adherents of the Boston-Edgartown Axis. I scuttled him on this point by indicating that I am a Long Islander of the fourth generation but a Massachusetts scion of the eleventh. For himself he could claim only eight generations or thereabouts!

The personal log included a proportion of text that was exceedingly intimate, trivial, or nonsensical. I began the preparation of this book by deleting much, but by no means all, of such matter. Then I inserted under the proper dates liftings from the letters I had written from the *Daisy*. Next, I transferred from my so-called scientific notebooks various items that seemed to possess general interest, leaving out, for the most part, the observations on birds which had already been published at length in the volumes referred to above. Finally, I added or expanded from memory the accounts of certain happenings that had acquired significance only with the passage of decades. The events are factual and the thoughts contemporary. If part of the emotional or intellectual content of the book seems boyish, that is as it should be.

Since *Logbook for Grace* begins and ends with the brig *Daisy,* I should add in this preface a few items of post-history.

For two and a half years after my return to New York, Grace's undelivered letters continued to come back to me from Cape Town, Buenos Aires, Tristan da Cunha, South Georgia, the Falklands, St. Helena, Ascension, and various West Indian Islands.

During the first World War, the old·brig was restored to merchant service. Laden with beans for Europe, she sprang a leak in the eastern Atlantic on October 29, 1916. The ocean water caused such an incontinent swelling of her cargo that the decks bulged and the planking was sprung. Her hull was verily rent asunder by expansion of beans, and she sank.

As I know through periodical reports from my friend the cooper, all but a handful of my shipmates have departed this life. One or more were killed by sperm whales on later voyages. Others, including Victor, the fourth officer, sailed from New Bedford on a Cape Verde packet that was never again reported. Many came to lonely ends in hospital wards. Captain Cleveland, however, not only made further whaling cruises but even learned to navigate a motor car. On August 8, 1917, he sailed into Buzzards Bay for the last time, in the bark *Morgan.* He was welcomed by eleven other veteran shipmasters of New Bedford, but shortly thereafter he was gathered to his fathers. In either late December, 1925, or early in the following month, his son and only descendant was drowned with all hands in the loss of the schooner *Mary E. Curtis.* Only the nameboard of this craft was ever found. Mrs. Cleveland lingered into the tenth decade of her life. When I last saw her, shortly before the end, she remarked that she had begun to dread "the prospect of growing old."

The cooper, José Correia, has survived to take part in

several scientific cruises for the American Museum, sometimes as my fellow-worker. Within ten years I have seen or heard from two of the West Indian sailors, one of whom was Conrad. And I have picked up from the breeze a recent rumor that John da Lomba, the mate, still lives as unofficial king of the tight little Isle of Brava, a fate so appropriate that I hope it is true.

In forging a unit from the yellowed pages of the original log and other notes, I have had the assistance of two able and sympathetic collaborators, Mrs. Margaret L. Davis and Miss Constance D. Sherman. Miss Sherman worked with me throughout the finishing stages, and I owe much to her enthusiasm and critical acumen.

My sister Augusta set down the music of the three airs, notwithstanding the difficulty that I usually began my renditions to her in one key and ended in another. Mr. Serafino Bogatto, out of the kindness of his heart, has inscribed these melodies in his own musical calligraphy.

The lady who is to me both the subject and the object of the tale has been my recourse in countless problems of judgment, while her matchless vitality has constantly revived my own drive. She has read the proof with me, just as for thirty-five years we have read all our proof together. The letter bag on the *Daisy*, of which more will be learned later, was a symbol of her enduring foresight for my welfare and success. As she was responsible for my voyage, so she has been no less responsible for the ultimate, if somewhat tardy, printing of the record. Its particular form, however, was a surprise to her.

Perhaps the only individual fit to judge the yarn from the point of view of an ancient and qualified salt is my friend Clifford W. Ashley, painter and writer of distinction, sperm whaleman by virtue of a cruise in the bark *Sunbeam*, and creator of beautiful books relating to the vanished calling. Far more shipwise than I, he has generously read my manuscript, checking usages that distinguish the seadog from the landlubber, and making a large number of welcome suggestions.

So at last the history has been spread where it can be saved for our grandchildren, already in number more than a whaleboat's crew.

—ROBERT CUSHMAN MURPHY

Crystal Brook, Long Island, 1946.

logbook
for
Grace

1 Caribbee Summer

ROSEAU, Dominica, July 1, 1912. The *Guayana* has faded from sight and even her smoke no longer hangs over the northern horizon. Behind my eyelids I still see you, standing straight and tall and proudly smiling, with the small figure of the skipper's wife beside you.

I have waited for the skipper to say the first word, pretending not to notice his brimming eyes, but thus far his only sound has been a murmured, "My soul and body!" Parting is an old, old story to a whaleman, born and bred. And yet, the prospect of a year's absence, perhaps without communication, must carry a very different portent to him at sixty-eight than to me at twenty-five.

JULY 4. On the second, we tried in vain to telephone from Roseau to Portsmouth so that the skipper might order one of his whaleboats from the *Daisy* to come fetch us. Failing to get a connection, we returned to the brig in black Benjamin's unpainted, ramshackle little sloop, but the going back was very different from the daylight voyage that you and I made together along the green coast.

This time the *Lily Laurie* was piled high, until her boom would barely clear—fifty barrels of flour, twenty divided among fish, vinegar and limes, forty-five cases of oil and the luggage of her fifteen passengers! The latter numbered several Dominican boys recruited for the *Daisy's* crew, three black women, and a little girl named Diana, besides the young Virgin Island master of the sloop, Captain Cleveland, and me.

We left Roseau at nine o'clock in the evening of July 3, a glorious tropical night, with all the big stars blazing. The moon, half gone, arose about eleven. The enthralled swains, clustering about the *Lily Laurie's* bow, sang snatches of a whaling song, for to their simple hearts our coming voyage seemed El Dorado. The skipper of the sloop chattered all night with an old crone who was smoking a clay pipe, and very serious they were about everything, too. In his native isle of Anguilla, the skipper has a dusky bride whom he has not seen for six months, but he is now on the verge of sailing home, and he punctuated his conversation by whistling a prothalamium. Or perhaps he merely whistled for a steady wind.

Little Diana slumbered as only a child does. Near her, on the hard oil cases, I dozed rather fitfully, felt the cool gusts blow down from the round ebony hills, and saw the water flicked into whitecaps. I heard the wise old woman who smoked the pipe say to the skipper from Anguilla that she could always tell at a glance a married man from a single man. When put to the test, she placed us all correctly.

At six o'clock on the morning of the Glorious Fourth, we reached our mooring in Portsmouth. I found in your packet for this date the bundle of firecrackers, and I banged 'em off to the tolerant amusement of the black British Colonials.

I celebrated also by obtaining one of the Dominican Hercules beetles for which you and I had hunted in vain. It is five and three-quarter inches long! In the evening I was chatting in what you and I called the Grand Hotel Mahogany Fourposter with dapper Port Captain Tavernier, when a boy entered and said, "A lady have a spin-saw insect she wish to sell you, sir." (The name stems from the absurd island legend that these beetles clamp their long jaws on the bough of a tree and fly around it like a whirligig until they saw it off.)

"How much?" I inquired.

Back went the boy, and in again. "One pound sterling, sir," quoth he.

"Tell the lady," said I, "that I will gladly pay thruppence for her astounding natural phenomenon."

Once more a round trip, and the report: "The lady reply that she cannot deliver the insect for thruppence, but she will be happy to accept sixpence, sir."

The haggle was now progressing well, so I sent for the black girl and her imposing bug. It was such a beauty that I gave her a whole shilling, to her palpable delight and the envy of bystanders.

JULY 5. While the *Daisy*'s anchor was being catted up, to the hoarse strains of a chanty, I bought a gross of ripening bananas for one shilling fourpence. At eight o'clock of a calm morning, we drifted slowly out of the roadstead of Portsmouth, and lay within sight of Morne Diablotín until the setting sun turned its cloud cap pink. After nightfall, blackfish puffed around the brig.

Captain Cleveland advanced the third mate to the vacant place of the second mate who had been killed by a sperm whale before the *Daisy* transshipped her oil at Barbados. Fourth Mate Almeida, your fiery red and bearded friend who looks like a Cape Verde Island version of the god Thor, now

becomes third mate. Here is the form, entered in the log, as it
applies to Mr. Vincent, the Tagalog from Mindanao, the Malay of burly body but delicate hands and gentle manners:

> *I have this day promoted Vincent Lunda from 3d officer to*
> *the second mate's berth, and for his services he is to have the one-*
> *thirtieth lay of the net proceeds for whatever oil and bone may be*
> *taken from this date forward.*
>
> > Benjamin D. Cleveland
> > Master and agent of Brig "Daisy"
>
> *Witness*
> R. C. MURPHY
>
> > > his
> > > Vincent × Lunda
> > > mark

I rejoice, my Grace, that your lively voyage with us in the
trade wind from Barbados to Dominica, when your stomach
proved better ballasted than mine, will make flesh and blood
to you of these names, and enable you to picture the *Daisy*'s
crew and gear.

JULY 6.   Land now below the horizon. Weather calm until evening, when a catspaw permitted us at least to point for
Guadeloupe. At this hour, songs came from the fo'castle, to
the accompaniment of a guitar and an old copper bugle.

In mid-afternoon I took the time from the chronometer
when the captain barked out the instant of his sight, and we
then worked out the longitude and were in agreement. "Scientist" would be a bit of an anomaly on a whaleship's papers, so
I am recorded as "assistant navigator," which may also be an
anomaly! It is at least a sly poke, because when a skipper's
wife goes awhaling with him she also is customarily recorded
in the articles as "assistant navigator." Anyway, to complete
the agreement, I am down for a one two-hundredth lay of the
net proceeds, which is more than a wife would get!

The Old Man—a term which passes in the third person
here at sea, although it is strictly taboo ashore—enjoys rib-

bing the scientist. He is entertained by the technical words I frequently enter in my notes, and he occasionally asks me the "scientific name" of a particular bird or fish. At table today, when all the officers were present, he ordered the steward to make some griddlecakes.

"Griddlecakes?" inquired our Dutch West Indian, black grubslinger, "what's them?"

"Griddlecakes, Steward," explained the captain, "is the *scientific* name for flapjacks."

We have not as yet signed on our full crew, and some of the men on board are still technically not shipped—merely picked up at Roseau and Portsmouth. Several of the New Bedford old hands, including all but one of the curly-haired young Cape Verders whom you called "cherubs," deserted at Dominica, and even the local police couldn't find them. A seasoned Bermudian boatsteerer decamped along with them. Fortunately, the men with the most conspicuous stigmata of very undesirable maladies were among the runaways.

The recruits from Portsmouth include a coal-black youth of tender years, named Conrad. An elder brother brought him off and put him under my especial charge. He had already made up his mind that I was either owner, captain, or first mate of the *Daisy*. "He's a good Latin scholar, he is," said the brother. However that may be, Conrad speaks extraordinarily good English. He also wears a silver crucifix around his neck, and makes the sign of the cross whenever he sees lightning.

The quiet of the daylight hours followed a night in which we seemed to tumble about like a rotary churn. Since my berth, converted from the cabin settee, runs athwart ship, I had to change ends whenever we tacked.

JULY 7. This morning I made out ship's papers for Captain Cleveland and we officially took on seventeen new hands. Feddy Lundy, Attenaze Jean Baptiste (a Martinican),

Elise St. Rose, and John Paul (without the Jones) were some
of the noble neophytes who stepped up and made their marks.
Feddy Lundy, however, could write his own name, thus:

Feddy Lundy

The sperm whale lookouts had been set on the day we
left Portsmouth, and today Conrad was ordered to the foremast head. The poor little devil had never even imagined
being aloft, but he gulped and started up the ratlines, one of
the boatsteerers following to encourage him by fanning his
backside with a rope's end. But when Conrad reached the
futtock-shrouds, his nerve forsook him, and he clung like a
Dominican gecko to the foreyard, while his knees made the
rigging shake. Neither coaxing nor dire threats would budge
him, so John Paul, an equally inexperienced but more self-
confident lad, was sent up to relieve him.

Feeling it high time to show my own nonchalance and to
give the specious impression of a long seafaring background, I
shortly afterwards made my own maiden climb to the mainmasthead. It was accompanied by much concealed sympathy
for Conrad, because the distance was ten times as far looking
down as looking up. The motion was extremely disconcerting,
particularly the sentient and malevolent snap at the end of
each roll by means of which the vessel endeavored to catapult
me off into the sea. However, there were already three men
up there, two at the fore and one at the main, and with outward casualness I finally crawled through one of the rings of
the lookout hoops and calmly (?) surveyed the horizon. The
deck looked small and queer, and usually far off to one side,
but the strangeness soon wore off and I began to enjoy my
vantage point above the shimmering ocean.

The lookouts, more properly called mastheads, are the eyes of a whaleship. Perched on small platforms a hundred feet or more above the deck, armed with rather foggy French binoculars and fortified with a promise of five pounds of tobacco to the man who first raises a whale that is later captured, they stand their two-hour watches from dawn until dark. It is not likely to be a comfortable berth except in the smoothest weather, for the motion at water line is augmented a hundredfold by the towering mast, and you go careening around above the groaning rigging until it seems that the sticks will surely snap off. The Old Man, however, vows that the iron hoops, which encircle and protect the mastheads, encourage drowsiness among the "mokes" and the "gueez" (Portuguese). The words are his own complimentary terms for West Indians and Cape Verde Islanders, respectively.

I dare say that a hard-worked whaleman is now and then likely to doze even in this most precarious situation, especially on some calm, overpowering, sun-drenched afternoon when, as Herman Melville wrote,

> "For every swing we made there was a nod from below from the slumbering helmsman. The waves, too, nodded their indolent crests; and across the wide trance of the sea, east nodded to west, and the sun over all."

Today is Sunday, which I realize because each fo'castle hand has been allotted one bucket of fresh water to wash his clothes. I have made an arrangement with Johnny, the cabin boy, to take care of my laundering throughout the voyage. Johnny, whose complexion is café au lait, hails from Brava—a most heavenly tropical paradise, according to his nostalgic and doubtless quixotic memory—but is now a resident of Falmouth, on Cape Cod.

Just after supper, a masthead bellowed "Porpoises!" and we crowded toward the bow from where we could watch the

beautiful play of long gray-and-white bodies under the stem.
A line was bent onto a harpoon in transit, and Mr. Vincent
clambered into the martingale stays and presently darted.
But he missed, and frightened away the whole shoal.

The Old Man emitted a volley of mighty oaths, which indicates a talent that he carefully conceals ashore. Even at sea,
I observe, he has a strong distaste for profanity when used by
others. He seems, indeed, to be a soul who is always deeply
repentant of other peoples' misdeeds.

JULY 8.   Calm again. Many Portuguese men-o'-war,
boobies, frigate birds, tropic-birds and noddies, and a few
doves and hummingbirds presumably on interisland flights.
Several pairs of tropic-birds, trailing their comet tails, passed
between our masts and then flew in oval orbits around us with
a rapid, steady beating of the wings. One screamed, or blew
his bos'n's whistle, when close enough for me to see the satiny
gleam of the plumage. Another dived from a great height, like
Phaëton, the son of Apollo, whose name this bird bears.
When it reappeared at the surface, it rested with wings up-
raised and the standard of its long tail pointing toward
its home in the sun.

The skipper and the cooper—the latter a native of Fayal
and one of the three bona fide white men on board this craft—
have made and installed a shipshape set of bookshelves for
my library, which is now all accessible and secure behind bat-
tens. The volumes might be called a motley assemblage, comprising the following:

Cambridge Natural History, the volumes on fishes, birds, and
     mammals
Parker and Haswell, *Zoology*
Howell, *Physiology*
Flower and Lydekker, *Mammals Living and Extinct*
Beddard, *Book of Whales*
Gregory, *The Orders of Mammals*

True, *Review of the Delphinidae* (porpoises)
Melville, *Moby Dick*
Tower, *History of the American Whale Fishery*
Starbuck, *History of the American Whale Fishery*
Weddell, *A Voyage towards the South Pole*
Catalogue of Birds of the British Museum, the volume on alba-
    trosses, petrels, gulls and terns
Journal of the Right Hon. Sir Joseph Banks during Captain
    Cook's First Voyage on HMS "Endeavour"
Ridgway, *Nomenclature of Colors*
Lönnberg, *Notes on the Vertebrates of South Georgia*
Darwin, *Voyage of the "Beagle"*
Moseley, *"Challenger" Narrative*
New Testament
Dante, *Divina Commedia*
Bunyan, *Pilgrim's Progress*
Horace, *Carmina*
Oxford Book of English Verse
The Oxford Shakespeare
Typewritten and bound summaries and translations of in-
    formation about South Georgia from the writings of
    Guyot, Cook, Forster, Sparrman, Bellingshausen, Kluts-
    chak, Szielasko, von den Steinen and others
Also, several fat notebooks, still blank and white, but des-
    tined to contain the great literature of the future!

Hanging and lashed beside the shelves, is the rotund sack in which you, my darling, by incredible labor and wile, seem to have arranged orderly files of communications from your beloved self and countless friends for nearly every date in the calendar of the long year ahead!

While the skipper was nailing up the shelves, he waxed reminiscent. As a lad of fourteen, he, Ben Cleveland of Martha's Vineyard, shipped as cabin boy on his first voyage in a whaleship of which his elder brother was master. One day during a gale, a great wave piled over the quarterdeck and swept the captain overboard. The sea was so wild that lowering a boat was out of the question. Young Ben, who was standing his trick at the wheel, with another man to lay hold when the hard kicks came, could not even look astern where his brother drowned.

JULY 9.   Calm. For four days and nights we have been endeavoring to beat up toward the coast of Dominica from our position near Guadeloupe, but, owing to the lack of wind and the adverse current, we are as far off as when we started.

The West Indians today complained about their food. The Old Man listened to what they had to say, then went forward and tasted everything. He pronounced each dish excellent except the bread, which was soggy, and this he promised to have improved. Several of the fellows were inclined to be saucy, so the skipper sent aft for a pair of handcuffs.

The green West Indians won't eat baked beans, and do not like soup or stew. Feddy Lundy cried out to the Lord to provide for him, saying he was "in a way to starve." He also told us that "mother was a proper cook," and that "she even own a cook book, she do." Captain Cleveland assured him he would be sent back to his mother damn quick when we returned to Roseau.

Elise St. Rose, reared on Dominican fruit, fish, and cassava, was even more outspoken. He recalled his rights as a freeborn British subject, albeit a black one, and, just before diving down the fo'castle scuttle, he shouted at the Old Man, "I shall tell my king of you!"

The sudden appearance of a school of skipjacks caused the trouble to evaporate. Lines baited with white rag were paid out from bowsprit and stern, while we moved slowly through the water. Several fish, weighing about five pounds each, were soon being scaled and gutted on deck, and their solid, beef-like flesh for supper put everybody in a cheerful mood.

It appears to go against the principles of the Old Man to be amused, in which respect he has good Victorian precedent.

Nevertheless, he is not without his tolerant streaks. During the evening he once again became reminiscent, and told me of the proverbial difficulty of keeping the large crew of a whale-ship in cheerful mood during the long periods that often pass between the sighting, taking, and cutting-in of whales.

Why, after all, should these equatorial children take delight in the experiences that will somehow carry me through until you and I are once again together? Their comfort is far less than mine, their work more arduous, their privacy nil. In the face of unfamiliar food, they remember only their palmiest days ashore. Hope of money, all too likely to dim with experience, is their sole lure. Their thoughts and desires are centered on whales—whales and a port. They follow the calling not for its own sake, but only for what it may bring—the lay, one-hundredth, one hundred-and-fiftieth, one two-hundredth, or whatever the humble cut may be. They are poor observers of things in general. Living creatures interest them when they can eat them or boil them down to oil, but they are as unconcerned with the dazzling plunge of a tropic-bird as with the glowing, luminescent waters of a Caribbean evening. Sunsets, and the constellations of night skies, they do not appear to see. Perhaps their first thought of a star will come when the *Daisy*, her hold filled, turns her bow away from the southern ocean. Then we shall all be gazing nightly toward the line until changeless Polaris pops up to guide us home.

JULY 10. Today we sighted Dominica again, but soon drifted out of range, without wind to hold steerage. It gave enough of a fix, however, to check our reckoning. The Old Man regards himself as in a bit of a hole, and yet I don't know why, because our present vagrancy is due only to the fact that he is waiting for John da Lomba, his right-hand man, to come down from New Bedford and join us as a sort of super-mate.

We broke out ship during the morning, which means that

we cleared rubbish from the steerage and elsewhere, and sorted and restowed supplies. Skipjacks made us another visit, and a bloody one. Most of those that escaped our hooks were bitten in half by huge albacores, so that the water around us turned red at the same time that the deck was gurried with fish cleaning.

JULY 11.   Once more we made the Dominican coast, but again stood off because July 17 has been chosen as the date for sending a boat ashore. With nothing to keep me busy, I spent most of the afternoon in my canvas chair atop the poop, lost in Dante's *Paradiso*.

JULY 12.   At half past five this morning a squall blew up, and the whitening waves, lifting high the *Daisy*'s stern, made her pitch as I had not seen her before. Martinique lay to starboard, Mont Pelée waving a long flag of clouds. Dominica loomed dead ahead, with all its highlands enveloped. Presently the sun came out, or rather, up, and a more beautiful daybreak has never been known since Creation. Flying fish, not by dozens, as you and I have seen them, but by tens of thousands, scudded along with the spume, shining like happy souls in the heaven of the sun, of which I had been reading last evening.

> —"Quant' esser convenia da sè lucente
>   Quel ch'era dentro al Sol dov' io entra'mi,
>   Non per color, ma per lume parvente!"

How shining must that be which in the sun, whereinto I had entered, reveals itself not by hue but by light!

During the night Mr. Alves, the elderly and slow first mate, who has been stuffing his belly despite warning cramps, had such a violent attack of indigestion that the skipper and I feared he would pass out. However, even we, his doctors, failed to kill him.

JULY 13.   We cruised all day in rugged and uncomfortable waters between Dominica and Martinique, twice running very close to the shore of the latter island, and then headed off, by the wind, for the night.

Coming about makes the *Daisy* seem a living being. "Ready about! All hands on deck," bellows the Old Man from the quarterdeck, an order echoed by the mates, boatsteerers and forecastle occupants whose watch is on deck. "Keep her off a bit and let her go," is the ensuing word to the helmsman, and the brig spurts ahead as the sails catch it full.

"Helms alee!" is the next song. The brig is in stays, and square sails are now quivering in the cross-cutting wind.

"Tacks and sheets!" and the forecourses are cast loose, to flap freely. When the vessel has swung around so as to be head to wind, the fore-and-aft mainsail boom is eased over, as the great canvas fills. Then, "foresail let go and haul," and the *Daisy* rapidly gains momentum, while the perspiring boys relax.

But, for the most part, this waiting and tarrying and getting nowhere is beginning to be monotonous. Bring on your whales!

> 'Tis a boresome game to watch a cockroach crawl
> Across the somersaulting *Daisy*'s cabin wall.
> 'Tis dubious joy to rove the many-sounding seas
> With the wild, uncouth, though baptized, Aborigines.
> 'Twould be bliss (for us) a keen harpoon to whack
> Into a sparm whale's blubbery, unexpectant back.

JULY 14. Sunday again. Cruising off the windward coast of Dominica, a soul-satisfying view and probably the most like Polynesia to be encountered in the New World. The cliffs and headlands pile up far more boldly than those of the leeward shore.

We carried away our fore-topsail, signalled by a quick, crackling, puffing report. With incredible speed and skill the three officers set to work on the hatch with their spikes and sewing palms, and it was soon mended and in place again. Later we had to reef the mainsail, but we still scurried along, rolling down to the bulwarks, the waves overtaking and passing us in long combers. The cabin chairs are all lashed in place and the fiddles are on the table, but at mess we mostly balance our plates in our hands.

JULY 15.   Squally; high winds and driving rains. A big gray grampus stuck out his snout close by, and appeared to eye us. Sitting still has become strenuous exercise on board.

JULY 16.   Perfectly calm, as to the air, but with a very heavy, dead ground swell, and no breeze to hold the masts steady. Consequently we both pitch horribly and roll scuppers under. A downpour of rain before breakfast has made the deck so slippery that the men skid from rail to rail.

I trapped five large rats between decks, and slew cockroaches without number. Sport, with what Shakespeare would call "small deer!"

In afternoon the mastheads announced a shoal of blackfish about a mile off. We crowded sail and headed in their direction, which was also toward Martinique, lowering two whaleboats on the way. Both of them soon skimmed in among the black shining backs, fins cutting water, and the rowers pulled until their oars bent. I could see everything clearly through my glasses. Twice one of the harponeers darted his iron and missed. Then Mr. Vincent, the Tagalog, broke tradition, took the harpoon from his own bow oarsman and plunged it into the back of a bull on the first trial. A free ride followed, the victim pulling the ocean chariot in circles until it became exhausted and could be pierced horribly through and through with a lance.

Third Officer Almeida's first blackfish tore out the iron and escaped, but he soon made fast to another. We hoisted the carcasses aboard with a tackle, and I took their measurements and cleaned up the skulls, while their blubber simmered merrily in the try-pots. The head or melon blubber, from "junk and jaw," makes watch oil worth $15 a gallon, whereas the body blubber yields a product now marketed at only 53¢ a gallon.

Both animals were males, but Mr. Vincent's was much bigger than the other. To say that the great blunt-headed brute measured more than fourteen feet in length will give you no adequate idea of his size, which equaled the bulk of three oxen.

The Old Man is in high spirits, less because of the value of the catch than because everybody is busy, and exalted by the spirit of the chase, and therefore contented. A whaleship is a fighting craft; it is manned for battle, not merely for ship-tending, and "Satan still finds mischief for idle hands to do!"

The skipper and I get along famously, thus far. Before breakfast, he is inclined to be grumpy, as he admits, but for the rest of the day he is as gentle as a lamb, unless something riles him—bawdy language among the men, for example. That usually leads to a gentle admonition to all concerned that he'll be goddamned if he'll stand for one such word from any Christless bastard on board, afore or abaft the mainmast.

After supper I jolly him into a talkative mood, and he yarns about the sea, islands of palm or ice, whales, porpoises, birds, fish, and mighty sea-farin' men. Since 1883 he has commanded ten whalers, including the famous barks *Bertha*, *Lydia*, *Swallow*, and *Wanderer*. He has his own saga and his odyssey. Calms put him in low spirits. The harder the wind blows, the merrier he becomes.

This evening I astounded him with a trick of my own, by bringing him a glass of water that seemed ice cold. Too simple! I had merely soaked the felt and canvas cover of my canteen, hung it from the shrouds in the night wind, and allowed the process of evaporation to chill the contents. A little magic up one's sleeve is a great asset on a voyage.

During the dog watches, which are the short, overlapping watches of early evening, I chat also with the three mates, the cooper, steward, and truthful Johnny, the cabin boy, whose whole world seems to be one of make-believe. (I am now indentured to the last-named to the extent of a dollar a month, for washing.) Most of these men can read and write, and the cooper is positively profound. But, if the letters they prepare are in English, they come to me when they can't spell a word, and they bring scraps of newspapers and magazines for me to read to them. This evening I learned that the officers, both Portuguese and Malay, together with two or three of the boatsteerers, used to gather at evening under our window in Dominica in order to hear you play your violin.

JULY 17.   We came ashore with a boat's crew and, as it turned out, spent the night at Miss Jolly's "Cherry Lodge"— that is, the skipper and I stayed there, the crew being put up at a boarding house of lower order.

John da Lomba, it appeared from letters, was still in New Bedford, so the captain sent a cablegram ordering him to come at once. We are therefore booked to remain in West Indian waters for at least ten days more.

The captain had told Mr. Alves, second in command of the *Daisy*, to lie offshore and, if we had not returned before nightfall, to stand off and on until the following morning. As soon as we arrived on the Roseau waterfront, however, local police began to round up the *Daisy*'s deserters, many of whom had come in from Portsmouth during our absence. They had drawn up a petition to the United States consul, stating that during the "week's sail" from Barbados to Dominica (in reality, as you know, the trip had taken less than twenty-four hours) they had been served only dry bread and salt meat; that they "had suffered untold agonies from the captain's cruelties"; and that the mate had informed them that they would be shot and cast overboard when we were once well out at sea.

All afternoon squads of black police could be seen marching one or another of these wretches to the lockup in the old Roseau fort. Before sunset five of them were behind the bars; the rest had apparently returned to Portsmouth or had shipped on other vessels. Captain Cleveland didn't want these five men especially, and he was becoming hot under the collar because it was growing late and the *Daisy* lay ten miles offshore, a long pull to make before dark.

But British Colonial decorum is not conducive to speed. First His Excellency, the Royal Inspector of the Leeward Island Police, was called. He was a quizzical, deliberate gentleman whom I had met before. Next the Sergeant-at-Arms, the American consular representative and his secretary, the Magistrate of Roseau, the Master of the *Daisy*, and the fort guard of ten uniformed and heavily armed men, were all officially sent for, and seated in state in the small courtroom before the magistrate, who was the bodily representative of His Majesty George V, by the Grace of God of Great Britain and Ireland King, Emperor of India, Defender of the Faith, etc. Finally, the five haggard deserters were ushered in before a line of Enfield rifles. Their names were asked in turn, and His Majesty's Inspector of Police stated to the court that the names of said prisoners agreed with names of the *Daisy*'s crew on the consul's shipping papers.

His Honor the Magistrate gazed long and hard at the five men before him. "How many of these men are there?" he ultimately inquired.

"Five men, sir, Your Honor," replied the Inspector of Police.

At this juncture, Captain Cleveland reiterated a request that proceedings be hastened, because, he said, he had left no accomplished navigator on his vessel and it was of the utmost importance for him to reach her before dark. The Englishman, always courteous, leaped to oblige him.

"You are sure there are five of them here," said His Majesty's Magistrate, by way of throwing new light on the subject.

"Five, Your Honor," volunteered the secretary of the American consular representative.

"Who is the master of this vessel, the United States whaling brig *Daisy?*" asked H. M. Magistrate of Captain Cleveland, who had already been introduced to him by several different persons.

"I," grunted the captain.

"You are the master?" queried H. M. M.

"I *am*, sir," said the captain.

"A Bible is required," stated H. M. M., and then, as a New Testament was passed to the captain, he added, "Kindly swear," etc.

The captain swore aloud for the benefit of the court and also under his breath to relieve his feelings, and the oaths were not the same. He laid down the book, but it was necessary for him to pick it up again and kiss it before proceedings could continue according to Hoyle. The captain then briskly told the story of how he had left his brig in the Portsmouth roadstead, and how the men had departed without leave.

He didn't want them again with any great longing, but the law required him to take them in order to save the United States Government the expense of transporting them back to the ports from which they had severally shipped.

The deserters were next questioned. Their fine fabric soon fell to pieces before the grave and verbose questions of the magistrate. The only tangible reason why they didn't want to go back was the fear of being shot. A document was written, ordering them all on board, and we were just about to depart when stay, not so quick—one of them, a Cape Verder, suddenly found himself ill. His legs were weak; his knees had troubled him for months—brutal work on the *Daisy* had injured them, perhaps for life. If he walked to the boat now, the exertion might bring about a condition that would necessitate amputation.

British justice must leave no stone unturned, so His Majesty's Magistrate sent, in His Majesty's name, for a reputable surgeon. In the course of three quarters of an hour or so, the doctor hurried in. The speed of the proceedings was most pleasing to Captain Cleveland, whose brig was offshore in the darkness in charge of a timid old Portugee mate who had never looked through the vane of a sextant. The sick man was stripped, carefully examined, and pronounced sound, in fact remarkably healthy. Two shillings thruppence, his worldly wealth, was taken away from him as a punishment for shamming and used in part payment of the physician's bill. The United States Treasury, represented by the American consular agent, stood for the balance of six and ninepence.

It was now pitch dark, and all thought of returning to the brig was abandoned. The five offenders were led back to their cells, and supplied with a supper to be paid for by Uncle Sam. The captain quartered his boat's crew in the already crowded cabin of a fat and shiny Negress, while he and I repaired again to "Cherry Lodge."

JULY 18. The journal to date, my darling wife, has gone to you by registered mail. The one vast consolation in this delay is that I am now assured of hearing from you before our final departure from Dominica, perhaps by the courier service of John da Lomba who, by all accounts on board, must be a Homeric hero among whalemen.

The *Daisy* lay quietly in the offing this morning. There being no further need for great haste, the skipper dickered with the police authorities and shipped several new recruits from a group of minor offenders languishing in the Roseau jail. The boys were glad to leave their cells for a forecastle, the officials were delighted to get rid of them for a year at least, and the Old Man still needed to round out a full crew for the sanguinary work ahead. It is specified in black and white, however, that "the Master of the *Daisy* may deliver again to His Majesty's gaoler any unruly or otherwise undesirable members of this troop at the time he enters port to pick up his mate, da Lomba."

Almost awash because of our extra load, we rowed out to the brig with our cheerful felons and erstwhile deserters. The latter were a sheepish lot, thoroughly tired out from a mixed period of starvation and debauchery. They seemed slightly perked up to escape from public gaze, after being conducted in irons to the Roseau dock. All had gone well with the *Daisy* and we joined her two miles off the coast. In the logbook the Old Man duly entered that our night ashore had been a "forced put."

JULY 21. We are off Martinique, and for the first time since I came on board it really seems like Sunday. We have finished supper, and I am sitting in my chair on the deckhouse. The low sun is on the far side of the mainsail, and a caressing breeze gives the temperature of Eden—just right for no clothes. The ultramarine water sparkles and each little wave, scarcely more than a ripple, breaks into a white thread. Soft, lofty clouds hang above Morne Diablotín and Mont Pelée; elsewhere the sky is clear and pale. Two of the officers, seated on the carpenter's chest, are reading a Portuguese Bible; forward, the green hands are clustered around a crude dial, drawn on a bit of plank, learning to box the compass. The skipper is wearing a new blue shirt and a jaunty Panama hat. A Sabbath calm is everywhere. Old Triton may blow his wreathed horn when ready, for I am listening.

But why must the ridiculous dog the heels of the sublime? For some minutes, here in the lee of the mainsail, a faint, putrescent odor has been wafted to my nostrils. I now discover that it is essence of blackfish long deceased, and that it comes from my own hands and forearms. I have been cleaning up macerated bones during the day, and the ripe smell has survived soap and water. Perhaps I used too little of the latter.

Fresh water is a substance for niggardly employment on shipboard; there are in our case thirty-five men to be supplied. The fact that the drinking water is warm, stale, and often bilgy, doubtless helps in the conservation and, moreover, the forecastle hands must obtain it with a slender, cylindrical "thief" to be inserted through the bunghole of the scuttle-butt and drawn out by a lanyard. The amount of time and labor involved discourages wastefulness.

Bilgy water is the result of tight bungs; it means that the gases of organic decomposition have had no vent. It stinks horribly. You go thirsty as long as you can, then hold your breath and swallow a glassful. Fortunately, the water eventually works itself clear, and all ship's water improves after a month or more in the casks, or so the Old Man assures me.

I toiled hard today, between half past six this morning and the middle of the afternoon. Late yesterday we killed four of the blackfish or potheads. The boats brought back only the melons of three of them and, as the sex had not been noted, they were of no value to me. The captain delivered a little homily regarding specimens in the future. The men are eager to help, but they didn't understand. However they towed home the whole carcass of one, a cow, which was just what I wanted. I made careful measurements, prepared the skull, and, best of all, took out and preserved a perfect embryo.

Incidentally, the heads, six thus far, have produced twenty-five gallons of the most precious oil of the sea. My

personal credit on the ledger of this voyage has run up to
about $1.78.

During the past two days I have overhauled most of my
equipment, restowing things in the order in which they are
likely to be required. My shotgun and two rifles are lashed
neatly in a cabin gunrack, where I can get them at a second's
notice. The first trip to draw fluid from my bonded alcohol
barrel, 'tween decks, was made with considerable loud conversation between the Old Man and me concerning its dangerous contents. Its only labels are in red paint, applied in
Barbados. They read STRYCHNINE and POISON, separated by a Jolly Roger emblem. Only two of us are in the
know, and we have agreed always to refer to the substance as
"strychnine." Dr. Bashford Dean first put me up to this precaution by telling me that sailors would cheerfully drink the
rum or alcohol in which the captain's body was being shipped
home from the China Sea!

If your mind ever turns, my Grace, to fancied hardships
or privations of your husband somewhere on the deep, find
the *Voyage of the Beagle* and read the "Retrospect" of its final
pages. I copy, from the book on my knees, one paragraph of
Darwin's words:

> "Many of the losses which must be experienced are ob-
> vious; such as that of the society of every old friend, and of
> the sight of those places with which every dearest remem-
> brance is so intimately connected. These losses, however,
> are at the same time partly relieved by the exhaustless de-
> light of anticipating the long wished-for day of return. If, as
> poets say, life is a dream, I am sure in a voyage these are the
> visions which best serve to pass away the long night. . . . The
> effect ought to be to teach him good-humored patience, free-
> dom from selfishness, the habit of acting for himself, and of
> making the best of every occurrence."

JULY 22.   Blackfish were sighted this afternoon halfway
between Dominica and Martinique. When the lookouts sang, I

went to the masthead and remained there two hours. The gam lay about a mile off; most of the animals were quiet, with backs awash. We lowered two boats but, when they drew near, the blackfish became gallied and started rapidly to windward. Finally, at a long distance abeam, I saw through my glasses one boat make fast and shoot ahead. As it was drawn up toward the straining animal, it began to jerk characteristically from port to starboard and back again, and then to spin end after end. Soon, however, the lance was driven home, and even at that range I could see red water. Perhaps sharper eyes on the dim horizon saw it, too, for presently a man-o'-war bird glided into the scene, spiralling grandly with the whaleboat as a center, and approaching close to the kill.

In the meanwhile, a portion of the blackfish gam, mixed with a few porpoises, had come toward the brig. There were seventy-five or a hundred of them swimming along leisurely, and grouped, for the most part, in threes or fours, the individuals of each such squad almost touching sides. While we were lowering a third boat, they approached so near that I could look directly down upon them from where I was, 130 feet above the water. The dorsal fins of the blackfish were exposed much of the time, though sometimes the creatures lay idly for many seconds with the head low, the fin and the flukes both under water, and only the angle of the high tailridge above the surface, while they rose and fell with the swells. Whenever they came up to breathe, the black junk was thrust out to the eyes and the corner of the mouth; the slit of the blow holes opened like a pair of lips, and a slight shower of spray accompanied a gentle puff.

One huge old blackfish was in the van of the herd. He was the first to see the vessel, at which he changed his course, after stopping for a moment. The others did likewise, although some turned to the left, some to the right, crossing ahead and astern. When the boat approached, the wary crea-

tures "let go," as whalemen say, that is, they sank straight
down without altering the inclination of the body. I could see
them lowering, changing from black to green, and from green
to indistinct shadows as the water deepened above them.
Presently they reappeared some distance off, and lured the
boat vainly on. The futile game was continued for an hour or
more, the boat pursuing for upwards of a mile. By the time it
was recalled by our signal, the gam was once more all around
the *Daisy.* One blackfish raised its hinder end clear out of
water and deliberately lob-tailed ten or a dozen times, with
the flat of its flukes, making loud reports and causing the
spray to fly.

The first two boats killed three. Dead blackfish sink
like lead, as I observed several times when a carcass attached
to a line was cast off from a whaleboat before being hoisted
on deck.

The Old Man informs me that these West Indian blackfish have been hunted for a century by the New England
whalers that rendezvous at Portsmouth, Dominica, in the
spring of the year. One schooner not long since captured forty
off the coast of the island. Nowadays, the wasteful whalemen
mostly try out only the soft, rich blubber of the melon and the
pan of the jawbones, deriving from two to five gallons of oil
from each animal. Formerly, the sailors used to cut the meat
into strips, salt and dry it, and barter it for fruit and vegetables with the Negroes of Portsmouth.

JULY 23.   More blackfish taken today, so that time is
passing not too slowly. However, we can never come back until after we start, and I am eager to cross the real threshold of
this separation. When we leave the Indies for the cold south, I
shall feel, in a way, homeward bound. My courage will then
strengthen as the days and weeks pass, if only your last letter
assures me that your heart is high.

When the Old Man wants a hand for any task, he calls

sharply from the break of the poop, "Here one!" Three or four of the more quick-witted boys leap toward him, but the first never gets the job unless it is pleasant enough to be in the nature of a privilege. If it is a dull order, he picks the last man to respond; if it is nasty or laborious, he is apt to call by name some member of the watch who has not stepped forward at all. This puts a premium on willingness. The crew has caught on to the idea, with a corresponding step-up in alacrity.

"Scrabble, now; no lolloping," he shouts, after an order. Then, with a grim look which doubtless stands for a twinkle, he is likely to add, "Never chuck anything to windward except ashes and boilin' water."

The Old Man has been watching everybody with the acumen of a judge at a horse show. Two of the Dominican jailbirds are already marked for return to durance vile, a fact suspected by nobody but the skipper and myself. One of these men is a superior fellow, perhaps the smartest in the forecastle. But by that very token he is doomed, for the Old Man, noting the influence he has already gained over the others, has sized him up as a ringleader and a potential focus of any trouble that may arise between forecastle and quarterdeck. Grumbling he doesn't mind, for that is regarded as a normal and proper state during easy periods. "It's when they're quiet you must watch out," says he.

The second man destined to be handed back to the Roseau police is obviously a bad one, an enormous, long-sparred Negro of about twenty years, who has an unduly small head. This fellow is mean, and a bully. The third officer has already taken away from him a concealed, sharp-pointed knife. But he still retained another weapon, of which he was neatly deprived this afternoon by one of his own shipmates. Nobody saw it but I, and nobody knows that I know!

I was reading on the quarterdeck, when "Pinhead," as the cooper calls the big black, strolled across the waist of the

brig toward the scuttle-butt. Just before picking up the copper "thief," and lowering it through the bunghole, he looped
over a belaying pin on the rail a pair of iron knuckle dusters,
which had four knobs on the business side. Then he turned to
drink. At that moment, Roderick, a small, bright, and very
very British Dominican, who had been a tailor's apprentice in
Roseau, chanced to pass the spot. He spied the iron bruisers
on the pin, comprehended the situation, and, without looking
about or changing his pace, he deftly lifted them off and
dropped them overboard.

Pinhead gurgled over his draught and then turned to
gather up his persuaders. A more dumbfounded scoundrel
could not be imagined. Nobody was near him, and I doubt
whether he realized that anyone had passed. His nearest shipmates were two sitting on the carpenter's bench, abaft the
try-works. They had obviously not moved, and I knew that
they had seen nothing. Your poker-faced husband was still absorbed in a book—except for the periphery of his eye. Toward
the bow was a cluster of idlers, with innocent Roderick in the
midst. For a while Pinhead continued a furtive and scowling
search around the stillion in which the water cask stands, and
then gave it up.

Pinhead's problem, however, is lost in a deeper one of my
own. I, personally, saw this man conducted from jail to
whaleboat by a squad of men bearing rifles. Can you tell me
how or where he has since acquired a dirk and iron knuckles?
The answer is "No, sir."

JULY 24, EVENING.   I have been on deck in glorious
moonlight, and am far more lonely than any ordinary night
could make me. The old skipper, too, is desperately homesick.
He hasn't said a word, but has been writing to his own lady-
love, and his malady is as obvious to me as though it were
whooping cough. How many other heartaches does a whaleship house? And who, near and far, white, brown, red, yellow,

or black, may be thinking of one of us this very moment?

For several days we have been seeing hummingbirds flying across the twenty-five-mile strait between Martinique and Dominica, sometimes in the teeth of a strong trade wind. That the tiny beings do this has been a revelation to me. Furthermore, instead of progressing in a beeline, as they appear to in their swift flight ashore, they dip with a rhythmic wave, about once every second, as they cross the wide water from island to island.

It is wonderful, too, to watch the long, narrow, native dugouts traverse this same dangerous expanse. They carry relatively enormous sails, are ballasted with several cobblestones, have only inches of freeboard, and are each manned by three or four Caribs. It gives one an inkling as to what fearless and unsung seagoers have accomplished with primitive gear since the dawn of history. I have been amazed to see such craft racing past us in a rugged sea, the occupants stopping their bailing, if not their balancing, long enough to give us a hail.

The Old Man has been reading my copy of Moseley's record of the great *Challenger* cruise. Because he has visited very many of the islands named, his comments and discussion are exceedingly interesting. I'll start him next on Darwin's voyage, even though he does say Galapáygos in the singular and Galapáygoses in the plural.

It is late (8:04 P.M.), so I must turn in. Quarter past eight has been my most dissipated bedtime hour since coming to sea!

JULY 25.   My Swampscott dory hangs on the starboard side forward, from davits that ordinarily carry a whaleboat. Astern of her is the cutting stage and a removable section of the *Daisy*'s bulwarks, a space always kept clear for the cutting-in of whales. Still farther aft is the starboard whaleboat, the mate's. On the port side three more, the bow boat, waist boat, and larboard boat, are lined up along ninety-odd feet of our length. The fifth is a spare, not now active, and suspended on "tail feathers" athwart the stern. I am sitting in it while I write.

A whaleboat, when ready for service, is a marvel of order and efficiency compacted within thirty feet of length. Constructed of flawless white cedar, seaworthy and graceful, sharp at both stem and stern, it rows lightly and sails like a yacht. It spins smoothly on the sea following the terrific dodges of a harpooned whale, and it withstands the stress of being hoisted by its ends when filled with a crew of six men, and sometimes half full of sea water as well. Within it is a place for every necessary thing, but nothing more. A mast, with sail and spars, lies ready to be stepped. Forward, along the starboard side, are the harpoons, and opposite them the razor-edged lances, all protected by wooden sheaths and cleated one above another in racks. At the bow is a built-in chest containing the brass bomb gun and its charges, and stowed in the stern are the "waifs" or signal flags, and a lantern, matches, flint, and steel, packed in a cask of hard bread. Distributed elsewhere are a keg of fresh water, the boat's compass, a blubber spade, knife and hatchet, grappling iron, line-drogue, paddles, piggins and bailers, and a few other necessities.

The harpoon line, coiled scrupulously in wooden tubs and shielded by tarpaulin covers from moisture that might mildew the manila, is not placed in the boat until just before lowering, when the larger, or two-hundred-fathom tub stows in front of the stroke oar thwart and the smaller amidship. When attached to a harpoon, the line runs first from tub to stern, there passing once and a half around a heavy post, called the loggerhead, from which slack or tension is controlled, and thence forward between alternate oarsmen and out through a notch in the stem, the harponeer standing astride it.

You saw these boats in their static stage, but I have now had my initiation as a crewman, and a lifetime on Long Island Sound has stood me in good stead. Shortly after noon the mastheads announced schools of blackfish and smaller animals, which the Old Man called "cowfish," so I slid down into one of the boats and took number two oar, next to the harponeer. It was rough, with short, choppy waves cutting across a long swell.

It gave me a new point of view to be down on the water amid the quarry. The crests rose high above us, shutting out the other boats from sight except when they mounted simultaneously with ours. We pulled back and forth in pursuit of dark fins that appeared now here, now there, always scooting rapidly. The third officer, steering, urged us on. Blackfish are alleged to be most easily approached and struck in rough weather, but this was certainly not so today. The first mate said afterwards that porpoises stampede, or gally, blackfish just as they do whales.

The porpoises themselves were no less wary. They came along with nearly every roller, half a dozen abreast, their squads reminding me of the deep rows of identical chariot horses in an Egyptian relief. But they always turned down their snouts and vanished before we could intercept or overtake them. Sometimes one would switch sharply and glide for many yards lengthwise of a high wave, just within the crest. From the trough below, we could see the torpedo-like form, with the light of the sky behind, as it shot out of the danger zone and then turned again to resume its course.

By the time the brig was nearly three miles to leeward, we set up the mast, hoisted the lugsail, and soon were cutting the water merrily. Every few seconds we would be caught on the steep front slope of an overtaking swell, to be carried forward at breathless speed for fifty or seventy-five feet, just as swimmers are borne on their surfboards.

Semper paratus is the motto of the whaleman, and no emergency baffles him. A few minutes before we drew alongside the *Daisy*, the tiller of our whaleboat snapped, yet almost before we could luff into the wind our helmsman had unlashed a spare tiller and clapped it into the rudder post.

But I began this entry with a reference to my own special craft, surely the only Swampscott dory that has ever had the honor of going awhaling. Before the hunt began, we swung her on deck where the cooper strengthened her sides with several new stanchions. Then I painted her a dull chrome, ran a black stripe around her upper strake, and applied her name, "Grace Emeline." So I shall often be down on the great waters alone in your namesake, just as you will be alone in my heart, during the long year ahead.

JULY 26.   When we approached the coast of Martinique this afternoon, the *Daisy* sailed through a marvelous display of birds foraging over a shoal of porpoises. Most of them were brown noddies, terns that never plunge into the water but merely stoop toward the surface and, with inconceivably swift coordination, seize in midair the tiny fishes that leap out to escape their submarine enemies. It was a chain of eaters and eaten. The porpoises were after big fish, the latter after little ones, some of which the noddies caught on the bounce. Among them were also twenty-three man-o'-war birds, equally on the lookout for anybody's disadvantage. Thus does a fierce competition in the water and the air above work toward a kind of cooperation. No wonder that sailors imagine a sort of league between porpoises and birds, because they play both ends against the middle. Only the poor fish seems to lack a friend!

The captain's mess is often a reasonably festive board, despite what might euphemistically be called the plainness of the viands. The Old Man, either one or two officers, the cooper, and I make up the first table to be served, together with one or two of the boatsteerers or harponeers in the stead of officers on duty. As soon as we finish, the places are reset for half a dozen more. Finally, the steward, cook, and Johnny regale themselves at the same table. This takes care of all the occupants of after-cabin, main cabin, and steerage. All other members of the crew eat on deck or between decks, carrying their own plates and cups to the galley.

Ever since our table was graced by so elegant a lady as yourself, the manners have maintained a certain uplift. Mr. Vincent, the Malay, who is by far the most sensitive of the officers, seems to have permanently discontinued employment of his knife for conveying food to his mouth. He now handles a fork quite daintily. The skipper's natural habits are, of course, no different from mine, but his example never influenced Mr. Vincent. It took the feminine touch. If you had stayed longer, I would expect finger bowls to be added to the *Daisy*'s expense account.

Johnny served us baked beans and coffee for breakfast today, and clam chowder, macaroni and apple pie for dinner (the noon meal). The clams were canned and the apples desiccated, but the steward had done a good job and both tasted like the fresh product.

"Johnny," I asked, "do macaroni trees flourish in the Cape Verde Islands?"

"Plenty," he responded, with a reminiscent look in his eyes. "Two beeg ones grow by my fader's house."

The Old Man winked at the cooper, but nobody else saw anything out of the way.

By some chance, we fell to talking about ancient surgery in Hawaii and South America, where it is alleged that broken skulls were repaired with pieces of scraped coconut shell or plates of silver. At this, Mr. Alves, a native of Brava, showed us a slightly bulging scar on his bald dome, above the forehead, and stated that the frontal bone had been trephined and a chunk of it replaced by calabash shell. When eight years old, he had fallen off a high wall, knocking a hole through his skull, and a Portuguese surgeon had performed the successful operation.

This mate, about three quarters white, is an unaggressive fellow, old for his years, but he has surely seen most of the watery world and can be cajoled into telling good yarns. In youth he had been on sealing expeditions beyond the Roaring Forties. He is now feeble and has a lame foot, and he needs the moral support of Mr. Vincent or Mr. Almeida to make the crew jump to orders.

Later, Johnny the Romancer, whose tales are never to be doubted, informed me that Mr. Alves is a man of multiple family prowess at Brava. His first wife and her children live in one house, and across the road is the residence of a second attachment, with a brood of younger half brothers and half sisters of the original progeny. Johnny declares that the two households dwell as amicable neighbors and that, when home between voyages, the patriarch divides his attentions with exemplary impartiality. This, at least, is how I translate what Johnny actually told me in verbicide which he believed to be English.

JULY 27. I have broached the delicate subject of the date of our return next spring. The Old Man says that he "hopes" to be back by this time of year, but that he can't make any definite promises, or even plans. It will depend altogether on the catch, winds, etc. I would say that you might come down to meet me, unless I send other word from St. Helena, but I haven't yet any idea what date to name. Moreover, the captain doesn't know whether in the West Indies we shall first touch Barbados or Dominica. I wouldn't want you to be waiting for weeks or months at either. But I shall probably be able to forward directions later, either by a spoken whaler or from some port.

Use reams of carbon paper, and mark your envelopes "Return after four months to Mrs. R. C. M." Send one letter in care of the U. S. Whaling Brig *Daisy*, Jamestown, St. Helena. Send a copy to Tristan da Cunha; it *might* arrive. Address one to South Georgia via Norway and a duplicate via Buenos Aires, because the modern whaling steamers go by both routes. But don't post anything to South Georgia after November. You might wait until the morning after Election Day, and then tell me the first and second in importance of all possible items, namely, that you love me and who is the President of the United States. A letter should be at both Barbados and Dominica by the first of April. Whenever you send off a batch, make them just alike, for I may receive one but shall surely miss the others.

JULY 28. It has been frightfully rough, and very un-Sunday-like, except for plum duff at dinner.

The Old Man discovered a box full of crusts and half loaves and, to the tune of randy, sulphurous, and prolonged expletives, has bounced the steward for wasting flour. He will pay him off and ship him back, third class, from Roseau to New Bedford.

The steward, named Henry Charles Spratt, is a black Dutchman, hailing from the tight little Antillean mountain of St. Eustatius. You will remember him as the peg-leg who hopped in lively fashion around the deck on a turned timber pin which, I suspect, has come down through the generations from Long John Silver himself. While the Old Man was roaring a litany that would put to shame a Cuban stevedore, the steward tried vainly to wedge in an explanation that he had been saving the box of crusts for a bread pudding. Under ordinary circumstances, Spratt is not to be easily out-talked because he can use fluently at least six languages, namely, English, Dutch, French, Spanish, Portuguese, and Papaimento!

Subsequently, the Old Man went after the cook on general principles, in his galley, which stands on the port side of the main deck. While he railed, Cooky chewed his quid and said nothing. Under the blue sky and above the bluer sea, I fancied that a still bluer haze from the skipper's oratory enveloped us for the balance of the day.

JULY 29.   The Old Man has picked a former cabin boy, now in the forecastle, to be steward after our call in port.

It has been squally, with varying trade winds. At four in the afternoon, a rainbow formed, brilliant and low-arched, the most beautiful I have ever seen. It seemed strangely near us, as though one might almost stretch out and touch it, and the ends of the bow had the curious appearance of lying horizontally on the surface of the water. The bow continued, with occasional gaps in its arc, until four minutes after six. During this period it steadily heightened, of course, and at the termination the two pillar-like ends were the last traces.

At five minutes after eight in the evening, the full moon being perhaps 20° above the horizon, a splendid lunar rainbow appeared, its right limb passing through the Great Bear down to the horizon, the left limb incomplete. The Dipper stood upright or "pouring its water," and the arc looped around Merak. It showed no prismatic colors but only a soft, argentine glow—the wraith of a rainbow. It endured for six minutes, the last visible segment being that within the constellation. Would to God I were sharing such visions with you.

The fret is on Mr. Almeida because we are still hanging around bad waters as the crest of the hurricane season approaches. He has lived through one—barely—off these same Antilles, and he keeps mumbling that we should get the hell out of here.

JULY 30.   The time for hearing from you, and then for a long severance, is at hand. Tomorrow we go ashore. It is hard to be writing the last few lines that may come to you for many a month. I'll leave a bottle note at any uninhabited island we touch, and drop others overboard at the Equator and the Tropic of Capricorn. Perhaps one of them will some day come in the mail to our grandchildren!

My friend Correia, the cooper, described for me today the passing of our late second officer, Antão Eneas. I took down his story verbatim.

"About Mr. Eneas, it was like this. The morning of March 29th was clear and calm. We raised a school of sperm whales. Captain Reed ordered three boats lowered down. They were Mr. Alves' and the second and fourth officers'. Mr. Vincent stayed on board.

"Two boats pulled about a mile from the ship, but Mr. Eneas's boat stopped short of a quarter mile off. When the whales came up, all three boats made fast within five minutes. The second officer's whale did not run, but stayed with a pod of others only two hundred yards from the ship. Mr. Eneas was at the bow with his lance. He stood still, waiting for the whales to separate, because they were crowded around him.

"Then the whale his boatsteerer had harpooned came head on for the boat. It struck the bow and lifted it five or six feet high. We saw Mr. Eneas go head down into the water. We saw the flukes of the whale thrashing at the same time and place. The rest of the crew tumbled out of the stern of the boat.

"Then we saw five men in the water hanging onto the boat. We lowered down Mr. Vincent's boat. When we hauled the five men into it, we looked around for Mr. Eneas, but he never showed up. The fourth officer, far away, lanced the whale on his own line, and then came over and picked up the line from the smashed boat and killed Mr. Eneas's whale too. The mate's whale got away. The rest you know."

"So ends" for Mr. Eneas, who was forty-four years old. Some day his wife in Santo Antão may hear of it, if any sailor happens to send whaling gossip home by letter.

And do you think that the report to the consul at Barbados played to the gallery? I give here a full copy of it:

"Antone Enos died at sea on the 29th of March, 1912, on the voyage from New Bedford to Barbados. Sworn to by Edwin J. Reed, Master. Attested by Chester W. Martin, American Consul."

That's my idea of understatement.

All this reminds me that you never saw the shipping papers that have sewn up your husband for durance at the Old Man's pleasure. They state my age, my stature of six feet three inches, my American nationality, and my lay of one two-hundredth. They were attested on June 10 by Mr. Martin and allege that "Robert Cushman Murphy acknowledged that he had read, or had heard read, the said agreement and understood the same, and that, while sober and not in a state of intoxication, he signed it freely and voluntarily for the uses and purposes therein mentioned."

The Consular Service evidently never learned about tautology.

Captain Reed, who had commanded the *Daisy* since she left New Bedford in October 1911, was discharged at the time I signed on. Captain Cleveland seems to feel no great admiration for his predecessor. "Pampers his crew," says he. "He's so soft-hearted he'd ship morphine to the sinners in hell."

JULY 31. The first month is dead and gone. Hereafter, time should fly more swiftly.

Last night broke our record for roughness, but I slept

well, nevertheless. In the small hours of the morning I was on deck awhile and the black crests loomed high overhead when the brig was in the troughs between.

Peg-leg, the departing steward, was ready with his chest when the whaleboat was lowered off Roseau. He took a cheerful leave and is not in the least downcast. The two poor devils who are going back to jail were notified to get their few belongings only after the rest of us were in the boat alongside. If they had any strong sentiments on the matter, they showed none.

Mr. da Lomba has come, a scrawny, raw-boned, energetic, six-foot octoroon, likable at sight. He is another Brava Cape Verder, but an American citizen. He appears to be suffering from several ills to which the flesh is heir, yet he is so full of vim that I could see his personality electrify our whaleboat's crew from the instant he greeted us at the water front. He was enthusiastic about having met you with Mrs. Cleveland on Buzzards Bay, and said, "My God, she swim like a feesh!"

I have read and reread your wonderful letters—all but one marked to be opened after sailing.

It is amazingly hot here on the island, one of the most insufferable spells ever known, according to the Dominicans. The oppressive air suggests a hurricane, and the skipper is feverish to be on the way.

We lunched at "Cherry Lodge," and then I persuaded the American dentist to give me a final picking over.

I have bought a large envelope and am now in the town library winding up. It is all very unreal, dull at the moment and yet also full of hope. I have nothing more to write except that I love you with all my heart. A faint breeze is beginning to move in from sea, and I can see the *Daisy*—my only home until we meet again—in a rainstorm off the coast.

The time has come for joining the skipper. Farewell!

Weary with toil, I haste me to my bed,
The dear repose for limbs with travel tired:
But then begins a journey in my head
To work my mind, when body's work's expir'd:
For then my thoughts—from far where I abide—
Intend a zealous pilgrimage to thee,
And keep my drooping eyelids open wide,
Looking on darkness which the blind do see;
Save that my soul's imaginary sight
Presents thy shadow to my sightless view,
Which, like a jewel hung in ghastly night
Makes black night beauteous and her old face new.
  Lo! thus, by day my limbs, by night my mind,
  For thee, and for myself no quiet find.
       W. S., SONNET XXVII

AUGUST 1. I had to hurry my final words without half adequate expression, and I obtained your second packet of letters only after we were under way. It had been in Mr. da Lomba's chest. Nevertheless, I had some sleep in the latter half of the night, and my earlier wakefulness was more triumphant than sad. If all goes well, the separation will become something for us to remember happily all the days of our life.

We took our departure from Roseau just before nightfall last evening, with a light fair wind. During the darkness we left Guadeloupe astern, and today we have had a fine breeze as we cruised by Montserrat, the Rock of Redonda, Nevis, and one of the long low extremities of St. Kitts. Now, at sunset, St. Eustatius lies dead ahead and more distant Saba off the lee bow.

Can a single incident of our weeks together in the Antilles ever fade from memory? The *Daisy*, on her northward course, will soon be abreast of St. Thomas, where we waked up in the harbor of Charlotte Amalie on the last day of May and, through the porthole of the *Guayana*, watched the sun rising over our first tropical island. And then our walk along the white ribbon of road by the sea, in an aisle of coco-nut palms, to the limestone cottage of the colored woman—she of the flaming headdress—who muttered "Pretty faces," and asked whether you were my wife or my sweetheart!

And St. Croix, with its cane fields, ripe mangoes, and giant silk-cotton trees, and the lizards we caught with grass nooses. And little Montserrat, where we climbed the cone and met the girl who curtsied and ceremoniously presented you with a lime, while kestrels were hovering all about to pick up grasshoppers from the flowery fields. And Antigua, where we learned to mix cocktails with a swizzle-stick, and heard the Negroes shout the "grey gaulin" song. And the French islands, where Louis Napoleon whiskers on black boatmen, who shrugged their shoulders and gesticulated, gave proper ambiance for the birthplace of Josephine. And St. Lucia, where we were driven grandly in a landau, up and down and down and up, to the base of the Pitons. And the crowds and the stone windmills of Barbados, the inky John Bulls who asked at the careenage "Do you require a cab, sir?", the hospitality and the delectable flying fish at every meal—until they ceased to seem delectable, the velvet swims (but watch out for sea urchins!), the bats I added to my collection merely by whizzing a horse-whip through the twilight air, and the grassquits that flew in through the windows to eat the butter and sugar off our dishes!

And, best of all, Dominica. The Little Africa of Ports-mouth; the "hotel" with mahogany four-posters, magnificent chests and highboys, but very little to eat; the tarantulas on the counterpane and geckoes on the ceiling; the Tantalus-tempting cannon of iron and bronze, lying higgledy piggledy and forgotten at tideline below the ancient French fort; the respectful, so British Negroes who were concerned for my health or life whenever I stepped into the open air, day or night, without a helmet on my well-thatched noddle; the church in which the sexton of stentorian voice assured us that "the bat, the owl, and other insects" dwelt in the belfry; our river picnic, under an arbor of the Green Mansions, in a Thames wherry with the port captain, his sister just back from five years in a Paris convent, and their uniformed oarsmen of the same dark complexion as themselves; our rides on tough little steeds into the luxuriant, showery hills, where the honeycreepers lisped and the *siffleur de montagne* sang for us; the fricassees of "mountain chickens," which turned out to be huge frogs, but none the less palatable. And the glorious June evenings, when we dangled our feet from the pier while the gentle land wind fanned us, and turned our gaze from Spica to Altair to Arcturus to blue Vega and then, always, to the Southern Cross.

This night, as we pass and smell the romantic chain of black shadows, it all goes chasing and tumbling through my keyed-up brain, like the patterns of a kaleidoscope.

AUGUST 2.   The night has carried us past St. Bartholomew, St. Martin, Anguilla, and Seal Rocks, where the exterminated West Indian seals used to swarm in myriads. Now, in the forenoon, Sombrero, low and flat but with a tall lighthouse, stands on the starboard beam as the northeastern signpost of the Antilles. It is the last spot of land we shall sight for many and many a day.

I finished work on my blackfish skulls and packed them away in a cask. We put up a tringle and strung curtains in front of my couch, which now makes a compartment like a Pullman berth, though little more than half as wide.

Bound for the icy south, it seems strange to be actually headed toward home and you. But, for a windjammer, the shortcut is the long way 'round. The *Daisy* must sail well up into the withdrawn northeast trades of the summer season before she can make the easting needed to carry her past Cape São Roque, Brazil, against the equatorial current and the steady southeast trade winds of the other hemisphere.

2 Sargasso

AUGUST 3.   Ocean, and nothing else. We are still on our first tack, moving sweetly over the smooth Atlantic. It is uncomfortably warm below, but on deck the breeze is sufficient to temper the curse, even in the full blast of the sun.

Do you remember how thrilled we were when we learned that the *Daisy*, now of New Bedford registry, was built next door to my home on Long Island? I have been gleaning her history from Captain Cleveland and his *List of Merchant Vessels of the United States.*

From Old Man's Harbor, where I grew up, to Drowned Meadow—port of John Paul Jones—is two-and-a-half miles, and from Drowned Meadow to Setauket is but two more. At Setauket Harbor *Daisy* was launched in October 1872. Nehemiah Hand, with whose descendants—grandchildren, perhaps —I used to play, was her builder. She was the twenty-sixth and the seventh from the largest, of the thirty-three staunch wooden hulls that came off his ways between 1836 and 1882.

Technically the *Daisy* is a half-brig, of 384 gross tons, 123-

foot overall length, two-decked, framed with oak and chest-
nut, planked with yellow pine, and copper-fastened. Original-
ly, she was one of fifty or more sail that carried the house flag
of William H. Swan and Sons, a firm which still operates a
ship chandlery in New York and Norfolk. Her first master was
Captain Ozias McCarty and, in the golden days of sail, her
strength, capacity, speed and ease of handling made her a
highly profitable merchantman. Captain Edward L. McCarty,
who succeeded his brother as skipper, died aboard her off the
coast of Brazil, when he and most of his crew were stricken by
the "swellings" (beriberi).

I am awed when I tramp the deck and consider the harbors that have seen my brig in merchant service. She has received or discharged cargo, for example, throughout the Atlantic world, from ports of the Baltic and Mediterranean to
most of those in America between Boston and Buenos Aires.
Good stock sailed in her during the seventies, eighties and
nineties, and lifelong friendships were established on her
cruises. More than once, though, men died aboard of the
"Barbados distemper" (yellow fever) after she had sailed from
the tropics.

In 1907, the *Daisy* was bought by a New Bedford group,
in which Captain Cleveland is principal owner. She was then
refitted as a whaler, with accommodations for a crew four or
five times as large as that of a merchant vessel of her tonnage,
and the Old Man has taken her on several voyages in the
southern oceans, including expeditions for sea elephant oil to
Kerguelen Island and South Georgia.

As a whaler, the *Daisy* is a property of thirty-two shares,
all held in Massachusetts. Captain and Mrs. Cleveland together control nearly one third of the whole, nobody else own-
ing more than one sixteenth. When the brig was last registered, on May 12, 1908, the holdings were as follows: Benjamin D. Cleveland nine thirty-seconds, Emma A. Cleveland

one thirty-second, Henry P. Burt two thirty-seconds, John V. Spare two thirty-seconds, Frank B. Sistare, Trustee one thirty-second, James A. Tilton two thirty-seconds, Irving L. Wordell one thirty-second, Henry L. Tiffany and William F. Read one thirty-second, William N. Church two thirty-seconds, all of New Bedford; Charles P. Maxfield two thirty-seconds, Henry B. Gifford two thirty-seconds, D. C. Potter two thirty-seconds, William M. Allen one thirty-second, Henry H. Allen one thirty-second, all of Fairhaven; Arline F. Collins two thirty-seconds, James T. Smith one thirty-second, both of Dartmouth. Sea captains, a school teacher, a carpenter, a seedsman, manufacturers, and tradesmen are represented among these owners.

The *Daisy* was last surveyed and dry-docked in November, 1903, and God alone knows whether she is now insurable. But, let it be a comfort to you that my own life insurance examiners regard me as a better risk here at sea than for the same year of exposure to microbes and accidents in the quiet environment of New York! Furthermore, to hear the Old Man talk, you would conclude that a whaleship is the only safe spot in a parlous world.

"*Daisy*'s as sound a craft as ever slid off the ways," says he. "Whaleships always come home—that is, nearly always. 'Course, the *Canton* was lost at age seventy-five—beginning to get old, maybe. But the *Maria* rounded out ninety years of cruising. *Daisy*'s only a youngster," etc., etc.

AUGUST 4. Latitude at noon, 21° 56' N., away up east of the southern Bahamas.

At half past three o'clock this morning I was awakened by a hullabaloo on deck, and got up in time to see the capture of a shark that had taken the buckskin bait of a troll line. The third mate, on watch, landed it. After daylight, Mr. da Lomba took out the spine and drove a wire rod through it so that he might make a white walking stick at his leisure. He also excised and dried the soft limy otoliths from the fish's inner ears, telling me in a roundabout way that these are crushed in salt water and drunk as a diuretic. Old Doctors Gray and Grindle are far, far away, and since the personal plumbing systems of many of the lads are in anything but A1 condition, I suppose the mate and the Old Man will have to function as the best available doctors, even if not the best doctors! The tout of the ship supply firm at Barbados summed up the matter this way:

> Our Jolly salts have sorry faults
> Concealed beneath their breeches.
> They bring disease from overseas,
> The scurvy sons-of-bitches!

After considerable persuasion on my part, a large chunk of white meat from the shark's back was forthcoming at dinner, more or less in the style of creamed codfish without the cream. It was excellent, and one or two officers at the captain's mess were served twice, but the men forward wouldn't look at it. We also had chowder, "salt horse," boiled yam and cabbage, fresh biscuit and "ladies' butter," which is the Old Man's half-contemptuous term for Danish butter out of a tin —provided especially for you and Mrs. Cleveland. Such other butter as we see is fished in amorphous gobbets from a barrel of brine. Incidentally, I fetched up half a fruit cake from your trunk of supplies, so our meal was altogether in the nature of an orgy.

AUGUST 5.   A finback whale, a kind politely ignored by Yankee whalemen because nothing can be done about it, was reported by the mastheads just before noon. We are now passing through scattered rafts of orange sargasso weed.

In the afternoon watch the Old Man gave the order to "break out slops." Now this word is neither slang nor vulgar; it is good Shakespearean English, meaning clothing, and its use illustrates the conservatism of sea parlance. The process involved unheading casks in the capacious half deck and sending up blankets, coats, overalls, oilskins, caps, boots, brogues, underwear (to be worn later), and thread and needles, for the tattered crew. There was also a sheath knife apiece, with the point broken or ground off square, according to regulation. The hint is that knives are strictly tools, not weapons. Before evening our boys looked like a new outfit, in their whole and fairly uniform garb. It was my job to make out their debit accounts, against a lay which is still mostly problematical.

A whaleship differs from any other kind of warehouse in that most of its stores come out of, as well as go into, casks. Not only slops, but also spare sails and rigging, flour, salt beef and hard bread, beans and tobacco, are all headed up in casks of various sizes that cram the greater part of the hold. Those that would otherwise be empty are filled with fresh water, which keeps them tight and sound and maintains the vessel in ballast trim. The water may be pumped overboard when space is required for oil. The Old Man was once officer in a ship when most of its water had been used up, toward the end of a good, greasy voyage. All hands were put on short rations, and the "thief" was hung at the mainmasthead. Everyone whose thirst demanded a sip had to go up and get it, and then return it to its high place before the next man could climb, come down, wet his whistle, and clamber up and down yet again.

Our hold, with its dim light and mouldy smell, might pass for the cellar of an age-old brewery. Some of the casks, which are the special charge of my friend, the cooper, have a capacity of fourteen barrels. These are mingled with smaller casks, and the narrowest interstices contain very slender oaken pipes called "wryers." They are all chocked snugly with cordwood dunnage, and they are inspected frequently for displacements or leaks, the men peering about with open whale-oil lamps or with candles on prickets that can be jabbed into the timbers when both hands are needed. The flames emit more smoke than illumination. Besides the finished casks, there are plenty of shooks and hoops from which the cooper can fabricate more.

AUGUST 6.   Exceedingly hot. There is no visible life in or above the quiet, warm, glaring water except that inhabiting the flecks of sargasso weed. But we are still moving north. Oh for a tiny, private corner in one's world!

AUGUST 7.   At three o'clock this afternoon we went over on the port tack for the first time since our departure, and now, just when we were almost out of the tropics, we are bearing away from you again, a point to the south of east. We are sailing, however, toward an Arc de Triomphe such as Paris never knew—the biggest and most gorgeous rainbow I have seen yet.

After supper and sunset, which came together, an indescribable panoply of color filled the western sky, a blazing afterglow above which carmine, orange, yellow, lavender, blue, green, and purple bands reached almost to the zenith. The darkening east was no less beautiful than the fading west. I sat on deck until the stars came out.

About eight o'clock we ran into showers, precursors of a rainy night. The wind veered, so we came about and again are northbound.

AUGUST 8.   Latitude 26° 54' N., about off Palm Beach, but what a way off! We are slightly east of the longitude of Bermuda, skirting the western edge of the Sargasso Sea, and it has been a sperm whale day!

Blackfish are all very well, in their trifling way, but nobody any longer gets excited about them. Today I have learned the difference. The mastheads don't shout "Thar she blows!" as the books tell us. No, for spermaceti they go plum crazy, and sing at the top of their lungs.

It was overcast and cool this morning, with a fresh

breeze until noon. About nine o'clock I was startled by a strange, wavering falsetto solo from aloft.

"*Blo-o-o-o-o-o-o-ws!*" It held the note for several seconds, pouring and climbing from the throat of the boatsteerer who had first raised the whale. "*Blo-o-o-o-o-o-o-o-ws! White water! Ah, blo-o-o-o-o-o-o-o-ws!*" with all four mastheads now screeching. The men on deck began to give a sympathetic response to the cry, and the watch below came scrambling from the forecastle, pulling on breeches and carrying footgear. Undertone *blo-o-o-ws* echoed the songs from above until the whole crew sounded and acted like a chorus gone mad.

It wasn't necessary to ask where the whales lay, because a glance upward showed heads and field glasses craned all in one direction. The Old Man took in vain the names of the two members of the Trinity with whom a Yankee seems to be on speaking terms, and snapped a few further well-punctuated orders to the man at the wheel while he picked up his own binoculars and clambered aloft. I presently followed him, when all but one of the mastheads had come down to join their boats' crews. Each boatsteerer looked to his own whaleboat. Line tubs were uncovered and lifted in, the gripes cast off, the harpoons and lances unsheathed, and everything else made ready.

We drew up slowly toward what proved to be a school of young sperm whales, lying to leeward, blowing and splashing at the surface. I could see the slow, forward-slanting spouts that distinguish sperm whales from all others. Presently they went down, and for ten minutes or so everything was silent except for the Old Man's softly echoed orders about course and sails. Then subdued "*bl-o-o-o-ws!*" rang out again, as the whales reappeared about a mile and a half ahead. The falls were cast off, the cranes swung in, and, at the word of command, the four boats were lowered almost silently to the water, with boatsteerer and boatheader at bow and stern.

The four other men then descended, by way of slide boards and tackles, and each took his own thwart, with the boat-steerer or harponeer at the bow oar. A few strokes put the little craft safely away from the brig, which by this time was idling, square sails aback. Then the masts were stepped, sails hoisted, and our fleet of four boats was soon in full pursuit.

With twenty-four men down, only ten were left on board and three of these were aloft. Six shiptenders on deck, how-ever, were almost equal to the full complement of the *Daisy* during her years as a merchant vessel. She was brought once more into the wind, and we slowly trailed the boats. But the Old Man was growing more disgusted by the minute, first at the small size of the whales, which all appeared to be calves, and second because several killer whales, the back fins of which stood high, were following, worrying, and even jumping over the sperm whales that were most distant.

Over and over again, I saw Mr. da Lomba's boat sail on a pod of calves, only to have them sound just out of darting range. Mr. Alves' boat finally got fast. Its sail and mast came down, harponeer and mate changed ends, the boys hauled up, and, with scarcely a struggle worth mentioning, a bull calf was lanced. A yellow waif on a staff was thrust into its eye, the harpoon line cut, and the boat rejoined the chase. By this time the pod was well gallied, doubtless by the killer whales. The Old Man, muttering somewhat incoherently though still profanely, hoisted a signal flag that recalled all the boats.

The waif, the original meaning of which is "something flapping," marked our lone catch, a six-barrel critter not more than twenty-five feet long. We picked it up and began to cut-in before dinner. Its total value may be $96, which will make your plutocratic spouse 48¢ richer.

This minnow of a whale didn't seem to rate a chanty, and the windlass that hoisted the blubber was worked in silence, save for its own creaking. During the cutting-in, a shark, accompanied by a pilot fish, swam around and around the vessel. The small, banded pilot never left its big companion for many seconds. Occasionally, it would dart aside for a morsel of food, but would then hasten on like a child afraid of losing his nurse. Its favorite position was close alongside the shark's dorsal fin, but sometimes it swam beneath its "protector." Just as a large piece of blubber was being cut away, the shark rushed up, pushed its head above water and buried its teeth in the luscious fat. The officers on the cutting stage paid no attention to it. Many large squids drifted out of the whale's gullet to float away, and the amount of blood let into the water was tremendous.

I made some photographs of the process, which I shall describe when we take a man's-size whale, and I developed plates in the evening, getting to bed at the unprecedented hour of half past ten.

AUGUST 9.   Sperm whale cakes for breakfast, and they were decidedly on the edible side, perhaps because we have tasted little fresh meat for six weeks.

The boats pursued a lone whale, this time under the power of oars in the glassy calm. At long range in the stillness, I could hear the boatheaders getting the utmost out of their men by a quaint mixture of flattery and imprecations (the Old Man doesn't count profanity in the whaleboats). The officers wielded their twenty-three foot steering oars, and the quintets of boys doubled themselves to a long, whippy stroke in a regatta of four craft, but they never came within half a mile of their quarry.

We boiled blubber most of the day, being short-handed for several hours while the boats were down. The brig appeared not to move an inch in the broiling calm. Sea bugs, of a group which comprises the only oceanic insects, skated alongside, and triggerfish came up out of the depths and pirouetted along the *Daisy's* bilge. Some of them were accompanied by very tiny clinging remoras or suckerfish, and I wasted time trying to catch the bigger fish for the sake of their leech-like companions, which may be an unknown species.

Sperm whale meat for supper, which somehow turns my thoughts toward chops, baked potato, onions, and other things we don't have here, including a bucket of spring water.

AUGUST 10.   Sunrises, sunsets, rainbows both matutinal and vesperal, and nights crystal and starry enough to make one gasp, leave nothing to be desired in the way of a spectacular setting here where I am. But the ship does not move. As a change from reading, I have just opened a bottle of figs. Still calm and hot. Here we lie, after the moil of the cutting-in, with limp and slatting sails, approximately where we were two days ago.

This morning a shark, accompanied by a single large pilot fish, paid us a visit. We lured the pilot to a hook and have since sucked its bones at the captain's mess. No fish ever tasted better. Man has to live on ship's fare for only a few weeks really to learn what a predatory animal he is, and how deeply he craves the flesh of freshly killed fellow creatures. While five of us lingered over our small but toothsome portions, Mr. da Lomba told of better luck on a former voyage. He had driven a harpoon, said he, clean through a shark from deck. Then, tying the line short, he had left his victim struggling on the toggled iron at the surface while he hooked, one after another, the eight pilot fish that had been accompanying it.

Evening began with heavy rain and as it pattered on the deck above my drowsy head, I thought of a secret which old Tibullus told me when I was a sophomore. About the same date, I communicated it to you, but it was still three years before we learned its full significance. Do you remember?

Quam iuvat immites ventos audire cubantem
et dominam tenero continuisse sinu
aut, gelidas hibernus aquas cum fuderit Auster,
securum somnos imbre iuvante sequi!

However, instead of actually following "the road of un-troubled sleep, the rain my lullaby," I lay in my bunk only until the mainsail had been well washed, then slipped above in the watery air and caught a basinful of cool rainwater, which quenched a nine-days' thirst as nothing else could have done.

AUGUST 11. No change. We lie like "a painted ship upon a painted ocean."

We caught several triggerfish, which our sailors call leatherjackets because of their thick, tough hides. It surprises me to find them at the surface over a depth of two thousand fathoms, and far from reef or shoal. Some of them were a foot long and meaty, but I have seen no more of the elusive little remoras which were so intriguing.

AUGUST 12. A tiny breath of air—hardly a breeze, but we have gained enough headway to cross the Tropic of Cancer into the North Temperate Zone.

At last I am beginning to be familiar with the composition of our crew, because in this latitude and longitude we are proof against either desertions or recruits!

The Old Man was surely kept hopping over desertion documents while the brig lay at Dominica. Several papers, sworn to before H. A. Frampton, United States Consular Agent at Roseau, attest that James Alick (boatsteerer), Pedro Batista, Leviro Andrade, Elias da Luz, José Lomba, Julio Correia, Manoel Merães, João Rosa, Manoel Andrade, Francisco Gomes, and Henrique Barros "absconded from the said ship Daisy, on or about July 1-3, 1912, at the ports or places named, without my knowledge or consent, Benjamin D. Cleveland, Master."

Some of these men were among those subsequently apprehended and returned, but two or three of them deserted yet again, with or without the connivance of the captain. I haven't quite straightened out just who is still aboard and who is gone for keeps.

The names may or may not be correct; no Yankee whaling officer ever spells a Portuguese name twice in the same way. First names, especially, in the ship's log and other papers show a bewildering variety, being different each time a new entry is made.

Anyway, the ranks that had been thinned both at Barbados and Dominica were reinforced by the following eleven black British subjects, one black French citizen (Jean-Baptiste) of Martinique, and one Cape Verder (Gaspar):

	Age	*Height*	*Lay*
Conrad S. Peter	17	5'10"	1/185
Stephen Ismael	20	6'01"	1/185
Gifford Paul	21	6'00"	1/185
Roderick H. Charles	22	5'06"	1/185
William Stephens	21	5'06"	1/185
John Paul	18	5'04"	1/185
Edward Bazzie	22	5'09"	1/185
Elise St. Rose	21	5'07"	1/185
Joseph Jimmot	21	5'11"	1/185
Feddy Lundy	21	5'07"	1/185
Edward Evelyn	25	5'08"	1/180
Attenaze Jean-Baptiste	29	6'00"	1/185
José Gaspar	30	5'10"	1/100

Evelyn had been to sea in a schooner, and he struck for a slightly higher lay than that of the green hands. Gaspar had papers proving whaling experience, and he was shipped with the rank and lay of a new boatsteerer.

"William Stephens" in the list above is elsewhere recorded as William Elwin.

Now, to go back to the beginning of the voyage: The following twenty-seven men, in addition to Captain Reed, were listed as crew when the *Daisy* sailed from New Bedford on or about October 31, 1911, for the first part of her whaling cruise. These names also, both first and last, have been badly scrambled in the records, and some of them have become "Americanized." I spell them here in what my friend the cooper tells me is the proper manner. The lays are not given in the list I have seen.

	Birthplace	Age	Height
João Alves, 1st mate	Brava	53	5'06"
Antão Eneas, 2nd mate	Santo Antão	43	5'09"
Vicente Lunda, 3rd mate	Manila	29	5'08"
João C. Almeida, 4th mate	Cape Verde Is.	28	5'07"
Vitor Ribeiro, boatsteerer	Brava	25	5'11"
James H. Alick, boatsteerer	Bermuda	38	5'09"
Emiliano F. Ramos, boatsteerer	São Nicolau	22	5'08"
Antão Neves, boatsteerer	Cape Verde Is.	23	5'11"
José G. Correia, cooper	Azores	29	5'07"
Henry C. Spratt, steward	St. Eustatius	39	5'03"
José Almeida, cook	São Nicolau	28	5'07"
João Rosa, "boy," later steward	Cape Verde Is.	22	5'06"
João Pires, cabin boy	Brava	22	5'03"
Francisco da Cruz	São Nicolau	24	5'09"
Manoel G. Andrade	Cape Verde Is.	24	5'10"
José da Lomba	Cape Verde Is.	21	5'08"
Pedro Batista	Cape Verde Is.	22	5'09"
Francisco Gomes	Cape Verde Is.	23	5'10"
Antão Dias	Cape Verde Is.	26	5'10"
João Delgado	Cape Verde Is.	19	5'05"
Julio Correia	Cape Verde Is.	23	6'00"
Elias da Luz	Cape Verde Is.	26	5'07"
Leviro Andrade	Cape Verde Is.	21	5'07"
Henrique Barros	Cape Verde Is.	22	5'06"
Manoel M. Merães	Cape Verde Is.	25	5'11"
José Fonseca	Cape Verde Is.	24	5'07"
Antão Lopez	Cape Verde Is.	22	5'10"

An additional boatsteerer, named Francisco Nicolau, was

picked up somewhere after the brig left New Bedford. He, together with Captain Cleveland, Mr. da Lomba and me, swell
the total list to forty-four men. One of these, Mr. Eneas, was
the mate killed by a whale last March. Since all hands now
number thirty-four, the remaining shortage of nine represents
the net loss from desertions and discharges. Some of the latest French leaves are not yet accounted for on the books, and
must be sworn to at our next port of call.

Among our entire crew of thirty-four, there are only three
Caucasians, namely, the skipper, the cooper, and I. The
cooper, Jose Gonçalves Correia, is old-stock Portuguese
from the island of Fayal, Azores. Mr. Vincent is a Filipino and
all the others are blackamoors of various dilutions. Mr. Alves,
Mr. da Lomba, one boatsteerer, and several boys in the forecastle are so nearly white that their complexions are described in the shipping papers by the euphemistic term
"light." Thus we are all recorded under three categories—
white, light, or black! Mr. Vincent, the Malay, is grouped with
the lights. Only a light can be successfully tattooed.

"Book names" are one thing, and names as they sound in
speech or appear in the *Daisy*'s log entries are quite another.
Thus our top boatsteerer, Vitor Ribeiro, is actually known as
Victor Robinson. He now ranks as fourth officer and boatheader, but when only three whaleboats are lowered he is still
to serve as harponeer for Mr. Vincent.

João Pirez, the cabin boy, is known to everybody as
Johnny Perry. (There are more "Perrys" than Smiths in the
New Bedford City directory, and they're mostly Portuguese.)
The sailor named Antão Dias is never called anything but
Ferleão. None of the Portuguese can tell me what this
nickname means.

AUGUST 13. During the night a gentle, blessed wind
arose and it has lasted all day. We have been moving at
a fair pace toward Bermuda, near which the Old Man ex-

pects to pick up the variables that will give us our easting.

For a long while I scooped up bits of the bladder-floated gulf weed with a dipnet, in order to sort and pickle samples of the animal life that dwells in these drifting gardens. There is probably not much still to be learned about its composition because the creatures have been collected thousands of times and they always turn out to be the same lot. Nevertheless, to me they have hitherto been only names and pictures, so I gathered up a concentrated aquarium of the weed and its inhabitants in a big enameled tray and then went to work on 'em.

There were fifteen or more kinds of tiny animals living in the floating orange forests, of which one was a sea-slug, one a worm, one a hydroid, one a fish, and four or more crustaceans. Of the latter, two were diminutive crabs and two long-whiskered prawns. You don't see them until you poke around, because they all look like part of the vegetation. It is astonishing, for example, to shake an unearthly little fish, the size of your thumb, from an empty sprig of weed that you have already been examining for several minutes.

I found two of these mousefish or sargasso fish, strange little composites of mouth, belly, and excrescences. They are painted with facsimiles, and fringed and pimpled with reproductions, of various parts of the weed. Two tasseled fish poles on the head are probably used as bait to lure prey toward the gulping mouth. They have both arm fins (the pectorals) and foot fins (the pelvics), and the latter stick forward under the belly like spread feet perpetually ready to hit bottom. The arm fins work like hands, bending at a wrist and folding ten long finger rays around anything of which they wish to lay hold. As they clamber around in a clump of sargasso weed, like lizards in a thicket, it is no wonder that they are difficult to see because the pattern of brown, orange, gold, and white resembles both the vegetation and its other animal inhabitants and, moreover, the fish can change the basic hue of the skin to match the general tone of the background and can even imitate the detailed pattern of the weed.

Our late lamented steward is getting his revenge on the Old Man by having failed to report that the tea and the saleratus were both at the point of giving out. Now the rumor is that we shall get along without either until we touch at the Brazilian convict island of Fernando Noronha. However, that's a place at which I have always hoped for a short sentence!

At five in the afternoon, a single large sperm whale was sighted close aboard, off the lee bow. Four boats were lowered, but the whale had already been going rapidly to windward and he soon hurried faster than ever, remaining at the surface and spouting often. During a violent thundersquall the boats lost him altogether.

The Old Man tells me that such single whales are nearly always old bulls, and that once, in the Japan Sea, he captured one that yielded 130 barrels of oil. That is almost fabulously large. Even the hundred-barrel sperm is an exceedingly rare fish. Mixed groups of sperm whales, numbering fifty or more, are the way the skipper likes to find them. Then, unless they become gallied, they rarely swim at a faster clip than four or five knots and the boats can cut out the large animals from among the lesser.

AUGUST 14.   We are moving northward at a snail's pace, and there is not enough to do. I read by the hour on such a day as this, but there is an end even to reading. I have finished Moseley's narrative of the *Challenger* voyage and now I have traveled far with Darwin in the *Beagle*. Aside from being delightful, both of these books play right into my hands when it comes to getting the most out of this cruise.

But a Yankee whaler offers peculiar opportunities for boredom and dissatisfaction during the long periods in which no game is sighted, because she is a hopelessly over-manned craft—except when taking and cutting-in whales. The Old Man and his officers simply can't think up enough jobs on board to keep our big crew sufficiently occupied for everybody's peace of mind.

I tried hard today to capture one of several beautiful dolphins, with blue-and-silver bodies and yellow tails, which played in the shadows under our counter. They proved very deft, however, in removing bait from a hook, and only nibbled at the latter instead of approaching with the brave rush with which they tackle a flying fish.

In the light of the new crescent moon this evening, I sat on deck and wangled Mr. Vincent into talking about life in the Philippine Islands under the old Spanish régime.

AUGUST 15.

> To-morrow, and to-morrow, and to-morrow,
> Creeps in this petty pace from day to day,
> To the last syllable of recorded time.

The joint sentiments of Mr. Shakespeare and your husband. During the past twenty-four hours we have gained but four miles of northing, resulting in a net loss because in the same period we drifted twelve miles westward. This afternoon, however, a slight breeze has sprung up.

I take the slow drag as philosophically as I can, trying to recall that there are only 7,000 hours, more or less, still to go! A little plot of ground where I might run a hundred yards, perchance to a spring of fresh water, would help. But best of all would be a room where I could shut a door, if only for an hour. You haven't an idea, until you go to sea, how strange it is to be imprisoned within a space 30 by 125 feet with thirty-three other men, mostly black, and to have to share even your cabin with the presence of one man and the sight of several others. However, all the disadvantages I suffer apply equally to the Old Man. In fact, it is I who am in *his* cabin.

Tonight there is a fine, cool breeze; it feels as chilly as

Long Island Sound. If it only holds out, we shall soon reach the northernmost point of departure of our southward (!) journey.

AUGUST 16.   Today we sighted a sperm whale afar, but did not lower. A tired semipalmated sandpiper, migrating southward, flew around and around the *Daisy*, finally mounting higher than the trucks, and then headed toward the West Indies. The foremast hands informed me that several other birds of the same kind had been resting on the bowsprit during morning. The position is lat. 31° 22' N., long. 60° 14' W., nearly three hundred miles east by south of Bermuda. If the bird was on a normal course, its direct migration path would take it from Nova Scotia to the Lesser Antilles, and it had covered just about half the distance. However, I have already observed that these small shore birds are quite capable of resting on a calm ocean surface and of taking off again.

AUGUST 17.   The "wind of the western sea" brings rain with it now, and at last we are making easting before it.

Several members of the crew became involved in a shindy on the forward deck. My heart skipped a beat when I saw our Martinican sailor, who had another man by the throat, grimly reach for his sheath knife and hold it close to his adversary's jugular vein. These two were separated by Mr. Almeida who, as third officer, is the chief strong-arm reliance of law and order. Four other fellows, however, continued to maul and slug one another indiscriminately, even after the Old Man himself bawled at them to desist. The second and third mates, Vincent and Almeida, each of whom is huskier than any man in the forecastle, together pulled this knot apart and, incidentally, knocked out one boy with a purler that banged his head against the carpenter's bench.

The Old Man, in vile dudgeon, then held court in the rain and dressed the bedraggled culprits down, ending with dire threats about the penalty if this sort of thing should ever happen again. Then he had the knife-puller handcuffed and put down in the stuffy lazaret on the afterdeck, with the hatch clamped on above him. Orders are that he is to be left strictly alone, to think matters over, until sunrise tomorrow.

Such a quasi-murderous brawl is, of course, the result of ennui and of lack of adequate employment. Everything on board this craft has been scrubbed, scoured, painted, slushed, polished, served, thrapped, tautened, or replaced, as the case may be; oakum has been picked, seams tarred, and countless unnecessary or trumped-up tasks performed. Even so, and despite the fact that four men are always busy at the mastheads, one at the wheel, and six or eight are sleeping out their off-watch, there are still too many on deck with leisure to think of their miseries and grievances.

A more sympathetic, or even a more whimsical, captain, and a more intelligent and imaginative set of officers, could doubtless accomplish something toward bettering the morale. I suspect, however, that the reform would have to start far back, because the general living conditions, as regards quarters, food, recognition of service, and hope of a reasonable reward, are about as poor as anything I would care to think about.

It is too early, of course, to figure out how much cash the half-shanghaied wretches will have at the end of the voyage. However, if we should take $40,000 worth of sperm and sea elephant oil, the second mate's share would theoretically amount to slightly more than $1,300, and that of a green forecastle hand to something like $250. But in each case, advances, slops, tobacco, and other supplies would be deducted. I should really hate to be present at the actual pay-off in New Bedford next summer!

In the old days, when horsewhips and corsets were still end-products of a great industry based upon whalebone, the prospects were much better. The same was true when sperm oil and spermaceti were worth twice or thrice what they are today. And yet, even then, the traditional regime of most whalemen before the mast was to be richer at the end of a voyage chiefly in experience. Those with sufficient character became successively boatsteerers, officers, and masters, perhaps ending up where Captain Cleveland is now—principal owner of two whaleships, lord of a tight little mansion on Pleasant Street, and doubtless possessed of much more pelf than will ever stand to the credit of a museum biologist!

The business principles of Yankee whaling offer one of the earliest and most persistent examples of industrial cooperation, even though they have now fallen upon degenerate days. Every ship is stocked and equipped by the owners, and the profits of the cruise are distributed in the ratio of two thirds to the capital invested and one third to labor (that's where the Old Man gets his cut from each side!). No member of the crew receives wages or a guaranty of any sort, but to each is allotted a lay of the net proceeds. In general, the captain's lay ranges between a fifteenth and an eighth, according to his whaling record. The mate and three lower officers, the four boatsteerers, the cooper, steward, cook, carpenter (we have no carpenter on the *Daisy*), experienced seamen, and green hands receive proportionate lesser shares, down to the "long lay" of the cabin boy (and of your adoring husband), which is in the neighborhood of one two-hundredth.

Thus the profit of each individual depends upon the success of the cruise. Ships have sometimes failed to pay for their fitting out. On the other hand, the *Onward* of New Bedford, once returned with a catch of oil and bone worth at prevailing prices $395,000 of which the master's lay was $40,000, and that of the least member of the crew about $2,000.

Those were large sums of money in the good old days, when a man was practically as well off with a million dollars as though he was rich! If nothing was due a sailor at the final accounting, the "generous" owners usually gave him a five dollar gold piece, anyway.

The net profits of a voyage include everything of value that may be taken. There are no exclusive prizes for skipper, owner, or anyone else; whether a stick of timber salvaged from the sea, or a haul of ambergris, each member of the crew has a pecuniary interest in every addition to the cargo. Even the proceeds of the galley soap grease are divided pro rata. A man's lay is further protected by a method of figuring which takes no account of the whales actually captured during his term of service. He is paid off, rather, according to the proportion that his service bears to the whole voyage. Thus at the end of a two-year voyage, a man who had been a member of the crew for only six months would be entitled to one-fourth of his allotted lay, even if not one whale had been sighted during his particular half year aboard.

Barn swallows, bound from somewhere "up home" toward their winter range in South America, visited us at noon today and perched in the rigging while they preened their feathers thoroughly. The position was lat. 31° 31' N., long. 58° 40' W. This is, roughly, 360 geographic miles on the seaward side of Bermuda and more than a thousand miles from Cape Hatteras, Cape Cod, and Halifax, Nova Scotia, all of which are about equally distant. At seven o'clock in the evening, at least six of the birds were still sitting and snuggling along the royal brace.

AUGUST 18. A rainy Sunday morning. Several of the barn swallows spent the night with us. They had better be on their way swiftly, if they hope to reach land, because the *Daisy* supports no flying-insect fauna, except cockroaches far too big for swallows to eat.

A school of whales was announced after dinner. At first the Old Man and Mr. da Lomba thought they were only killers, but presently they were distinguished as sperm whales mingled with and surrounded by killers. The latter were jumping in a most spectacular display, and the whole area was white water.

The aggregation was approaching the brig, so we waited with sails aback until the whales, blowing furiously, came close. Then we lowered four boats and, from the mainmasthead, I had a superb view of the hunt and death.

Most landlubbers suppose—as I did formerly—that a Yankee whaleman captures his prey by maneuvering the boat somewhere near the whale and then throwing the harpoon at it. Nothing of the sort! The harpoon is not "thrown"; it is planted. It rarely leaves the hands of the boatsteerer until the boat has been beached on the whale's back. "Wood to blackskin," is the muttered or grunted order by which the boatheader holds his harponeer's eagerness in check while the craft is sailing, or being pulled, onto the whale.

At half past one o'clock the first of our boats made fast. At that moment a tropic-bird flew into the field and for some minutes circled about, watching the boats and whales. The killers had disappeared. At quarter before two, another boat made fast and went shooting ahead, lowering sail immediately as the whale sprinted at the surface. Six minutes later, the third boat planted its iron. By this time, the first boat had lanced and waifed its whale. The fourth boat, Mr. Almeida's, was unlucky, and never succeeded in making fast.

At the first signal of "fin out," the shiptenders began to haul up from steerage and 'tween-decks the heavy fluke chains, cutting tackle and other gear used during the flensing, and the helmsman endeavored to keep the brig to windward of the boats. Mr. da Lomba was, however, a mile or more up wind, and his boys consequently had the added labor of towing their carcass to the *Daisy*. They looped a bowline from the flukes around the loggerhead and bent backs to five oars, but at each stroke the blades seemed to drop into the same hole in the water. I think that their progress would have been livelier if they had followed the time-honored custom of towing their whale head first, but there seem to be differences of opinion about that. At any rate, it took Mr. da Lomba two hours to bring in his prize. By that time the blue sharks had followed their noses in from all directions and were clustering about our catches like hyenas around a dead lion. The water was alive with them.

It was late afternoon before Mr. Vincent's whale was finally lanced. All three of the animals taken were small, and the Old Man couldn't have had a more disgruntled expression on his mug if he had filled his mouth with sour pickles.

Conrad, as it turned out, had furnished the principal excitement of the afternoon. The boy was one of two green hands in Mr. da Lomba's boat. After the iron had been successfully darted, and the oarsmen had turned to face the bow and to haul toward the harpooned whale, Conrad suddenly bowled over in a faint. Emiliano, the boatsteerer, splashed a piggin of sea water over him, without effect, but Mr. da Lomba, putting down his lance at the bow, strode aft over the thwarts of the boat already whizzing along on its Nantucket sleigh ride, picked up a paddle and began to belabor the lump that was Conrad. Happily, the treatment revived him before it killed him. Conrad yelped, popped up, seized the line, and began to haul like a veteran.

Mr. da Lomba reported all this in a routine, unemotional manner to the skipper, and I pieced out details from other members of the boat's crew. It seemed to be a familiar circumstance to the officers, and no particular stigma against a youngster fast to a whale for the first time. The Old Man clearly wanted to explain to me that paddling a sailor whose behavior endangered the lives of his fellows was no infringement of the modern laws that forbid flogging.

The operations of bringing a dead whale alongside the ship, and of attaching it, are called sweeping and fluking. After the line from the carcass has been passed on board, a heavy chain, made fast around a bitt on the forward deck, is paid out through the starboard hawse pipe. A light rope is then dipped under the whale's "small" (the tail end, just in front of the flukes), and is used in turn to pull the chain around. As soon as the slack has been drawn in, the whale floats on the starboard side of the ship, with its flukes toward the bow and its head stretching along past the waist. The process is simple enough in quiet weather, but today there has been a small choppy sea and the fluking was accomplished only with a good deal of hard labor by the crew and of still harder language by the Old Man.

As soon as our prizes were safe alongside, the fall blocks were dropped to the four boats and all hands laid hold and swayed back until the precious craft were triced up into position on the cranes, the salt water streaming from plug holes in their bottoms. Then it was "Supper the watch," and nobody needed urging to a meal so long overdue.

As darkness closed in, the nearest whale lay on its side, fin out, limberly yielding to every swell, with its great blunt head stretching toward the quarter and its closed eye and infinitesimal ear-opening occasionally breaking above the surface. I could still see the troop of hungry sharks filing silently along its length, fondly rubbing tail fins against the gray hulk, as though they were anticipating the feast of the cutting-in.

AUGUST 19. We lay hove-to throughout a night that grew calmer as the hours passed.

At half past four o'clock this morning, every soul was on deck and on duty. My only job, however, was to sit at some good point of vantage, such as the mate's boat on the starboard quarter, and watch proceedings.

In the dim light of early dawn, two pieces of apparatus

were immediately brought into use—one the cutting tackle, the other the cutting stage. The latter is a scaffold which, when lowered from the ship's waist, is suspended directly above the whale. On this rocking platform the officers stand while performing the cutting-in. The cutting tackle is a cluster of enormous blocks hung, by hawsers as thick as a man's leg, from the head of the mainmast, the strongest structure on a ship above the deck. Through these blocks are rove the hawsers which lift many tons of blubber from the water to the main hatch.

A great iron hook, weighing about a hundred pounds, was lowered from the cutting tackle and inserted in a prepared gash in the blubber just behind the sperm whale's eye. This was accomplished easily this morning because of the quietness of the sea, and tension applied to the line at once raised the carcass high in the water. Then the officers, leaning against the rail of the stage to steady themselves, began to cut a flap of blubber around the inserted hook, using for this purpose razor-edged blubber spades, which have handles fifteen or twenty feet long.

In the brightening morning, the officers jabbed and jabbed from the stage, sometimes seeing where they struck, and sometimes, when the whale was engulfed in boiling foam, only guessing. Their spades dulled rapidly, and on the quarterdeck, with the laziest Portugee on board to turn the grindstone, my friend Correia, the cooper, was kept busy renewing edges until the last cut had been concluded. "Sharp spade, Cooper!" the four officers were continually bawling out from the stage, while the cooper cursed under his breath at their recklessness in chipping the spades against bones or a harpoon imbedded in the blubber.

On the deck of the *Daisy*, at the other end of the cutting tackle, no less heavy work was going on. Double hawsers ran through the great blocks to the windlass on the topgallant fo'c'sle, and there, under the eye of the Old Man himself, the greater part of the crew rocked the windlass and hoisted the strip of blubber as it was loosened from the whale. This was at least the cheery part of the business, work that could not be done without song, and, to the accompaniment of squeaking bearings and clicking pawls, the husky chorus rang out:

> Come all ye brave sailors who're cruising for sparm,
> Come all ye bold seamen who sail round the Horn—
> Our Captain has told us, and we hope it proves true,
> There's plenty more whales 'long the coast of Peru.

Back at the waist, the stress of the windlass soon began to rip the first strip of blubber from the whale's body. Scrambling sharks made the water crawl as each fish tried to bury its teeth in exposed fat. Now and then a shark would flounder right out of water, on top of the whale, until a descending blubber spade put an end to its ambitions.

Eventually, the windlass grinders pulled up the strip of blubber until the paired blocks of the tackle were almost in contact, high above the main deck, block-a-block, the long, tough blanket-piece of skin and fat hanging from that point to its attachment on the whale, which had rolled over and over in the water as its blubber had been peeled off along the scarf. The jabbing of the spades went on incessantly, and the water for an acre around the brig was stained by outpouring blood.

When the blanket-piece had been hoisted higher and higher, until it could rise no further, the third mate, armed with a long-handled, double-edged sword called the boarding knife, cut a pair of holes through the blubber down near the level of the deck. A chain looped in and out of these was connected with a second hawser, the "port falls" of the cutting blocks. When this new attachment had been drawn taut on the windlass, the boarding knife slashed through the blubber just above it. The upper piece swung free across the deck, to the peril of anyone who chanced to be in its path, but it was soon controlled and lowered down the main hatch into the slithery blubber parlor, where men with short-handled spades reduced it to mincing pieces that could be stowed in pens.

Then the second blanket-piece hung in the gory sea, the chain which held it grinding on the plank-sheer of the waist, and the identical procedure was repeated until this, too, rose dripping over the deck, ready to be severed. And so on, down to the small of the whale, which was cut through and hoisted aboard, flukes and all.

Before the stripped carcass was set adrift, the intestines were well punched with the long spades, and the officers smelled their blades with the unrealized hope of detecting ambergris. Most of the sharks, squirming like massed maggots, went off with the carcass, which floated high as a result of eighteen hours' decomposition.

The other two whales were also cut-in during the day, and the mincing and boiling of blubber was begun in six-hour watches. But in the afternoon and evening I was so busy developing photographic plates, and writing up my notes of the morning, that I kept no close tab on the process.

Our position at noon was lat. 31° 32' N., long. 56° 09' W. A large schooner passed, and I made ready to send you a letter by her, but she failed to approach within hailing range.

AUGUST 20. Boiling blubber.

When the raging furnaces of the try-works raise the temperature of the forehold to an uncomfortable pitch, the cockroaches, accompanied by cockroachesses or henroaches (take your choice), move aft into quarters of a rising social order. Unfortunately, they do not pause at the steerage, inhabited by boatsteerers and cooper. Neither are they content with the officers' domain. No, they keep on their sternward trek until, in the end, there is no room left for the Old Man and me in our after-cabin.

The breed of cockroaches with which the *Daisy* has

become inoculated during her sojourn in the tropics is unlike anything known in the purlieus of even the most venerable sinks and drains in your effete part of the world. Of course, one of our cockroaches is not to be feared alone, at least by a man in fit physical condition and armed with a belaying pin, but three of them together could easily best and drag off a he-Airedale in the prime of life.

Cockroaches take to all perishable stores, which means anything not soldered or welded inside seamless metal plates. Leather or paper comes under the heading of food, and the covers of my books are already beautifully chased with hieroglyphics and other symbols pertaining to the language of the exceedingly ancient insect family of the Blattidae. Today I found in the run, beneath my cabin, a three-gallon stone jug supposed to be full of ship's molasses. It was strangely light, so I sent it on deck, where it was emptied of ten thousand (estimated) deceased cockroaches. The pioneers had eaten through a deep cork, and the drowned bodies of them and their successors had continually raised the level of the fluid for later invasions of an endless horde.

Furthermore, these cockroaches are intensely personal in their advances toward sleepers. I frequently awaken in the morning with the gesture of dashing a large brute off my lips, only to find that it has just flown to the bookshelves, from where it grins at me or even laughs until its antennae shake. A few of them get their just desserts by being cooked alive in our tastiest dishes. If they play 'possum in the flour, for instance, it is their own fault that they subsequently turn up in the duff. The other day I saw the cooper skillfully use the point of his knife to flick one out of his plate of steaming lobscouse. It went sailing across the cabin, like its own ghost, passed out an open port, and vanished in the deep.

Now your immediate and naïve conclusion will doubtless be that the cockroach is an undesirable member of the navifauna. Quite wrong! The cockroach is the least of several possible evils, and he has the merit of being a predacious beast who will brook no rivals. Lesser vermin of every sort, including their eggs and babies, are his natural prey and he'll go anywhere to get 'em. I have recently read Shakespeare's admonition in *The Taming of the Shrew*—"Tush, tush! fear boys with bugs." I am sure that our boys bring them, of various species and predilections, but, thanks to the beneficence of our trusty cockroaches, they cannot keep them. Furthermore, when we reach South Georgia, even the cockroaches will be betrayed and frozen out, and we'll come home uninfested!

AUGUST 21. The boiling is finished, the golden oil has been run into casks below, the gear stowed and the *Daisy* thoroughly scrubbed and tidied. I don't know where the canard originated that a whaleship is a dirty craft. She becomes a bit greasy, sooty and redolent in the natural and fortunate course of events; but she also gets cleaned up like nothing else except a man-o'-war.

There is a strong breeze astern and we are speeding eastward and rolling scuppers under. I have read *Hamlet*, in which, as in everything else by its author, it is possible to find allusions to one's present job—

Whose sore task
Does not divide the Sunday from the week.

The Old Man has been poring over his Bible for at least two hours. He is rather full of pious instincts, and might be called religious but not churchly. All the sects familiar in the vicinity of New Bedford seem, for one reason or another, to have won his displeasure, but Quakers lead the field in his list of preferred funerals. The Friends, incidentally, have been famously successful whalemen ever since the early days of Nantucket, and first among owners of whaleships, and it may be that Captain Cleveland has fallen afoul of some powerful rivalry during his long blubber-hunting career.

However, he has nothing but bitter words also for the Episcopalians, Congregationalists, and Baptists, *et al.*

I have now known him for just about six months, and this afternoon he finally popped the dread question, "Mr. Murphy, what's your religion?"

"Well, Captain," I responded, "I'm a member of the Unitarian Church, and—" but he cut me short with a comment that has smoothed all possible difficulties.

"Oh, I have *great* respect for the Unitarians. They don't believe a goddam thing and they live up to it every day in the week, Sundays included."

AUGUST 22. Lat. 31° 50' N., long. 50° 49' W. See where we have arrived now, in the heart of the Sargasso Sea, at least 1800 miles east of Savannah!

This morning I hooked and landed a big barracuda. Later, while I was down in the pitch-dark run, loading camera magazines, the boats were lowered. Within a very brief time, and before I had even arrived on deck, two of them harpooned and lanced an eighty-barrel bull, a sperm whale which makes his predecessors seem insignificant and which will, indeed, yield much more oil than all four of them together. As the creature floated alongside, I measured its extreme length, between markers on the *Daisy's* deck, as 55 feet 10 inches, which is certainly accurate to within less than one foot.

While the whale was being fluked, two blue sharks, each accompanied by three pilot fish, behaved very much like tugboats nosing an ocean liner toward her pier. They had every appearance of helping our crew in the task of sweeping the whale. Presently they were joined by a third shark which had six pilot fish as companions. By the time the cutting-in had started, the sharks were to be counted by scores and the pilot fish by hundreds. Most of the sharks were patient, so to speak, swimming slowly along the whale and around the brig, an exceedingly interesting though somewhat macabre procession. They were slender and swift-looking creatures, of an intense blue color on the upper surface of the body, with small but conspicuous teeth, and of an average—and remarkably uniform—length of about eight feet. The species is the common surface shark of the high sea in the tropical and subtropical Atlantic, and is rarely seen near the continental coasts.

AUGUST 23. Supper was late last evening, but the Old Man trusted Sargasso weather to the extent of stopping the cutting-in for the night. The men were at it again about five o'clock this morning, since when it has, of course, been everybody's watch on deck.

The sharks evidently lost their aforementioned patience, for during the dark hours they scooped many neat mouthfuls of blubber out of the whale, leaving white gouges in the black-skin. When the blubber spades recommenced their work, with a new reddening of the water, the sharks went berserk. Many of them jumped or wriggled on top of the whale, where they were methodically chopped to pieces by the officers on the cutting stage. Some were washed back into deep water badly mutilated but still able to swim, and these, even though their entrails were hanging out of the side of a body that had been cut away, would turn again toward the whale, bury their teeth, twist, yank, and swallow. I believe, though I am not quite certain, that one or more of these insensate fish were taking food in at the mouth and immediately losing it through a stomach that had been severed by a blubber spade. At any rate, the hacked-up brutes continued to feed until they died in the act and slowly settled into impenetrable depths beneath our keel.

Johnny hooked three sharks, using whale meat as bait, but we succeeded in getting only one of them on deck. Nothing could be more brilliant than the steel-blue of its wet back in the sunshine. It confirmed my estimate of the size of the creatures, and its jaws, together with a piece of its rough skin, have now become a catalogued specimen. Jaws and skin denticles are sufficient to identify a shark of any kind.

I was thinking, as I somewhat negligently sank a razor-sharp tooth of this shark into the end of my middle finger, that I have lacerated my hands a thousand times since embarking. Bones, scales, spines, teeth, not to mention the abrasive gear and rigging of this vessel, have cut and pricked and barked my skin almost daily. I make at least a moderate effort to keep the wounds clean and sterilized, and not one of them has remained sore. Perhaps, however, Shakespeare's advice has been best for a whaleman,

> —telling me, the sovereign'st thing on earth
> Was parmaceti for an inward bruise.

Johnny further demonstrated his usefulness during the cutting-in by capturing several dolphins, each a yard or more in length. The flesh of these, along with sperm whale meat balls and baked beans, was served at supper.

The biggest dolphin measured thirty-nine inches. I had a good opportunity to watch its color changes as it died, at which time rainbow tints seemed to pass in rhythmic waves along its mother-of-pearl flanks. The general aspect of the living fish, flouncing helplessly on deck, was burnished silver, blotched with old gold on the upper sides and back, and with round ultramarine spots along the lower flanks and belly. The long and high dorsal fin was a mixture of dark blue and green, speckled with ultramarine spots, like those of the belly. The mouth and the side fins were heavily edged with Antwerp blue. These hues are not figments of imagination, but might better be called "pigments of precision"! I noted them by direct comparison with the plates in Ridgway's *Nomenclature of Colors.*

AUGUST 24.   Lat. 32° 17' N., long. 49° 58' W. We paid scant attention to a school of blackfish sighted this morning, all being busy enough on board processing our whale. If the Old Man's estimate of eighty barrels proves correct, the bull will be worth at least $1300, of which my lay amounts to the munificent sum of $6.50!

Our former whales all being small, their heads were hoisted on deck entire. Then the "case" (the top section of the head, which contains the spermaceti) was cautiously slit open, and the limpid, fragrant spermaceti, mingled with stringy masses of snow-white fat, was bailed out with copper scoops and poured into tubs.

The head of a whale like the bull now alongside weighs many tons, for a sperm whale's head is reckoned as a third of the total length and more than a third of the bulk. The strain of such a head hanging from the blocks of the cutting tackle would be liable to break the hawsers, or even to force the foot of the mast through the keel and thus to scuttle the ship. So the head of a big whale must be handled quite differently from that of a small one.

This morning Captain Cleveland himself came for the first time out on the cutting stage. Working only with Mr. da Lomba, after the stripping of the body blubber had been nearly completed, he cut transversely into the enormous mass of tissue, presently exposing the condyles of the vast skull and finally decapitating the whale. The head was then attached by a line to the lash-rail and allowed to float aft until the swollen, grisly carcass was cut adrift.

Next, the entire fore and upper part of the whale's head, comprising not only the case but also a huge mass of fat called the junk, was severed from the skull. After that, case and junk were in turn separated one from the other by cutting cautiously through a fibrous layer known as the "whitehorse," which forms a sort of floor for the case. The junk was then hoisted on deck, to be chopped subsequently into oleaginous blocks and fed into the trypots. The great cistern of the case, with its hundreds of gallons of spermaceti inside, remained floating in the sea.

At this point, José Gaspar, one of the boatsteerers, volunteered to go overboard to make the fastenings. (It seems that the boatsteerers always volunteer for this job—but each in his own turn!) Girdled with a monkey-belt of braided marlin, from which a tether ran to competent hands on deck, José was lowered into the seething water. By timely yanks on the rope, he was kept from being squeezed between case and ship as they rolled together in the swell. On the cutting stage the officers stood with their long spades, sending one shark after another to Davy Jones's locker while the poor boat-steerer, now thrown high, now half drowned in foam and froth, completed his task of sewing a sort of spiderweb of cordage around the rear end of the case in order to form an attachment for a heavy line from the cutting blocks. This deli-cate bit of tailoring was accomplished with a "head needle" about two feet long. Finally the job was fulfilled, and José was hauled and bumped to the deck.

The hinder end of the case was then hoisted level with the planksheer of the waist. Its weight was supported more by water than by our cutting tackle, for the snout was still far beneath the surface. Mr. da Lomba then used a short-handled spade to tap the store of spermaceti from above, i.e., from the back of the case, exercising great care not to spill any of it. A few cupfuls that gushed on deck were promptly scooped up by slick-skimmers, meaning anybody standing by and not al-ready fully occupied.

Then, through a light tackle hung from the tip of the foresail yard, a long, narrow, round-bottomed case bucket, suspended at the end of a thin pole, was lowered through the slit that had just been made in the case. The pole was used to push the bucket in, and then to haul it out again, as from a well, filled to the brim and dripping with liquid spermaceti. This operation was repeated again and again, until the long pole rammed the "old oaken bucket" down fifteen or twenty feet, and drained the last few gallons. All of this luscious and valuable spermaceti was poured into butts and tubs, to be boiled separately from the body blubber. Finally, the great sack, emptied of its treasure, was cut away to plunge into the deep. The last of the fat was now on board; the drainage oil and spilth were "likkered" up from the slippery decks; the stage was raised to its inactive position, and the cutting-in was over.

AUGUST 25. Calm, hot and wet, starting with the threat of a rainy Sunday, but clearing up before noon. We boiled blubber most of yesterday and all through the night, and have now finished. We would be on our way if there were any wind to take us. Clothes-washing and fishing are the principal occupations on deck. Since the rain ceased, I have been sitting for several hours in the scanty shadow of the furled mainsail, rapt in a book, or several books in succession. Thus has the egregious development of my gray matter (if any) helped the hours to slip by, and I'm another day nearer you.

At home it is drawing toward the end of summer, but here in the Sargasso, where the northeast trades reign, there is little to distinguish one season from another.

During the dog watch, I had a long chat with my friend Correia, the cooper. He is a canny republican Portuguese, a leftist who has a strong, though calm and rational, dislike for kingship and priestcraft. He has not yet quite decided whether to become an American citizen or to return ultimately to his own little up-and-down isle of Fayal, Azores. He is a voracious reader, and our conversation was a pot-pourri in which we mixed the Arabian Nights, Victor Hugo, Garibaldi, Jules Verne, Francisco Ferrer, the Papacy, and the Hague Tribunal.

The magazines you sent by Mr. da Lomba are seeing service from cabin to forecastle. They ultimately pass through every pair of hands on board. Mr. Vincent can't read a word, even though he is second officer, but he pores over the pictures more than anyone else, occasionally asking the cooper for an explanation.

AUGUST 26.   Calm. We are still rapidly going nowhere.

From the stomach of a dolphin I took three entire flying fish that looked fit to eat, so, by Jove, we ate 'em! Then, after studying awhile, I read the tragedy of *King Richard III*, just to rest my mind.

Johnny, the incomparable cabin boy, who knows that I am a scholar worthy of trust in weighty matters, informed me in utmost confidence that he had seen a "sereia" early this morning. Discreet inquiry revealed that "sereia" is Portuguese for mermaid. The cooper, suspicious unbeliever, wanted to know where I had picked up the word, but I put him off. If I had been the happy observer, I would not have trusted my eyes, but, since Johnny tells me, it must be so.

There is every reason why my turn should come next, because during the year before I was born my mother painted, quite out of her imagination, a number of charming water colors of mermaids. What more potent reason could there be for the fact that I became a marine zoologist?

Even though I missed the vision that ravished Johnny's eyes, I can draw her, with apologies to a very old print.

AUGUST 27. Lat. 32° 20' N., long. 46° 12' W. Calm. A tropic-bird passed us, the first bird of any kind seen for many days.

I have found some laboratory animals on board, and have been running a series of experiments to while away several days of this trying calm. No, they are neither rats nor cockroaches, but familiar house spiders of a species that the spider specialists call *Pholcus phalangioides*. Their food supply is a mystery, because we have been two months away from land and have seen no small insects except a few fruit flies from bananas that have now all been eaten.

Anyway, the spiders occupy several rather shapeless webs in the shelves and corners of the after-cabin. The Old Man and I extend them Scotch hospitality, and Johnny, who does the house cleaning, has of course never noticed either the cobwebs or their builders.

These spiders have a whirling defense that is most astonishing. It is a reaction only to tactile stimuli, as when the web is shaken or the animal touched with a hair. Blowing of the breath, the heat of a candle, sunlight flashed from a mirror, or the odor of alcohol merely makes the spider crawl into a crack and hide. But if you touch it, however lightly, the pinwheel begins. The spider rotates its body upon its legs, keeping all its claws bunched together upon a strand of the web, while the long shanks are pulled out straight by centrifugal force, and you can see no more of either body or legs than of the blades of a whirring propeller.

The first response to the stimulus is brief, my spiders soon checking their motors and coming to rest in an average period of fifteen seconds. But in the second and third responses their tempers rise, and the spinning of the live whirligig becomes increasingly violent and of longer duration. The

third or fourth response (usually the latter) hits the maximum, the nice little blur lasting from two minutes fifteen
seconds to three minutes.

After this, a jerky, feeble reaction indicates the beginning of fatigue. The whirlings become slower and shorter.
If the nasty experimenter continues his annoyance seven or
eight times, the spider doesn't want to play any more; it
hunts out a hiding place and sulks.

Here endeth the first lesson in the study of animal behavior. Now for a sample of human behavior:

It is comical to see long-legged, gawky Mr. da Lomba trying, under the eye of the Old Man, to work out a sunsight. The
big Cape Verder never got no book larnin' and, in any case, his
heart is rather better than his head—except that in seaman-
ship and whalecraft he is as competent as any man could
possibly be. He sits on a stool in the cabin, knees crossed, a
slate in one hand, the fingers of the other constantly twisting
the curls of his bewildered head, while he struggles to add degrees, minutes, and seconds and to comprehend the use of
mysterious logarithms. He looks the picture of misery, like an
overgrown backward schoolboy. The captain—who is better
as practitioner than as preceptor—puts him half a dozen
times through the drill, then pretends to look for a club in
order to let daylight into John's cranium. All of this, of course,
is in private so far as other members of the crew are concerned.

The point is that Mr. da Lomba never will learn astronomical navigation. Yankee whaling and the whalemen of
Yankee ships are only dregs of their foregoers and, with current crews, the captain is certainly not privileged to die at
sea!

In the interlude between waking and sleeping, I am
sometimes overcome with a transient terror at the part that
luck or fate must play for every soul on board the *Daisy*. If a

man were to be stricken here with acute appendicitis, he
would simply die. A compound fracture of a leg or arm would
be horrible to contemplate. It is a grim sort of tribute that the
men already turn to me when they have minor injuries, because I dread to be forced to think of myself as the closest
available approach to a physician and surgeon. And when a
troglodyte with a swollen jowl climbs out of the dark forecastle, respectfully approaches me on the afterdeck, and asks
me to wrest out of his jaw the half-buried stump of a molar
—with the ghastly rocker, or turnkey, which is the *Daisy's*
whole dental equipment—then, I assure you, I have to put up
a hypocritical brave front to hide the quailing of a cowardly
heart. I have no craving to be loblolly boy of this brig.

The Old Man has been in aggravating pain for the past
several days because he wricked his back going aloft. I have
been rubbing it with some sort of horse liniment from the
medicine chest, and gently massaging the muscles. Either my
treatment or the mere passage of time has led to an improve-
ment, but what if the tough old boy should become really
incapacitated?

The lower jaw of the eighty-barrel sperm whale was the
first one we have saved. After the great masses of lush fat had
been taken out of the ramus, or pan, on either side, it was
roughly trimmed up but the fifty teeth were left in place.
When the boiling of blubber had been completed, the gear
stowed, and the brig cleaned up, this jaw was lowered into the
ocean and towed astern for several days at the end of a long
length of whale line. It was astonishing to see how clean and
white it became in the tropical water, all the oil evidently
being washed out of it and all the clinging meat macerated by
the warmth or devoured by tiny organisms. Before the gristle,
which held the teeth in their sockets, had softened too much,
the jaw was once more hoisted on deck and lashed to the bulwarks near the bow. Later in the voyage the white bone of

this jaw, and the creamy ivory of the great teeth, will no doubt be worked into scrimshaw by the officers.

AUGUST 28.   Calm.

I have been looking further into the medical equipment of this brig. The bulk of it consists of Epsom salts. There is also a supply of "pain killer." Various other bottles contain, or once contained, fluids for internal or external use, but the contents of some have dried out. Most of the bandages are in yellowed paper covers and appear to have been on board for years. There are one scalpel, some surgical needles, and a pair of forceps, but no sutures. The "doctor book," in which I have been reading chapters on the character and treatment of infected wounds, fevers, scurvy, etc., is enough to chill the blood. It was published forty years ago. The Old Man is at least consistent in the period of his essential literature, because his *South America Pilot* is as old as his medical authority.

I had hoped to be able to describe for you one of the famous boxes of numbered medicine bottles that were formerly supplied to whaleships. Captain Cleveland says that he carried one up to about the year 1900 and he has given me a version of a story I first heard from Frank Wood, in New Bedford.

It seems that a skipper was once called to minister to a sailor with the gripes. Consulting the label inside the cover of his medicine box, he found that No. 14 was the remedy indicated for that affliction. Alas! The bottle proved to be empty. However, this master was an ingenious and logical man, and one who remembered his arithmetic well from school days. Pulling the phials from their compartments for inspection, he noted that No. 6, a remedy for ague, was full to the cork. No. 8, likewise, contained an abundance of a green liquid, intended to alleviate stricture. Now six added to eight make fourteen. The skipper mixed a stiff dose and hastened forward to his unhappy patient.

Time lags on a hot still afternoon in a motionless ship.
Shall we ever reach South Georgia? There is nothing that re-
quires doing, nor anyone here I wish to talk with. I don't want
a nap and yet there is no use in staying awake.

I have just read *King John*, the most giggling of comedies
for the first half, and a bit scurrilous withal. The scene of
Hubert and Prince Arthur in the Tower then ends all laughter
with a bang, and steps up the pulse and respiration. The bastard, Philip, is one of Shakespeare's most likable characters.

Before I came below for the last time, early this evening,
I saw a strange ruby blaze on the water ahead of the ship. It
seemed several miles distant and the glow increased in a
rapid, awe-inspiring manner. I couldn't imagine the source of
such a balefire, and I was puzzled that nobody on deck made
a word of comment. Then it climbed a little higher, into a rift
of the cloud bank, and unveiled itself as the round and blood-
red moon.

AUGUST 29.   Still calm, and here we lie in midocean,
about as far from anywhere as from everywhere.

Today I went over various gear in anticipation of its use,
sharpened my knives, cleaned and lubricated instruments,
and then read *Twelfth Night*. We have scarcely moved all day.

The food on the *Daisy* sometimes makes me wish that I
might shift to the festive board of state's prison inmates. This
is despite the fact that we have discovered another tin of
Danish butter.

The Old Man has a disingenuous method of showing his
stinginess with sugar. With a loud grunt he makes a show of
putting about one-fourth teaspoon in his coffee. Then he stirs
it, gulps a mouthful, ruckles up his brow, and utters the
disgusted comment, "Too sweet!" while he passes his mug to
be filled to the top with fresh coffee. Finally, he looks
around the table, hoping that his meaning has sunk in. The
ruse doesn't work too well, however, and Mr. Almeida goes

right ahead shoveling three or four heaping spoonfuls into his drink, while Mr. da Lomba pipes up: "Will you shove that sugar bowl within darting distance?"

AUGUST 30.   Lat. 32° 21' N., long. 42° 46' W.

We have had a slight breeze and have actually gone forward a few miles. This morning we lowered two boats for a lone sperm whale, but he was going to windward and gave us the slip. In confidence, it is no grief to me, because I want to reach South Georgia before Thanksgiving Day. As so often happens, a tropic-bird—or "boatswain" (from the whistle), or "marlin spike" (from the long tail)—was sighted while the whale was in view. There is no limit, in the warmer oceans, to the flight range of these birds.*

AUGUST 31.   Lat. 33° 14' N., long. 40° 40' W.

A stronger breeze, but from a direction that does not permit us to turn toward the south, which the Old Man evidently wishes, although he has given nobody a hint about our next intended landfall.

I read from biological texts for two or three hours and then went on with my Shakespearean debauch: first the crazy, frolicsome, and boisterous *Comedy of Errors,* and then *A Midsummer Night's Dream.* There's a real play for you, worthy of the Queen of the Fairies, the finest of the comedies except, perhaps, *The Tempest.*

Toward evening a big merchant bark was sighted crossing our bow, bound as if toward England. I closed out a letter to you, so that it would be ready if we could speak her. But she had the wind fair, and we only came near enough to see her mementoes of rough weather, perhaps while rounding the Horn. Most of her foremast had been carried away and only a stump was still standing.

SEPTEMBER 1.   August has joined the ranks of the slain. Last night was squally; about midnight we had to take in sail in a hurry. Throughout the day, a strong southeast wind has held—coming from the very direction that has been set as the course toward which the helmsman should inch.

Another bookish day. Titus, Philemon and Jude, from the New Testament; then the *Winter's Tale*, doubtless the dreariest production of the Bard of Avon, even though it has some exquisite passages. But the theme is nasty, the noblemen are arrant liars, and the joyous end is a fraud and a swindle.

You probably never suspected that a whaling cruise would incubate a Shakespearean critic!

When I worked out the longitude, the result disagreed with the Old Man's findings. He made a few scathing cracks, so I did it again and turned out the same figure. Then the cocky old boy unbent enough to run over his own reckoning, which was on a schoolroom slate, and, behold!, he found his error and came out with my position. Keep your shirt on, Bob; the less said the better!

Anyway, it's high time you learnt how we do it, so here goes:

The Old Man usually shoots the sun, at which job he is far more skillful than I have yet become. I stand below, over the pair of chronometers, and note the time when he shouts. Then we pull down our copy of Bowditch and go to work.

This formula is the haversine method of determining the longitude, a word meaning "half the versed sine." Incidentally, it is the method that led Captain Sumner to the discovery of his famous "circle of position," on December 18, 1837. Here we are, seventy-five years later, and yet Captain Cleveland has either never heard of the Sumner Line, or at any rate, he knows nothing about its applicability to his daily problem except, perhaps, when he shoots the stars.

Observed altitude of ☀	43°	25'	00"
Correction for parallax, semi-diameter and dip	+	12	00
	43	37	00
Refraction	—	01	01
☀'s true altitude	43	35	59
Declination	08°	19'	50.7"
Correction for time and longitude	—	04	58
	−08	14	52
	90	00	00
Polar distance	81	45	08
Greenwich time by chronometer	5h.	40'	25"
Chronometer error		−11	28
Correct Greenwich time	5	28	57
Latitude, dead reckoning from noon sight	32°	03'	00"
☀'s altitude	43	35	59
Polar distance	81	45	08
	157	24	07
Half sum of the last	78	42	03.5
☀'s altitude	−43	35	59
Remainder	35	06	04
Log. secant latitude	10.07182—10		
Log. cosecant polar distance	10.00542—10		
Log. cosine half sum	9.29214—10		
Log. sine remainder	9.75967—10		
	1.12905—10		
Log. sine half sum of the last	.56452		
Apparent time	2h.	52'	11"
Equation of time			−02
Mean time of observation	2	52	09
Greenwich time	5	28	57
Difference in time	2	36	48

—which converts to 39° 12' 00" longitude W.

Furthermore, I find that he hasn't the vaguest idea what logarithms are. To him they are merely columns of figures to be used, which, after all, is sufficient for his purpose.

This morning Mr. da Lomba spent nearly two watches at the masthead. He reported sighting an ocean sunfish, which is a great lump of a creature shaped more or less like a peach pit, measuring up to twelve feet in both length and height, and weighing up to a ton.

He also saw a thirty-foot bone shark, which is the whaleman's name for the basking shark, one of the largest of all fishes. The name is due to the fact that the bone shark carries a sort of imitation whalebone on its gill-rakers, and feeds by straining small creatures out of the water, after the manner of a right whale.

In Colonial days an extensive bone shark fishery for liver oil was conducted along the Massachusetts coast, especially in the bight north of Cape Cod, and it was not unusual to obtain four hundred gallons from a single shark. Mr. da Lomba has captured them himself while whaling, and tells me that the harpoon is always planted as near as possible to the snout in order to prevent the shark from diving before it can be lanced. The tail is the dangerous end, the teeth of the bone shark being scarcely more abrasive than sandpaper.

I have requested Mr. da Lomba to bellow for me by day or night whenever any such interesting objects are raised again. I would have gone up the rigging like a squirrel if I had known that the mastheads had spotted anything.

SEPTEMBER 2. During the night we passed great numbers of luminous jellyfish that glowed with pale blue light. The good wind of yesterday died away before dawn and what little we now have is against us. A tropic-bird inspected us at sunrise and then fled from the apparition.

On such a morning I should like nothing better than a swim, but the Old Man forbids it for fear of wanton and scurvy sharks beneath our keel.

At noon the mastheads announced a derelict about a mile off. We changed our course and bore toward it, making ready every available fish line on the way. It proved to be only a small bit of wreckage, part of the wall and roof of a ship's deckhouse. It was caught with boat hooks and towed along. Immediately a great horde of fish spurted out from beneath and swam, bewildered, along the sides of the brig. They took hooks greedily and we captured fifteen—five dolphins and ten others. The planks were swarming with crabs, teredos, goose barnacles, and bristly nereid worms. Captain Cleveland, thrifty Yankee that he is, ordered the wreckage made fast and sent down men to break it up for firewood and the nails in it!

I caught up on my sewing—general repairs to work clothes—and then read *The Two Gentlemen of Verona*. Lines here and there reveal the ineffable genius, but some Shakespearean heroes are certainly detestable beasts.

Fresh fish for supper was a treat. Our vegetables of all descriptions, including potatoes and yams, gave out some days ago. Meals now, and for the future, until we reach some port as yet unannounced, consist of combinations of the following: salt meat; hash made of salt meat, hard bread and dried potatoes; baked beans; bread; bean, pea, and corn soup; canned tomatoes; coffee. The tea is all gone. Three times a week we have dessert at dinner—apple pie (dried apples), mince pie, bread pudding, or duff. Once in a while we have rice (ruined in the cooking) and on Sundays canned clam chowder. Then about once in two weeks or more, a tin of peas or beans is opened.

The officers and cooper say that victuals were never so poor on Captain Cleveland's ship before. They are quite dissatisfied. The captain admits they are the worst ever, and lays it to the fact that he thought Captain Reed had properly provisioned.

Two bells have struck; good night.

SEPTEMBER 3. The disadvantage connected with the fish I chortled over yesterday is that they boil the bones and skin to make an alleged chowder (really glue) for next day's dinner!

This noon, the air and sea being calm, Mr. da Lomba and I lowered the *Grace Emeline*, rowed around the *Daisy* at a little distance, and made several photographs of her. It was fun to be on the gently swelling ocean in the dory. For forty-eight hours the surface has been glassy, and a full-rigged ship, bound southward as we are, or also trying, has lain on the horizon. We two made up the stationary Labor Day parade on the Atlantic last night.

For boat or masthead work, I am chary of my bulky and infinitely precious Graflex. But, just before I sailed from New York, Jack Nichols generously insisted that I take along his old reflex camera as an extra. I have already developed plates from it, and it works as well as the other.

SEPTEMBER 4. A slight breeze, but from the wrong direction. If I could send a letter by the proud ship still in sight, I would not dare say what follows. But something begins to whisper to me that we are going to touch at the Cape Verde Islands, and that the log for all of August and part of September may be in your hands this autumn.

Today we have cut and passed endless bands of sargasso weed, lying parallel and up-and-down wind in the dark blue ocean, just as billow clouds are streaking to the horizon across the mazarine blue of the sky. This is Sargasso weather, such as Columbus described in September, 1492, when he wrote that the mornings were like April in Andalusia—lacking only the songs of the nightingales! Columbus did a good job, too, of fishing up and recording the appearance of the strange little denizens of the weed clumps, which are almost the only surface creatures in this remote hub of the ocean.

There is little or nothing from the land in the vast, deep

Sargasso Sea, which forms an area as big as the United States, all enclosed within the currents of the North Atlantic. I don't mean only that there are no mouldering fleets of galleons caught in the tangles; neither are there twigs or straws afloat, nor silt suspended in the water, which is clearer than any pool or spring on earth.

After dinner, when the breeze died away, I had the dory lowered and I rowed off alone for an hour. The appearance of everything was different than the view from shipboard. Channels of bottomless blue, banks of orange vegetation—or so it seemed. But whenever I attempted to pull "ashore," the masses practically dissolved ahead of me. I could feel no resistance, hear no swish of weed along the flanks and bottom of the *Grace Emeline,* nor could I catch a single elusive strand upon an oar. Solid rafts seemed always yonder; close by, all was fluidity.

I noticed also, when I reached what appeared to be the heart of a great band, that all the weed floated at the very surface of the calm ocean. Six inches below, there was none. And yet not a strand, or a leaf or a "berry" projected anywhere above the surface. In this respect it differed remarkably from the clusters of ordinary rockweed that float with the tide at home.

Sargasso weed, as was pointed out generations ago, has no reproductive organs. It grows from its tips, like cuttings of land plants. Forever and ever it replenishes itself in this way, while the old strands die and sink. So what I have seen to-day is merely another pattern of the changeless seascape through which the *Pinta, Niña* and *Santa Maria* once skimmed.

SEPTEMBER 5.   Lat. 32° 12' N., long. 35° 15' W. The day has been squally, with frequent showers.

I have read the Revelation of John the Divine and Shakespeare's *Measure for Measure.* The latter was a new play to me and I found it thrilling and wholly engrossing, and tricked up with magnificent passages. It was not designed for Sunday school reading, however.

As for the Revelation, it has colored the literature of two millennia, but what has it to do with Christianity? Tinsel and might, rather than love, are made the supreme attributes of deity. If the members of a recent Chicago audience had been more thoroughly versed in the Revelation, the joke would not have been on them when T. R. cried, "We stand at Armageddon and we battle for the Lord!"

SEPTEMBER 6. At evening the heavens opened wide, and the deluge found a way through deck and walls and trickled below. The aftercabin is a forlorn spot during heavy rain. The swinging lamp makes so timid a glimmer that one cannot write there, and the only thing to do is lie down. Fortunately, my special section, both bed and bookshelves, has always remained completely dry.

Today I read *Love's Labour Lost*, of which the lyrics are the only part up to scratch.

SEPTEMBER 7. Lat. 30° N., long. 33° W., by deduced reckoning, more familiarly called dead reckoning. No sunsights were possible.

This morning was ushered in by a brilliant double rainbow in the west, out of which came a 2,000-ton ship under short sail. I hastily closed a letter, but the weather proved too squally for a gam. The three-master passed half a mile astern of us—a beautiful sight, with her wings spread to the strong, driving gusts, and a large bone-in-her-teeth. I could make out neither name nor any other mark of identification, but the Old Man said quite confidently that she was a Spaniard bound for the Canary Islands. (Perhaps his inference was as subtle as that of the skipper who identified a Scotch ship out of Glasgow by noting that "there weren't no gulls follering her.")

Today has been my first truly rainy day at sea. The spattering winds came in tremendous puffs. Rack scudded across the white-gray sky, and spume filled the air just above a jumbled, unreal horizon that looked as though it was studded with half-visible trees and shrubs. All day there were gleaming cloud lifts and sky windows here and there in the pall. After dinner I put on my leather hip boots, sou'wester, and oilskin coat, and paced the deck in the downpour. How unfortunate are they that don't know the joy implied by the name of the old Sioux Indian, "Rain-in-the-face"! Toward evening there was a rainbow again, which lasted twelve minutes after sundown, and extended much higher in the air than any I had seen before. A golden sunset followed a final hard squall, betokening a fair morrow.

SEPTEMBER 8. Sunday, by the clam chowder and baked beans!

A bright day, glassy calm, succeeded by a motionless evening. We haven't made a really good day's run since we left the Antilles. I have been three months on my journey, yet I am now within three weeks' sail of New Bedford. We are not yet back in the tropics, and there are at least 6,000 miles to go before we shall begin to turn toward you and home.

The big ship lies becalmed, a few miles ahead of us. The nearest land is "the blue Canary Isles." Do you think that they were named for the birds? Tut, tut, not at all, not at all! The Roman voyagers found them full of dogs, so they called the islands Canaria, meaning "kennels." And the dicky birds were named after the islands. (I have just sprung this erudition on the Old Man and his officers.)

SEPTEMBER 9. Lat. 28° 36' N., long. 31° 45' W.

The calmest day I have ever seen on the ocean, and excessively hot. I had not known that the face of the deep could lie so flat and still, like a polished silver plate. The glare was blinding. The *Daisy* rested all day with furled canvas, while

our fellow ship did likewise, nearly hull down on the far horizon.

Here and there, patches of small organisms that the
skipper called "whale feed" or "tallow drops" discolored the
water, and the oceanic bugs or water striders, which are
rarely visible, left long wakes on the impressionable mirror of
the sea.

About the middle of the forenoon a moving speck half a
mile off the starboard beam was pointed out to me by the
mastheads. My trusty field glass, a daily reminder of your
thoughtful generosity, revealed it as a bird, probably a shearwater. Within a few moments I saw also several Mother
Carey's chickens, so we lowered the *Grace Emeline* and Conrad rowed me out toward the potential specimens. One of
them made the error of flying within gunshot and, when I
picked it up, it proved to be Leach's petrel, a breeding species
of the northern North Atlantic, now doubtless bound toward
its tropical winter range. I chummed for a while with grease
from the galley, in the hope of luring other birds, but none
approached.

It was very pleasant to be free on the placid water, a
mile from the *Daisy* and eight hundred miles from the coast
of Africa. When the petrels had flown off, so that they were no
longer a distraction, I saw that the ocean around the dory was
dotted with the tiny, translucent sails of a siphonophore
called the salleeman or "by-the-wind-sailer." Its scientific
name—which the Old Man demanded of me as soon as I had
come on board with specimens—is *Velella*, and it is a small
cousin of the Portuguese man-o'-war. Never before had I seen
the creature outside a bottle, but now it was an effortless
task, because of the perfect calm, to pick up examples by
their sails.

Each one rested buoyantly on an oval, gas-filled float
about two inches long and of a delicate bubble-blue color.

Running at an angle across the float was the stiff, upright sail, tinted with lavender, pink and yellow, but nearly transparent. The sail enables the silent, expressionless salleeman to run before the wind or, more likely, to point into the wind and tack, because otherwise a lee shore would be its ultimate bourne.

Seeing hundreds or thousands of these exquisite little surface dwellers all about me, and realizing that they are always there, though usually hidden from human eyes by the light and movement of a rippling sea, caused a strong and strange upwelling of sentiment, which I can best suggest by lines from *The Rime of the Ancient Mariner:*

> O happy living things! no tongue
> Their beauty might declare:
> A spring of love gushed from my heart,
> And I blessed them unaware.

Later in the day I read *Much Ado about Nothing* and *As You Like It*, and in the latter play I found the perfect description of this, my journal, the sole object of which is to keep you with me while we are absent one from the other:

> It is a melancholy of mine own, compounded of many simples, extracted from many objects, and indeed the sundry contemplation of my travels, in which my often rumination wraps me in a most humorous sadness.

SEPTEMBER 10.   My suspicions grow that we are going to touch at the Cape Verdes. We are running several points to the east of what would be our normal course into the South Atlantic. We are going short of more and more supplies, and the men started today another row-de-dow over the food. Furthermore, there are but two cans of condensed milk left—and the Old Man can't enjoy his coffee without it! Our hard bread and flour, according to the steward, would not last beyond midwinter, so we must be going to São Vicente.

You might assume that it would be a simple solution to ask, "Captain Cleveland, are we going to the Cape Verde Islands?" but you don't really know the tight-lipped, repressed, self-contained old panjandrum! He would go to any lengths in circumlocution rather than make a forthright statement on anything which, by definition, is only *his* business. It must be tough to be as lonely as that for sixty-eight years.

We are so far behind that I am fearful for the other end of the voyage. It may be protracted into next spring and summer. However, it is too early to begin to worry about that. I suspect that scarcity of food may drive us home on time, the sole consolation of being improperly provisioned.

The calm is past, and we have been skipping along on the port tack since before dawn. The wind comes from the east, and the mainsail keeps my chair and book shaded from noon until sunset. Today begins my third trip across Cancer, back into the tropics a month after leaving.

SEPTEMBER 11. The merriest breeze for weeks. We have a cheerful list, as we head straight for the Cape Verdes. Soon I shall have "crossed" for the first time. I had counted upon going the length of the Atlantic but not the breadth. The afternoon is nothing short of chilly, and the sun is now dropping close to a crinkled, dark gray sea.

SEPTEMBER 12.   Lat. 23° 17' N., long. 28° 49' W.

We are only 350 miles from the Cape Verdes. A sperm whale was sighted this morning, but the Old Man announced that we would not lower, although he still keeps mastheads posted. Mutton birds, a kind of blue-gray petrel, began to appear in small flocks. They probably represent the rare species that nests on certain high islands of the Cape Verde group.

At evening, for a few minutes, there was a lovely new crescent moon, as slender as a bow. I always watch for it, night after night, because it grows so rapidly, and time flies, and then, as it passes full and wanes away, I know that I am a month nearer you. The Great Bear and Polaris are dropping low again; we have crossed latitude 23°.

SEPTEMBER 13.   The spanking breeze still holds, and we ought to make port by Sunday, day after tomorrow. Not a word of confirmation yet from the Old Man!

SEPTEMBER 14.   More and more mutton birds, foreshadowing a landfall.

I am greatly excited at the prospect of dropping a large sheaf of the log unexpectedly into your lap a few weeks hence. For ten days I have surmised from our course that we were going to the Cape Verdes. Now it seems evident, for we are within two hundred miles and are bearing straight toward them.

As I look back over what I have been writing for you, it seems a depressing record to send—calm after calm, and one adverse wind after another, until we have finally entered the Mediterranean or North African trades. Moreover, you may conclude that I have spent nine tenths of my time loafing, because the story gives scarcely an inkling of the collecting, preserving, photography, and other useful tasks that have kept me reasonably busy.

Let me recapitulate a little. My daily life is somewhat like this: I bounce out of my berth at 6:30 and take a look-around and a walk on deck before breakfast. Then I work at something in my outfit, or pickle and label and pack away specimens, or get out nets to try a surface haul. The mast-heads always report everything of possible interest to me. All members of the crew are glad to help me when they can. They look for nothing in return, but I take an unfeigned personal interest in each man and I have plug tobacco to spare, especially since I use none myself. They can't get much yet from the Old Man, because he doesn't believe in allowing a seaman's debit to run ahead of his equity. What if a moke should desert or die, still owing the ship? Horrible thought!

When the sun travels around behind the sail, I open the

luxurious canvas chair you gave me (now considerably patched), and read on top of the cabin. I have told you mostly of my reading for sheer fun, which includes thus far fourteen plays of Shakespeare, but I have also done a good stint of biological and geographical study, and have pumped everybody on board who has had experiences of special interest to me. The Old Man and the cooper have been my best sources, though the officers and two or three forecastle hands have helped, too. Then there is always Johnny, for the fictional and romantic role! I keep my eyes open for every sort of phenomenon in the world around me, and my scientific notes, descriptions, catalogue of specimens, and tables of measurements bulk as large as what I have written for you.

After dinner I work out the longitude, and then read again, or go to the masthead, unless there is action in which I can share. Sometimes I elect to stand a two-hour trick at the wheel. In the evening I pace the deck, trying to imitate a long walk, while standing as straight as a lance handle and breathing down to my midriff. Then, unless there are negatives to develop, I turn in before nine. During about one night in three, however, something is likely to happen on deck, or in the waters round about, or in the heavens above, to bring me up again. My standing orders to the officer on watch are to call me if he sees anything whatsoever that might interest me.

The captain has made the environment as comfortable as possible for me. I wish I might say that he has done as well for the others, but I can't. He's a lone wolf, and he tries to work off his unhappiness by being taciturn at mess or else by a half-bullying spout of words, of which the officers and the steward are the principal targets. He knows that the men forward have real grievances, and yet every reference to them now drives him blasphemous.

His secretiveness, apparently, is an old story. Last voyage, two years ago, he cleared for Kerguelen Island, in the southern Indian Ocean, according to the cooper, but actually took the brig to South Georgia, in the western South Atlantic, without mentioning his change of plan to anyone! I found out long ago that I can't demand information from him, because he always comes back with some such explanation as that circumstances beyond his control have not yet enabled him to decide. He's a natural-born sea lawyer, beyond a doubt.

The fact that we'll be late in reaching South Georgia won't interfere particularly with my work. The weather, indeed, will be better; it is very blizzardy during September and part of October. I don't think it will make us much later next spring, either, because the sea elephant season lasts only so long anyway, and, besides, we are not provisioned for a longer trip.

Your letter bag has proved a joy unending. How did you ever accomplish such a task? Each morning I look for the next date of the postman's call, and he has never kept me waiting more than four days. Friends, relatives, colleagues, professors —usually the individual I would be least likely to guess—all have caught up with me, but the real red-letter days come when the message is from you.

SEPTEMBER 15.   A gray Sunday morning, with a strong wind into which we are pointing. The Old Man's recent reckonings also indicate a crosscurrent from a northerly quarter. So the *Daisy* is battling at last, and it is invigorating after the sleepy reaches of the Sargasso Sea.

The mutton birds are now common, and I have no longer any doubt that they are Fea's petrel of the Cape Verdes, named for the Italian who collected the first one about 1899. They fly singly or in pairs, never approaching us closely, although we passed within half a length of one that was feeding on the floating carcass of a squid. Their flight, almost grazing the water, reminds me of a marsh harrier foraging over vast windy salt meadows at home, alternately soaring and beating its wings, now rising, now just skimming the pulsing waves of green thatch, wandering capriciously and of a sudden darting downward for its prey.

At 2:20 o'clock of a dark and blustery afternoon, the prolonged cry of "Land ho!" rang from the masthead. Shortly thereafter we made out Santo Antão, about twenty miles ahead, its western point rising abruptly 7,400 feet to the clouds. The landfall seemed to snap the tension of the Old Man. He suddenly became very genial, broke his oysterlike silence, and talked as though we had known all about where he was taking us. He hauled out the chart of the archipelago, and began to chatter to me about the several islands he had visited on former voyages.

At four o'clock we were welcomed to the Eastern Hemisphere by a tired swallow that alighted on one of the whaleboats. The bird is the Old World equivalent of our barn swallow, though slightly different. It is interesting that the American form was the last land bird we saw in the western Atlantic, and the European form the first to greet us on this side of the ocean.

When the cloudy evening closed in, we tacked and stood offshore, with the plan of bearing in again during the latter watches of the night.

SEPTEMBER 16. No need to tell you that I was on deck at peep of dawn. A long line of stratus clouds lay on the horizon and to the south I could make out only a dark promontory of Santo Antão, lost in the bank. Presently, however, I realized that only my mundane point of view had prevented me from seeing more land. When I raised my eyes, I found that the cloud bank was nearer the bottom of the island than the top, and, far above it, stretched the ethereal blue crest of the mountain. Although of lesser area than Dominica, where I last set foot on land forty-seven days ago, this island is nearly 3,000 feet higher.

We spent the whole day working inshore and across the seven-mile strait that separates Santo Antão from our destination on São Vicente. The *Daisy* approached the islands from the north and northeast. Except for short periods in early morning and at sunset, clouds and mist hid the lower face of the Santo Antão hills, and it seemed to be raining in every valley. In a gorge west of Punto do Sol two slender cascades, several hundred feet in length, were streaming from high ledges. A thin coating of bice-green foliage lay on the slopes, although bare rock showed through in most places. A number of hamlets, consisting of stone buildings with red tile roofs, stood out against a background of verdant terraces and almost perpendicular garden plots. The surf broke furiously upon beachless shore-lines, and from the foam basaltic dikes rose like buttresses against the steeps above. Over the gray water, set agleam by threads of sunlight leaking through slits in the still grayer clouds, mutton birds were sailing back and forth, and flying fish were bursting out before the rushes of albacores.

You, my darling Grace, are a mighty traveler. You have visited both the Alps and the Rockies. But your young husband is a provincial lad, who has never before seen mountains as lofty as eight or nine thousand feet. He has found quite awe-inspiring today's close view of precipices rising so high from the wild Atlantic that they have given him a crick in his neck. The Cape Verders have a proverb which says: "To be dashed to pieces is a natural death in Santo Antão."

From what I can see of these islands, they bear no such forests as the Antilles. Nevertheless, some of them are noted for their fruit. They are also famous for their seafaring half-breed men, who illustrate what biologists call "hybrid vigor." In stature and physique the Cape Verders are superior to both the colonial Portuguese who furnished the white fraction of their ancestry and the undersized Congo forest slaves who supplied the darker heritage.

On Cape Cod, these people are indiscriminately called "Bravas," and it is from the little island of Brava that most Cape Verde whalemen, including ours, have come. However, we have also one boy from Fogo, two or three from São Vicente and another, Manoel Merães—the best sailor in the forecastle—from Santo Antão. Captain Cleveland has a particularly high opinion of the Santo Antão men who, he says, can all handle boats and swim like Polynesians, and who, until recently, kept themselves in battle trim by never-ending bloody feuds among their fastnesses.

The Old Man, by the way, has been as unctuous and soft-spoken as a deacon in search of contributions for the church, ever since we made the land. I certainly have not heard him utter a swearword inside the twelve-mile limit, and when something irked him today he merely murmured, "My soul and body!"

Poor Old Man! He leads a hard and lonely life, and he pays for his own scrimping. He has not been well, and the burden of an aching back during much of the crossing has worn him down. The diet on board is atrocious for a human being of his years. It is bad enough for the officers and me, but most of us at least have teeth. The skipper, Mr. da Lomba and Mr. Alves are probably the only souls on the *Daisy* who have passed the age of thirty or thereabouts. The Old Man and the mate soak their bread in coffee or water, swallow "leather and wood" without chewing, and then squirm with the mulligrubs. Well, we'll take in new food here, replenish the West Indian supply of bananas and coconuts, and within six weeks or so we'll be handy to constant sources of fresh greens, fresh fish, and fresh penguin eggs!

The well-watered appearance of Santo Antão hardly prepared me for the desolation of the neighboring island of São Vicente, which is hell with the fires burnt out. The reason is that it lies in the lee or rain-shadow of the larger island, which steals all the precipitation. Bird Rock, with its surmounting lighthouse, in the harbor of Porto Grande, was visible from afar. Behind it naked, brick-red ridges are piled up helter-skelter, with sharply marked strata lying at every angle, and all ending in peaked and crumpled summits. One such crest, facing the town, outlines the recumbent profile of George Washington, as unmistakable as though the features had been sculptured by a titan.

The strength of attachment to a homeland came to my attention forcibly when we drew near this forlorn island. Native sons on deck, who had beheld without emotion some of the world's fairest spots, began to dance with patriotic joy, and one of them explained to me: "My country; I not see him for t'ree years!"

We anchored just before dark, and the brig now rests with sails furled, in the quiet, moonlit evening. I wish that I could convey a real picture of the jagged and infernal surroundings. Dante, to whose pages I turned many times on the way across the Atlantic, would feel at home here.

SEPTEMBER 17.   When the rising sun shone into the red bowl of Porto Grande, bumboats with lateen sails were already hovering about at a little distance, not daring to attempt to bargain with the skipper of the *Daisy* until we had received pratique.

After breakfast the mildly comical officials, all in uniform and escorted by skinny, sad-looking gendarmes wearing swords, came out in a launch. I expected them to climb on board, greet the captain warmly, and behave in general as the British port officers do in the West Indies. Nothing of the sort happened. Britons have a continuing maritime tradition, and the master of a ship—even of a humble windjammer and blubber-hunter—symbolizes a relatively lordly estate in their system. The Portuguese have a great maritime past, but it is a long way past. Prince Henry the Navigator, Vasco da Gama, Fernão Magalhaes (whom we call Magellan), Frey Concalobello, have no living significance to them. The visiting officials of Porto Grande evidently regarded the Old Man as just another foreigner, and doubtless an unimportant and un-profitable one. They coolly ordered him down into their launch with his papers, and there the necessary business was transacted as an unceremonious and poker-faced chore. I could sense the skipper's flush of humiliation, but he doubt-less knew what to expect. The gold-braided visitors then chugged off, leaving two of the sword-bearing boys to serve as a prize crew on the *Daisy* during our stay in port.

The Old Man hastened below, coughed and grunted to unruffle his feelings, and then dug out a cigar box containing some black powder and an old toothbrush, with which he pro-ceeded to darken his moustache. I remembered then that this adornment had appeared iron-gray whenever he landed in Barbados or Dominica, whereas at sea it has always been snowy. Then he went up from his cabin and announced that one boat's crew would take him ashore, but that the other men would have leave and liberty money later in the day.

So in to the landing place we pulled, I all atremble from the very unlikely possibility that one of your letters might have come to this port. There was no reason why it should have, for I believe that the Old Man's decision to visit the Cape Verdes was made only after he had learned the sad state of our larder.

We were enthusiastically welcomed by a crowd of jabber-ing small boys. "Bless their young hearts," I thought, "they are speaking English!" As soon as the meaning of their words sank through, I made a mental correction to "virginal hearts," because the message pouring out of each mouth was the same:

"For five cents I show you nice gal!"

I learned later that these ardent receptionists are great linguists, to the extent that they can offer the same hospitable services in French, German, Russian, the Scandinavian languages, and the tongue of the Lascars.

The Old Man and I went to the home of Senhor J. B. Guimaraes, American Vice Consul and agent for our whaleships. He is a most agreeable and courteous gentleman, who speaks perfect English. In response to my questions, he immediately sent a note to the governmental authorities requesting permission for me to bring a shotgun ashore and to collect in the environs of Porto Grande. All ships' mail was at his office, so he called a ten-year-old boy to guide me thither, while he and the skipper discussed over a bottle of wine the acquisition of stores for the *Daisy*. I anticipated a silent walk with my small guide because of the language barrier, but he presently looked at me archly and asked, "Mebbe you like see nice gal?"

The son of Guimaraes, at the office, knew not a word of English, and the vocabulary of my courier proved to be limited to the aforementioned sentiments. So I made a stab at asking in French about letters for the whaleship *Daisy* and received a most grateful and fluent reply, which continued more volubly than I could well follow while several score packets of ships' mail were inspected. There was nothing for anybody on board. I was assured that registered mail from here was quite as safe as from anywhere in the world, so I obtained a large, muslin-lined envelope for sending manuscript to you, and also addressed and stamped a batch of postcards, mostly depicting the rocky countenance of George Washington. I thought last evening that I had discovered him on the mountain, whereas he actually proves to be one of São Vicente's chief claims to fame!

My knowledge of this place had been derived from the prosy pages of the pilot book and from Moseley's account of his visit in the *Challenger*, thirty-nine years ago. The town of Porto Grande has evidently improved since 1873. It is now a community of nearly ten thousand inhabitants, and very busy because of the constant train of shipping. Business centers in the fuelling station, where all day long, and sometimes all night as well, files of stalwart black women dogtrot up narrow gangplanks, each balancing a bushel of coal on her head until she can empty it into the bunker of a steamer. A small braided mat protects the scalp. I never saw a hand raised to steady or adjust the burden, something that seemed especially remarkable on the return trip, when the baskets were light.

This may be the only kind of headwork in which these women indulge, but it is at least exercise that bestows a proud carriage and a queenly gait. Why not sell the idea to proprietors of beauty parlors at home?

Vessels in African and Indian Ocean trade are provisioned here, although nearly all the meat, fruit, vegetables, and grain used or sold are transported from other islands of the Cape Verdes. Santo Antão supplies most of the fruit, which includes delectable oranges.

The country around the town is desert or near-desert. There was a short shower, however, this morning. I asked when this had last happened, and Senhor Guimaraes replied: "Oh, it rained last year." Nevertheless, there are rows of small but dense and healthy shade trees along the principal streets of Porto Grande.

Most of the urban buildings are substantial and attractive, and the streets are clean. Yet they are filled with black children wearing nothing more than one coral bead. Whole strings of such youngsters perambulate, led by the biggest and dwindling from hand to hand down to two-year-olds. There are also many mulatto girls who disport elegant coiffures, silk dresses with a white shawl over one shoulder, heavy earrings and bracelets, but neither stockings nor shoes! Toward the borders of the town, the human picture grows more unsightly, because one runs into filthy dumps, dirt-covered hovels housing large families, and frightful hags. Many of these outskirt blacks must be living at the very bottom level of subsistence, for this is different from a tropical island at which food of some sort may be had for the plucking.

My collecting permit was obtained within two hours! It is a beautiful document, no product of a typewriter but indited by a scribe whose joy is in penmanship. It instructs the police and all others that the *naturalista americano* is authorized to commit murder on the fauna of São Vicente, but it was delivered with an oral request that I refrain from shooting quail, which are just beginning to nest with the onset of the so-called rainy season. So, after a late forenoon snack on board, I came ashore again, armed and accoutred, and started into the country with Conrad as my henchman and game-bearer. He carried a vasculum and a haversack.

We covered many miles across stony, dusty plains, along beaches and up and down steep slopes. We snooped in white-walled cemeteries, and through copses of tamarisks near the sea, and collected a miscellaneous lot of insects, lizards, mollusks, birds, and plants. Among birds, I was looking particularly for the Cape Verde Island sparrow, found only in this archipelago and first collected by Darwin. We took four examples among the tamarisks. I shot also some whimbrels, a raven, and a white Egyptian vulture, or Pharaoh's chicken, a species that ranges all across North Africa to these islands.

The vulture I killed with a phenomenally long shot, near the Porto Grande garbage dump. A native boy was standing by, and he ran to fetch my specimen. I used all the Portuguese

I know in asking him, *"Como se chama?"* (what do you call it?).

Passaro branco (white bird), he answered, which seemed to reveal a limited imagination. Then he eyed me for a moment and inquired, "How you like me show you nice gal?" I drew the conclusion that every little bastard in or near Porto Grande is a full-fledged commission merchant.

We returned to town dusty and tired, laden down with spoil. Conrad tried to look nonchalant as he toted a great white vulture through the crowded streets. In the words of Hamlet, I ordered him to lug the guts to our waiting whale-boat, while I stopped for a whiskey and soda with Senhor Guimaraes. There I met no less a personage than the Governor of the island, a little man, dressed scrupulously in white, and extraordinarily unhappy looking. If Madeira is the "A" colonial post of Portugal, I judge that São Vicente must be the "Z."

SEPTEMBER 18.   I had to skin my Pharaoh's chicken last evening in order to be permitted to keep it on board at all. The Old Man vowed that the bird had fed exclusively upon human corpses.

This morning the record of our life from day to day has been posted to you. Mr. Alves, the mate, has obtained his discharge, the alleged reason being his lame foot, which was run over by a cart in Barbados. He may have been paid off in small part but most of his credit status was left for future settlement in the hands of Senhor Guimaraes. Long credit, but good credit, is taken for granted in Yankee whaling. Captain Cleveland needs practically no money because he can apparently purchase whatever he wants, anywhere, by drawing a draft on New Bedford.

Mr. da Lomba now becomes first officer *de jure*, which he had previously been *de facto*. Despite his intellectual limitations, he is the ablest and most masterful man on board. Per-

haps he inherits a few drops of briny blood from Tristan da
Cunha and other Portuguese mariners of the Golden Age.

The Old Man has taken on a lot of food—potatoes, yams,
tea, fruit, salted and tinned meat, onions, beans, rice, flour,
etc. He had to pay $30 a barrel (double the home price) for
salt beef, so he has ordered the ration cut down to one portion
a day. While he was ashore, the harponeers smuggled on
board a young, mongrel, long-tailed, female fox terrier,
warranted to kill rats. They have hidden her in the steerage,
and the Old Man is not to know of it until we are well out at
sea. A blue-eyed kitten has likewise been added to our floating ménage.

We are now waiting for clearance and shall soon be under
way. I am poring over several odd copies of the *New York
World*, all published within five weeks of the present date and
presented to me by Senhor Guimaraes.

Our Portuguese guards have liked their duty on the
Daisy. They have shown two main interests: (1) eating and (2)
sleeping; and have gained their ends by a thoroughly tested
system. Upon being left with us, they first unbelted their
swords, laid them on the carpenter's bench, and then sought
out the steward and Johnny in pursuit of provender. Next
they borrowed a pillow from the cabin, and one of them went
to sleep, while the other watched. Us? Not at all! He watched
the harbor so that he could awaken his fellow and don the
sword in case an official launch seemed likely to approach. In
due course he changed places with the first sleeper, but at
meal times they were always on the job together.

3 Southeast Trades

SEPTEMBER 19.   Once more we have broken ties with the world. Won't you be surprised about the middle of October, or sooner, to catch up with me as far as the Cape Verdes? I gave one of our departing gendarmes two hundred some-things—equal to 50¢—to stamp and post one more short letter to you.

The vicinity of these islands is subject to strange meteorological conditions, such as the harmattan or dust-laden wind from Africa and the sudden squalls of the rainy season (August to October). Such a twister struck us in the forenoon today, coming up with practically no warning against the northeast trade wind and almost flattening us. When the *Daisy* canted until water gushed in through the scuppers, I feared that we were about to be dismasted. Instead, however, the strong craft leaped ahead, while her spars groaned, and we pointed into the wind enough to ease the strain. Severe gusts continued for an exceptionally long while, whipping up the surface and eventually leaving us in a miserable tumbling calm for the afternoon. At the height of the storm, a flock of brown boobies passed us, following a shoal of huge albacores which, in turn, were hunting sardines.

Between afternoon and evening, as we came abreast of Brava, toward which many of our boys cast wistful eyes, a tropic-bird flew across the deck. Above and east of Brava the great cone of Fogo loomed up dimly, with a column of smoke or dust rising from it. This volcano, 9,760 feet, is the highest oceanic island in the Atlantic except Tenerife. It was last in violent eruption in the year 1847.

SEPTEMBER 20.   The nights are now becoming sultry again, except when the northeast trade wind blows briskly. We are south of the latitude of Barbados and we expect generally fair winds down to about 09° N. There, in the doldrums, we hope to find enough variable breezes to carry us somehow across the line and into the southeast trades.

I finished preparing my specimens from São Vicente.

SEPTEMBER 21.   Uncomfortably warm, and barely wind enough to keep us moving, until it freshened toward evening.

The dog, which I had almost forgotten, and which was concealed at São Vicente only for fear that the Old Man would turn thumbs down, was casually let loose on deck this afternoon. The men called her "Cadella." When the skipper came up from his cabin he looked momentarily startled, but then screwed his face into the grim, disapproving expression that usually indicates contentment, and announced:

"Fine! We'll keep her on the v'yage to kill the rats. Her name'll be Lizzie."

I thought to myself that nobody but a prosaic, hard-bitten old Yankee from Martha's Vineyard would give a pet such a handle. The Portuguese doubtless had the same idea, because they went right on calling her Cadella, as did the West Indians and everybody else. Within the next hour all hands had played with the pup until she was fagged, and her musical name rang out from topgallant forecastle to quarterdeck as officers, harponeers and seamen continued to call her.

These Romance peoples, I mused, have an innate sense of beauty, even down to humble half-caste sailors. "Cadella," with a lingering penultimate and a liquid "l"; a euphonious name, worthy of any lovely maiden! I turned toward the cooper, my mentor in all learned matters, and inquired: "Who was Cadella in history? Is it just a girl's name, or was she a queen of the Old Kingdom?" And, with completely unconscious solemnity, the cooper replied:

"Cadella ees justa *portuguesa* for bitch."

The kitten and Cadella have taken to each other at once, perhaps because they are both Portuguese. They tumble and play together all over the main deck. Like other members of the crew, they are not supposed to come abaft the mainmast except on official duty. So far they have had none. In temperament they both resemble their human compatriots of the Cape Verdes, being chummy and merry. I begin to understand the French simile *"joyeux comme un portugais."*

SEPTEMBER 22.   It has been annoyingly calm. This afternoon a sixty-pound albacore was first hooked and then harpooned from the bowsprit. Two irons were needed to secure it, and within three hours it had all been eaten.

SEPTEMBER 23.   Many happy returns of the day! It's a well preserved woman you are, at the ripe old age of twenty-four. I have been thinking of the birthdays that have passed since I first met you, and longing for this same date next year. Early this morning I took out of the letter bag the missive of five sheets, dated September 23 but probably written last March or April. As a tour de force of verisimilitude it is the trickiest and most wonderful composition! I can't believe that it wasn't written this morning, just as you state!

Our position is latitude 12° 46' N., longitude 25° 05' W., and the sun has thus beaten us in the race to cross the equator. The day has been dead calm and perhaps the hottest I have ever lived through. I have even acquired a new sunburn through my tropical tan.

At eight o'clock this morning Mother Carey's chickens were sighted. Since the brig was as good as anchored, I had the dory lowered, took Conrad as oarsman, and went shooting. The birds proved to be my old friends, Wilson's petrels, which nest in the far south and spend the winter (our summer) in the North Atlantic. They are now headed homeward so as to have eggs or young ready for me when we arrive at South Georgia. I collected also a jaeger, or robber gull, which is the converse kind of migrant, namely an Arctic bird bound southward for its winter vacation.

In afternoon all our whaleboats were down because an enormous school of blackfish surrounded us. The creatures were exasperating as never before; in the absolutely still water they lay with backs exposed—hundreds of them—and yet were so wary that not one boat could come close enough to dart an iron. The boys shipped oars, sat on the gunwales of the boats wielding paddles, and tried to sneak up silently on their prey, but their efforts were of no avail.

A butterfly flew across the deck this afternoon and a dragonfly bumped into the bunt of the mainsail. Have they flown to this position or are they stowaways that we have carried from the Cape Verdes? We are now approximately 125 miles from the southernmost islands of the group and 480 miles from the African coast.

In late afternoon I wrapped a couple of bottles of Mouton in a wet towel and exposed them atop the cabin just as a faint air began to move. This proved a partially successful means of bringing the temperature of the wine down from eighty-odd toward 66° F. The Old Man subsequently proposed the toast at your birthday dinner, and did it quite handsomely. The fodder has vastly improved since our call at São Vicente, and we have been enjoying an abundance of potatoes, yams, onions, rice, succotash, bananas, and oranges. Now, with good food and half a pint inside, I hope to dream of you for ten oblivious hours.

SEPTEMBER 24. Another calm scorcher, ending with the sudden, equatorial darkness and then a torrent of rain. Again I undertook bird collecting. More dragonflies were noted during the day. Since they appear to approach the *Daisy* from a distance, pass by, and proceed straight on until neither the naked eye nor field glasses can keep them longer in view, I am convinced that the insects have reached this position under their own power.

SEPTEMBER 25. Rainy. Lowered alone in the dory for observation and collecting. I stayed as long as possible, because the combination of rain and calm, and of heat and dim light below decks, makes life on board extremely dull. It is impossible to read in comfort at the very time that one has most leisure for books.

A shark, several pilot fish, and a number of big albacores nosed around us half the day, but all avoided being hooked.

Clearing weather and a head wind at evening.

SEPTEMBER 26. Nearly calm again. It seems a good many days since we have moved more than a few lengths, and there is still an equator to cross. It is a pleasure at least to sit above decks in my chair again, after packing up a box of jars containing specimens in alcohol and stowing away all my new bird skins.

Cadella, ferocious hound, now spends most of her waking hours killing cockroaches. She has learned to lie in ambush, like a cat, and to watch for the first brown and varnished ene-

my that rears its horrific head above the combing of the main
hatch. As for rats, she flees them! We turned two loose on
deck from a cage trap, and Cadella immediately decamped,
with her tail decurved. The Old Man has not failed to emphasize to his officers that she is purely a "Portugee dog." In fact,
his harping on this aspect of the matter has long since ceased
to be amusing.

SEPTEMBER 27. Lat. 10° 46' N., long. 24° 38' W.
Calm, with heavy swell all morning. A welcome northerly
breeze sprang up later in the day.

New papers show that Mr. da Lomba, now aged forty-
one, was shipped as mate at Saint Vincent on September 17,
1912, following the discharge of Mr. Alves. Apparently the Old
Man did not trouble to sign him on at Dominica; he just came
along for the sail! His lay is recorded as one-eighteenth, the
highest in the crew except the Old Man's.

	Officers	*Harponeers*
Starboard boat	Mr. da Lomba	Emiliano Ramos
Larboard boat	Mr. Vincent	Francisco Nicolau
Waist boat	Mr. Almeida	Antão Neves
Bow boat	Victor Robinson	José Gaspar

José Gaspar is the newest harponeer, whom we picked
up at Roseau. He is of light complexion, well set up and has
an attractive personal pride and dignity. In fact, he has the
bearing of a conquistador, and looks as I think some of the old
Portuguese maritime heroes should have looked.

Victor is fourth officer and boatheader. He has not yet
become "Mister" because he lives in the steerage (for want of
room aft), and because he still serves as harponeer—and the
best we have—if only three boats are sent down. Francisco

Nicolau, called merely Frank, is not in the pink of health and often remains aboard as a shipkeeper when a hunt is on. To my mind, Frank is cracking up at such a rate that the Old Man would have been wise to pay him off and discharge him at his home in the Cape Verdes.

The formality of address on a whaleship is just as strict as on a clipper or a man-of-war. It goes without saying that the skipper is never called anything but captain, although he may be indirectly referred to as the Old Man. The officers are invariably addressed as mister. In the privacy of his own cabin, Captain Cleveland may call the mate "John," because his relationship is almost that of a foster father, but on deck or at mess he would never think of using any other term than Mr. da Lomba. The only halfway departures from the code on the *Daisy* are the cases of our second mate, who is always called Mr. Vincent, although his full name is Vicente Lunda, and of Victor, which I have already explained.

Today I saw two kinds of Mother Carey's chickens as well as other sea birds near the brig. In the calm air we carried no forward motion, though we were rolling and tossing in a lively swell. The Old Man gave me permission to lower the dory, which was effected not without difficulty, and the cooper and I set off birding, with moderate success.

While we were wallowing in a trough, one wall of water hiding all of the *Daisy* save her topmasts and another racing toward us to lift us high, a big shark came up and circled the *Grace Emeline*. Thereafter it clung to us as we pulled toward the vessel, several times rubbing the planking and frequently thrusting out its back fin close alongside. It offered no violence, and I am probably guilty of overstatement when I say that it acted as though it wanted to eat us.

However, there is no overstatement in the report that we ate it, which on the man-bites-dog criterion should be news!

We led it all the way back to the *Daisy*, from the deck of which the harponeers fed it several small chunks of pork fat, ending with one enclosing a shark hook. Not only did we thus treacherously take the shark, but we also took three remoras that stuck to it, high and dry, to the bitter end, as well as two pilot fish that seemed quite leaderless after their boss had been hoisted out of water. They just waited for Johnny to lower hooks for them and each vied with the other to be caught first.

Later in the day I felt ill in my midship section—my first moment of indisposition on the voyage. It could not have been the shark meat, because at least six others had partaken of it with no ill effect. The Old Man, instead of going to his medicine chest, gave me some blackberry cordial and later had two large pieces of toast and a cup of tea prepared for my supper.

By the time the quick darkness fell, I knew that my troubles were passing. A fair wind is blowing up now, just as I am turning in for the night. I can feel and hear the indefinable sensation that tells me we are sliding forward.

SEPTEMBER 28. A beautiful, light, fair breeze has carried us southward all day long.

My illness has gone, but I have not felt energetic, and I did not walk on deck until the sun ducked under just in time to avoid facing the moon, which is now past full. I read in my berth while the light was good—*King Henry the Fifth* and *King Henry the Eighth*.

The chief drawback to a day below is that I have to stoop wherever I go and, indeed, whenever I stand. I want to live up to my promise to reach old age with the carriage and bearing of Daniel Giraud Elliot.

SEPTEMBER 29. A dull Sunday in the doldrums, with calms and showers, and whatever hope a rainbow at evening brings.

A flock of terns, probably of the species called the Arctic tern, flew past us, plunging beneath the surface for their prey and scattering pearls from their wings as they emerged. They had all gone on southward before I could fetch a gun to settle the question of identification.

SEPTEMBER 30.   At breakfast we ate by lamplight, for the first time on the cruise.

The day was very hot and calm, and up to noon we had progressed but three miles during the past twenty-four hours. Heavy showers, marked by no trace of wind, fell several times. After dark, however, puffy squalls blew up. I have just been walking the quarterdeck in oilskins. It was exhilarating to be in the spattering dark, to watch the foamy spots on the black water racing sternward, to feel the cool night wind and colder drops on my neck. The tattoo on my sou'wester sounded like rain on the old shingle roof under which I used to sleep.

OCTOBER 1.   Lat. 07° 55' N., long. 24° W. The fifth month of our pilgrimage begins. Brisk southerly or head winds, ending in a tumbling calm which is, of course, far more unpleasant than a dead calm.

At nine o'clock this morning a big sperm whale was sighted, going quickly to windward and blowing out conspicuous and regular spouts. While three boats were being lowered, he crossed our bow at close range and I had a superb view of him from halfway up the rigging. His progression was marked by a gentle rocking or pitching, the blunt junk and the hump on the after-back alternately rising and falling. The flukes did not break the surface at any stage of their stroke. The appearance of ease, smoothness, and speed was exceedingly impressive.

The first sign of the forward end on the upswing was usually the spout, which burst forth a split second before the tip of the snout was exposed. The spout was slanted in the

direction of the whale's course, and it fountained out for at
least two seconds, perhaps longer. Mainly condensed vapor, it
included also a basal spray of water due to the fact that violent expulsion of the breath began before the spiracle had
quite reached the open air. This is contrary to what the
books describe to us.

When the snout was at its high point, possibly eighteen
inches above the water, I could see the mound made by the
dilated lips of the single nostril as air was sucked back into
the lungs. Then the whole head rocked slowly down, the long
back rose and leveled, and the gleaming but curiously crinkled and rubbery skin showed clearly. Finally, the angular
hump pitched into view, for a moment exposing also several
of the lesser knobs and notches that lie along the crest of the
back between hump and flukes. When the hump was highest,
the submerged junk was lowest, and vice versa.

In less time than it will take you to read this, of course,
the whale was nearly out of sight. As he moved away majestically, a quatrain from Moby Dick came into my mind—one
from the introductory pages which Herman Melville credits
to an hypothetical "sub-sub-librarian." I began to sing it, not
knowing whether or not it ever had a tune, and devised the
following, which might go well if arranged for a quartet of
lusty young throats. What think ye, Grace and Captain Ahab,
of a song by Melville and Murphy?

Oh the rare old Whale, mid storm and gale In his o-cean home will be A
gi-ant in might, where might is right, And King of the bound-less sea.

The boats returned empty-handed after an hour's chase.

The leverage of whaleboat oars is extremely powerful because each rower sits at the end of his thwart farthest from

his oarlock. Midship oar, with its oarlock on the starboard gunwale, is the longest—18 feet. Bow and tub oars, respectively afore and aft of the midship oar, are shorter and of identical length. They both rest on the port gunwale. Harponeer and after (or stroke) oars, nearest bow and stern and both starboard, are the shortest of all and likewise identical. Thus one long and two shorts to starboard work against two of medium length to port. And how our boats skim and fly when they race all abreast toward the brig!

Getting through the doldrums and across the equator is a tedious and discouraging process. I hope that the South Atlantic will turn out to be more exciting, and that we may sight South Georgia before Christmas. Sometimes, when I think of the endless weeks of our southward course, I become fearful of the return. Last voyage the *Daisy* spent seven months on the way between South Georgia and New Bedford.

The Portugee cat has put the Portugee dog to shame by stalking and killing a half grown rat. However, Cadella is learning courage with experience and is beginning to take the orthodox terrier, or lethal, interest in rats.

OCTOBER 2. Evidently we are once more on sperm whale grounds. At half past six this morning the boats were down after a big bull, but again in vain. In midmorning, however, a school was sighted and the lowering, hauling aback, and all other maneuvers were repeated.

The three boats became widely scattered, and one went so far out into the dim horizon that we lost sight of it for a time. However, each crew killed its whale. It was half past three in the afternoon before we had the carcasses all alongside, and also before anybody had a dollop of grub beyond his early breakfast. Moreover, the meal was a quick and a poor one, and Mr. da Lomba got the cutting-in started without stopping for a bite.

All three whales were rather small, and the cutting-in

was completed at night. Then mincing and boiling were begun, while the last whale was still being hacked and stripped by artificial illumination. Between half past eight and nine o'clock in the evening we had supper in shifts. The meal was at least hearty—hash of salt beef, potatoes and onions, sperm whale steak, corn hoecakes and tea. Work is to be continued through the night.

OCTOBER 3.   I stayed up until all hours, watching every process, moving about the dusky, slippery deck, or sitting atop the cabin, in a whaleboat on the davits, or anywhere else that offered a good view. If there is any modern counterpart of an uncouth revel around a witches' brew, it is the scene of the trypots at night.

It was eight bells (midnight) when we had cut-in the final fish. The *Daisy*, with topsails aback, rolled gently in the quiet swell, while the officers on the cutting stage punched with their spades as best they could in the dismal light of lanterns and oil-soaked torches. The flickering glare showed the hulk of the whale alongside and the flash of bloody wavelets beyond. On deck a cresset, or bug light, of burning blubber scrap, and the fiery chimneys of the tryworks in full blast, cast enough illumination to reveal the great blankets of blubber and the greasy, toiling figures scurrying about amid the shouting of orders, the creak of tackles and the clank of chains. At six bells the last strip came over the plank-sheer. The severed head of the whale floated by the starboard quarter, lashed securely and ready to be handled at daybreak. Only the rite of the whaleman's ultimate hope remained to be carried out before the flensed carcass should be cut adrift.

The Old Man joined his officers on the cutting stage. Then, with methodical movements, he and the three mates thrust freshly sharpened cutting spades deeply into the guts of the whale, twisted them, cautiously withdrew them,

smelled the bright steel blades, and scrutinized them pains-
takingly in the glow of a lantern, while the crew looked on in
fevered anticipation. Back and forth along the stage the four
men trod and jabbed, until the vitals had been intimately explored. But nary a whiff of the longed-for odor of ambergris
was forthcoming. "And so to bed."

Our position at noon today was latitude 06° 30' N.,
longitude 25° 03' W.

The processing of yesterday's whales and the disposition
of the ultimate residues—oil and scrap—are still going on. It is
the only aspect of Yankee whaling that I have not yet described to you, so here goes:

After blubber is hoisted aboard until the main deck presents a discouraging appearance, heaped up with the overflow
of the blubber room; after one or more carcasses have been
cut adrift, and the spermaceti has been bailed from the cases;
after every member of the crew is at the point of collapse
from hustling, hauling, chopping, lashing, stowing, rocking the
windlass, and slipping galley-west on the greasy planks—then
you are ready to mince and boil. Some skippers have a pleasant interlude between cutting-in and cooking. It is known as
splicing the main brace, which means that each sweaty man
files to the quarterdeck and gulps down a tot of rum. But no
such happy custom prevails on the *Daisy*. The Old Man believes that there is already far too much drinking and profanity in the world.

The blanket pieces, above and below deck, are cut into
"horse pieces," which are flitches about two feet long and a
little wider than the thickness of the blubber. These are handled with two-pronged blubber forks and are heaped along
the port rail, ready for mincing. The strips are minced before
boiling so that the heat may penetrate every portion of the fat
and extract all the oil. Mincing is accomplished with a huge

double-handled drawknife. One man, holding a meat hook, pushes horse pieces along a table, while another slashes across and back with the drawknife, cutting the strip into thin slices. These, however, are not completely severed, but are left clinging together, like bacon on the rind, so that the whole strip—now called a "bible"—can be manipulated on a blubber fork.

The bibles are boiled in the tryworks on the forward deck, which consist of an enormous pair of iron pots in a brick support and fire-box, the latter being insulated from the wooden deck by a water bath. Beside the tryworks stands the cooler, a rectangular iron tank into which the oil is ladled from the pots.

The blubber is boiled until the minced strips, crisp, shriveled, and of a golden-brown color, rise to the bubbling surface, where they float like clinkers. They then constitute the scrap, which is the fuel of this self-supporting process. The boiled-out blubber of one victim is used to cook the next one. The bits of scrap are pitched off the pots, after a momentary drainage, and are subsequently fed to the fires beneath, burning with an avid and roaring flame, and leaving almost no ash.

After the boiled oil, now of a beautiful amber hue, has been passed through the cooler to the storage tank between decks, the ship gets once more under way, the lookouts mount to their perches, the decks are scoured, the rigging cleaned of its accumulation of grease and soot, and the watch, with the cooper in charge, runs the oil through a canvas hose into the bungs of the great casks. From the quarterdeck the Old Man, looking very sour—as he invariably does when he is happiest —casts his weather eye aloft and orders the mastheads to look sharp and raise another whale. And everybody longs for a repetition of the hard labor because, after all, every barrel of oil is a barrel nearer a full ship and homeward bound.

The boats were down again today, but had no luck because an enormous number of porpoises gallied the sperm whales. Mr. da Lomba said that porpoises were scurrying like fleas around their big cousins, and even jumping over them. After giving up the serious part of the chase, he ordered his boatsteerer to harpoon a porpoise for me, and I am now about to clean up its whole skeleton. It was uncanny to see sharks follow home the whaleboat containing the dead porpoise, whereas they ignored the clean boats headed by Mr. Vincent and Mr. Almeida.

For supper we had porpoise steak (only so-so), porpoise liver (really excellent), and boiled new white potatoes (a luxury to vie with ambrosia!). We ate also a beautiful fish, hooked this morning while the brig lay drifting. This fish, called the blue-lined runner or rainbow runner, looked more like the personification of speed than anything I have ever seen taken out of the ocean. It was forty inches long, spindle-shaped, smooth, and streamlined. Its fins were small and there were no projections to impede its progress through the water. Its flanks were racily decorated with two bright blue streaks, one of which passed over, and the other beneath, the eye. It contained a large double roe, as toothsome as shad roe.

Three sail were in sight on the horizon all day.

OCTOBER 4. Last evening, for the first time, I nearly killed myself. There will doubtless be other occasions! A petrel flew aboard, dazzled by a light, and, when I ran to catch it, I slipped on the oily deck and struck my head against the iron combing of the main hatch. I retained just enough consciousness to enjoy the display of shooting stars, comets, meteors, and other heavenly bodies in rapid motion, after which I was carried below. My head then fell into rhythm with the orbs and spheres, and continued to spin all night. By morning the revolutions had ceased, and I now have merely a large and tender swelling behind my right ear.

The men on watch did not forget my interests. They captured two Leach's petrels during the night and kept them for me. This morning I ringed one of them with a numbered aluminum band of the American Bird Banding Association and set it free.

No sperm whales disturbed us today, but we harpooned a big blue shark from deck. We have been running southward before a light wind, interrupted by several furious little tempests and downpours. As Shakespeare says, "Small showers last long, but sudden storms are short."

OCTOBER 5.   The bones of my porpoise are well macerated, and most of them are drying. The beast proved easy to identify from True's book. Its name, if you and the captain must know, is *Prodelphinus froenatus*. Are you any better off? I have photographs and a good sketch of it.

OCTOBER 6.   Sunday. A big bark that has been in sight for several days is now running parallel with us, but too far off to signal.

I have spent the whole day tinkering with my Graflex camera, the shutter of which refuses to work. It would be calamitous to lose the use of it. Unfortunately, the manufacturers publish no directions for amateur dismounting and assembling, as the gunmakers do for their arms.

OCTOBER 7.   Stormy, and too dark for meddling with the mechanism of the Graflex.

Just before nightfall we hooked an albacore, from the stomach of which I took a haul of specimens in perfect condition. They comprised small fish of two species, a crab, and a delicate and exquisite swimming snail of a sort that builds itself a raft of bubbles. It is related to the Mediterranean snail from which the ancients prepared the dye called Tyrian purple, a fact commemorated in the generic name of the creature, *Janthina*. This example, which the obliging albacore captured for me, is the first I have ever seen in the full glory of its living color.

OCTOBER 8. Lat. 04° 25' N., long. 22° 40' W. I still hope that we may sneak across the equator while it isn't looking.

The Graflex is mended, to my vast relief. I worked all morning over it, with the sympathetic interest and help of the Old Man. Its anatomy gave me no trouble but its physiology was most baffling, and I had a terrible task getting it together so that all parts functioned one with another. Anyway, the shutter no longer clogs, the whole instrument is cleaned inside and outside, and the springs and bearings are oiled. I have already tried it out on the Mother Carey's chickens that fly up under our counter.

These trailing birds are Wilson's petrels, still bound south with us. I have been feeding them small bits of porpoise blubber and have learned, to my surprise, that they can dive skilfully to a depth of several times their length, almost invariably recovering sinking food and then leaping forth dry into the air. This afternoon the flock of thirty or more little black birds performed a wonderful aerial dance. After following all day, they ceased to hunt food shortly before sunset and began to dash hither and yon in wild abandon, sometimes shooting upward as far as the masthead and then plunging back at high speed. Perhaps this behavior is prophetic of their courtship in the cold south.

We are now westing before crossing the line. The big bark, a craft of 1,500 tons or more, is still abeam, under nineteen swelling canvases.

From the middle of the afternoon a bank of cottony cumulus clouds has hung in the west. I have just been on deck, after supper, to see Venus, alone in the sky, glowing above the crest and flanked by two mountainous thunderheads.

Since eight bells this morning there has been a man in irons down in the lazaret, and a sick one at that. He was too ill for duty. After the Old Man had examined him, he fetched some medicine, which the sailor refused to accept. The skipper then offered him ten minutes in which he might make one of three choices—either to join his watch on the job, take the medicine, or be put in irons. The boy was stubborn and held out his wrists, after which he was assisted aft by two of his fellows. At mealtimes they lift the hatch, unlock one handcuff, and pass down hard bread and water. Now they have just given him his blanket for the night. What a prospect! Sick, manacled, lying on a coil of rope, in a sort of maritime dungeon that stinks of bilge gas and paint stores! I wish that there were something I could do about it. But, as the Old Man says, he remains there only at his own will.

OCTOBER 9.   South of 04° N. We are still making westing in a strong wind.

The prisoner remained incarcerated throughout the day, but toward evening reported that he was ready to swallow his dose. Shortly thereafter the Old Man came to the lazaret with a spoon and a bottle of God knows what. The boy was freed and walked to the bow under his own power, obviously in much better shape than yesterday. I dare say that thirty-six hours of going hungry may have been what his insides most needed.

OCTOBER 10.   Evening. This has been the most exciting day of my life. Even though the cabin lamp is a poor, dull flicker, I must pour my experiences onto paper while they are still fluid.

The morning broke gray and overcast, with a strong wind whipping the ocean. About eight o'clock a squall blew up, bringing a torrent of rain which was just at its height when a school of sperm whales rose a few ship's lengths to windward.

The boats were at once cleared on the davits and all hands stood by. The rain presently slackened and the weather brightened enough for us to see at least two pods of whales spouting off our quarter, and others astern. When the order, "Lower away!" was shouted and echoed, I slid down into the mate's boat and took stroke oar, replacing a Dominican who remained with the shiptenders.

Seeing that the spouts were fast pulling to leeward, we stepped the mast, after reefing, for the wind was brisk and the sea choppy. As soon as the whales had sounded, indicating that they were foraging and not alarmed, we zigzagged and jibed to hold our headway, while we lashed the line tubs to the thwarts, poured sea water over the rope, and put all gear in order. Then the blue waif at the *Daisy*'s masthead signaled "whales up" and gave direction. Mr. da Lomba pulled the tiller sharply; once more we jibed and made off before the wind, with the other two boats running abreast of us on either side. By this time it was raining a deluge again and we were drenched to the skin.

While we were bearing down toward the school, which was now steaming at the surface in preparation for the next dive, two good-sized bulls popped up unexpectedly just ahead and we were whisked upon them. The nearer of the pair crossed our bow and, while its gray body glided along a little under water, Emiliano drove the iron into the whale's right side, just in front of the hump. As the beast leaped forward, his whole massive head breached above the surface and his flukes grazed the keel as he cleared us and dashed to windward, making the wet line groan when it tautened and began to rub round the loggerhead.

Sail was dropped, mast lowered, and rudder unshipped, while harponeer and mate changed ends, the latter forsaking the helm for the still more ticklish business of lancing.

Our whale's run was for only a short distance. Coming up
with others of the school, he joined them, and we could see him
lying calmly at the surface. We four oarsmen now hauled line,
the boatsteerer holding the turn around the loggerhead and
coiling slack in the stern sheets as it was paid in. We pulled as
hard and as fast as we could and, when we neared the whale,
a strange sight was presented through the curtain of rain. Our
whale lay wallowing, the harpoon shaft projecting from his
blubbery back; beyond him were three or four half-grown
calves. On the near side lay a second bull, belly up, his jaw
and most of his head out of water, and our harpoon line
caught between two of his teeth.

Mr. da Lomba gesticulated frantically for the other boats
to come up, and we waited silently but in a shiver of impa-
tience. Before Mr. Vincent's boat could arrive, the bull which
had fouled our line, and which had probably been puzzled by
the obstacle, allowed it to slip from his jaw. We then hauled
up on the whale to which we were fast and, when the keel
pressed his side, the mate drove in the long keen lance to the
socket. Within the same instant the hump hove up, the great
flukes reared into the air, our bow went down with a jerk, and
we shipped a couple of barrels of water as the whale sounded.

"Forty-barrel bull," said Mr. da Lomba.

Forty-barrel bull! I recalled then what the Old Man had
told me long before, that no big sperm whale is likely to make
as much excitement for a boat's crew as a lusty forty-barrel
bull, enjoying the most active period of his watery life.

For a quarter of an hour we bobbed about quietly within
a small area, the line snubbed round the loggerhead, Emiliano
expressing the sentiment of all good boatsteerers by slacken-
ing it as little as possible and only at the last moment of
safety. Then the expected burst of vapor appeared to windward, the lopsided head began to seesaw with the pointed
hump, and we shot ahead on our sleigh ride.

The sun broke through the louring clouds, thawing out our goose flesh while we strained at the line and gradually gained on our unwillingly harnessed beast. But the whale had been goaded to alertness, and the lance puncture had been too far aft to affect his staying powers. Before we attained even pitch-poling distance, he sounded again, jerked us about, carried us back two miles before the wind, and then, without rising to the surface, plunged deeper, tearing the smoking line after him and soon exhausting the two hundred fathoms in the large tub. When the contents of the small tub began to follow, we were in a quandary. But in the nick of time one of the other boats sailed alongside; we bent on borrowed line, and saved our forty barrels!

In the middle of this fight into which I was putting all I had, I confess to a certain sympathy with the enemy. It seemed reasonable at least that after being pricked with the harpoon that still galled him, and pierced through with the horrible lance, the whale should wish to steer clear of us. This, however, was not at all the mate's idea of good form and fair play. Standing like an armed crusader in the bow of the boat, Long John da Lomba would scratch his head after the whale had sounded, and mutter, "I cain't understan' what make that animile so goddam shy!"

Our status, I thought from time to time, was that of the tin can on a dog's tail. We annoyed the whale, but were otherwise pretty helpless.

Time flies with a fighting whale on one's hands. The sun climbed to the zenith and its pleasant beams alternated with cold showers while we sped over the rugged, white-capped Atlantic, wearing the skin off our palms in this yet undecided tug-of-war. The whale battled nobly for his life. He tried sounding, spinning, and running all ways with respect to the wind. At one time he was towing three whaleboats, besides two drogue tubs, one of which is alleged to offer as much resistance as four boats. Watching one of these tubs dragged through the water at high speed made me marvel that the single tiny harpoon was not ripped from its anchorage in the blubber.

During a midday tempest, the roughest period of our chase, the whale pulled us cross-seas through the troughs and crests so that combers slopped over the gunwales. It was then that we kicked off our oil-skin pants (I was the only man wearing shoes), so as to be unencumbered for swimming. Over and over again the bow was pulled completely under water, because a boatsteerer hates to slacken line. Three times we half swamped and had to let the whale steal line while all hands bailed; indeed, the piggins and our sou'westers were employed thus more or less continuously.

I have a dreamlike mental background for the day's play —the choppy, spumy water and the varying sky, the heliotrope Portuguese men-o'-war that seemed to bob past us, the bright flying fish scared up, the inquisitive Mother Carey's chickens that fluttered astern; and, focus of it all, straight ahead, the rocking, shiny back of our forty-barrel bull, with an impertinent little harpoon sticking there.

The brig appeared to shunt about magically, being now abeam, now close aboard off the bow, now nearly hull down astern. Fortunately, we were moving mostly in wide circles, for otherwise we should have been towed out of sight and would have had to cut line. Time and again we slacked away and tried to give another boat an opportunity to sail upon the brute and plant a second iron, but he was all wariness. When the boats came ever so softly within three or four lengths, he would kick up his big flukes and be gone. Mr. da Lomba eventually shot a bomb lance into the whale's back, but the rubber-feathered end of it broke off and went whizzing over the sea, while the cylinder failed to explode. Three more bombs from a shoulder gun were likewise vainly spent, and the mate concluded that the charges were watersoaked.

The turning point of the struggle came when the frantic whale once more fell in with a gam of his fellows. The calming influence of neighbors was soon apparent, for he allowed us to draw right toward him. We pulled ourselves through an acre of sperm whales, big bulls that we might have touched with oars, cows at arms' length, and tiny calves, ten or twelve feet long, with huge remoras clinging to their flanks. Such company lay unconcernedly awash all about us, but we paid it scant attention because it is quite sufficient to be fast to one sperm whale at a time.

"Shush, easy, easy boys," whispered Mr. da Lomba; "trim the boat; don't shift your quids."

We hauled softly along the length of another whale and, when our line was as short as a dog leash, the mate braced his thigh in the clumsy cleat, raised his long powerful arms, and buried the five-foot shank of the lance in blubber and flesh. The tortured whale quivered and sank. We peered tensely over the side for his dark hulk, knowing that the sounding would be brief and that he might rise beneath us. The mate pounded and pried the twisted lance shaft into a semblance of straightness.

"Stern all!" Up came the whale under our keel. While we just avoided capsizing, the lance struck home twice or thrice again through the froth before the whale got under way on another lap of his race. Then everything was repeated. Once more we were drenched. Again we bailed and hauled and slackened and hauled and bailed.

Finally, the second officer's boat, which had been back to the brig, transferred to us a case of dry bombs. Late in the afternoon, when we once more entered a group of whales, the crucial opportunity was seized. A bomb was shot into the brute's lungs, where it exploded with a muffled crack. In his leap, he half filled our boat with water for the last time, but he no longer had the breath to sound. His spout, formerly so thin and white, reflecting tiny rainbows in the rays of the low sun, now became first pink and then crimson and gouted.

"His chimney's afire!" said Mr. da Lomba, with a heartless chuckle.

Mr. Almeida's boat closed in with ours. Lances were thrust between the whale's ribs, held there, and churned, until the creature went into his ghastly flurry, all the while belching squids from his gullet until we floated in a slimy pool of their remains.

He died and turned fin out after giving us nine thrilling hours. We chopped a hole through one of his flukes, attached a line, and rested, weary but content, munching hard bread, drinking fresh water, and awaiting the arrival of the distant brig which, happily, was then to windward. After all the bluster of the day, the sun set in a calm sky. Mars, burning red, followed closely on the same track, and was hanging like a lamp on the waters when the *Daisy* bore down and gathered us in.

OCTOBER 11.   Lat. 03° 20' N.

One other whale was captured yesterday, by Mr. Vincent's boat, but our forty-barrel bull is the talk of the ship. The Old Man admits that my baptismal experience of being fast to a sperm whale was as thoroughgoing as anything he has ever witnessed.

The men were in fine fettle during the cutting-in, and the lusty strains of "Sally Brown," "Whiskey Johnny" and "Blow the Man Down" rang out for hours across the empty ocean.

As I was awalkin' down Paradise Street—
  Away, ay, blow the man down—
A flash lookin' packet I chanced for to meet.
  Give me some time to blow the man down.

I hailed her in English; she answered me clear—
   Away, ay, etc.
"I'm from the Black Anchor bound to the Shakespeare."
   Give me, etc.

I tailed her my flipper and took her in tow,
And yardarm to yardarm away we did go.

I clewed up her courses, to'gansails and all—

—but I can write no more without peril of having Anthony Comstock bar my manuscript from the mails!

Sharks were about, as usual, during the cutting-in today. One of them was surrounded and practically concealed by a cloud of small fishes and, to my surprise, these were not pilot fish but were young blue-lined runners. It seemed amazing that the satellites, of which there were certainly more than fifty, could stick to their own host, so to speak, and also that they could move with apparent impunity among crowds of other sharks.

In afternoon, when boiling had been started, two boats were lowered to pursue one or more sperm whales raised in the distance. Neither was successful, but Mr. Almeida made the tactical error of taking time to harpoon and lance for my benefit a large, curious, beakless porpoise. It was no more than Mr. da Lomba had done a few days back, but the skipper stands in a far more personal relationship to his mate and right-hand man than he does to anyone else in the crew. He at once assumed that Mr. Almeida had been soldiering instead of tending to business. He flew into a violent and prolonged rage as soon as he saw the carcass in the boat, and I had a hard time persuading him to cancel an order that it should be pitched overboard.

Once off to a good start in giving vent to his spleen, the Old Man does not cool down soon or easily. His testiness and vituperation seem to feed on his own language. Without interrupting his supervision of the work in hand, he discoursed in a loud voice about deficiencies in the third officer's ancestry, complexion, character, courage, and ability. He accused him of unmentionable vices and called him various uncomplimentary names, from misbegotten cullion to panderly zany, but, as you may guess, I have replaced with euphemisms the more hairy-chested words that the Old Man actually used.

Altogether, it was a painful display of browbeating, received with eloquently disapproving silence by every soul on board. As for the feckless Almeida, who made no reply, I could think of him only in the terms of a couplet from *King John:*

> Zounds! I was never so bethump'd with words
> Since I first called my brother's father dad.

OCTOBER 12. The 420th anniversary of when we were discovered! I started to thaw out an exceedingly frigid atmosphere at breakfast by singing to the skipper, two officers, and the cooper the immortal words of the old commemorative hymn.

> Columbus he came over here in fourteen ninety-two,
> When New York was a vacant lot, if histhory be thrue.
> Who was the first to greet him when he landed on the sthrand?
> Who was the first to welcome him and grasp him by the hand?
>
> 'Twas Misther Dooley, Misther Dooley,
> He marched him up Columbus Avenoo!
> With head uncovered, said "We're discovered"—
> Did Misther Dooley-ooley-ooley-oo.

I am lame from the strenuous tenth, and the palms of my hands are galled raw. Nevertheless, I roughed out the complete skeleton of the fateful porpoise, which proves, after consultation with True's monograph, to be an exceedingly rare species, never before captured in the Atlantic Ocean. It is called *Lagenorhynchus electra* but, for the first time, the Old Man isn't interested!

We have been trying out blubber today while under sail and keeping on our way, and no bituminous-burning towboat ever left such a black trail across the sky. A smoke sail, suspended above the tryworks, has perhaps kept a small proportion of the soot out of the aftercabin. It has kept none off the faces of the boys, however, which now have a stove-pipe polish on their already dark skin. We look like a minstrel show on Noah's Ark. Last night the deck and rigging were aglare from the fiery chimneys and bug light. It would not have surprised me if other craft had left their courses, bent on rescuing the crew of a ship afire!

The noon position was latitude 02° 25' N., longitude 25° 35' W.

OCTOBER 13.   Lat. 01° 07' N., long. 27° 12' W.

The best breeze since we left the Antilles! We are running gaily southwestward and pitching among the whitecaps. The fore-royal has been furled. Shortly afterwards the main boom cracked, so the mainsail is down and a large crew is now fitting iron hoops to fish the spar.

There is a bottle below, all sealed and flagged and containing a note to you, my Grace, which I shall drop overboard as soon as we cross the line.

The weather has been prevailingly cool for a number of days, and a sweater feels comfortable in the morning and evening. We have already passed the heat equator, even if not the geographical equator.

My whale, of October 10, made forty-seven barrels. The other of the same date tried out thirty-one barrels.

OCTOBER 14.   Over! Longitude 28° 46' W.

A white booby crossing the deck indicates that we are approaching Fernando Noronha, or that St. Paul's Rocks lie not far to northward and leeward. Flying fish are extraordinarily abundant, as we run at a fast clip through the blue equatorial current, which is flowing across the Atlantic and toward the Caribbean, there to build up the headwaters of the Gulf Stream.

I have developed cold sores on both lips, a result, I suppose, of the constant salt water shower bath during the long whale hunt.

Three of our boatsteerers are hulling corn for samp—not, however, with lye, as we do it in New England, but by pounding with five-foot pestles in a mortar carved from a tree trunk. They are striking in beautiful rhythm and making a merry job of it, and each blow sounds a muffled note of music that seems to keep time with the rocking and leaping of the brig. The wind whisks the loosened hulls out of the mortar without waiting for a winnowing process. The three strong fellows, Antão, Emiliano, and Victor, are working, of course, for sheer fun, because the task would normally fall to deck hands. Is the teamwork of the singing blows—one, two, three, one, two, three—a sort of memory of a tribal dance among their dark forebears?

The corn porridge is excellent. Since leaving the Cape Verdes, we have also had a tasty variety of succotash, which the steward calls *curchupe*. It is composed of corn, peas, and sweet little red beans of a sort I've never seen before.

OCTOBER 15.   Lat. 03° 10' S., long. 31° 20' W.

All day we ran freely, canting well over to starboard and completing more than two hundred miles for the twenty-four hour period ending at three o'clock in the afternoon. Boobies and other passing sea birds told us that we were nearing land. At nine in the evening we made the revolving light of an island lying under the bright quarter moon, so we hauled aback our square sails and lay to for the night.

OCTOBER 16.   Evening.

Another letter has gone to my Grace! Won't you be astonished to see Brazilian stamps, and the postmark "Fernando Noronha," which most of our friends have never heard of? I did not dare send the log because it was doubtful whether we could register mail, but you will at least learn that thus far all's well. I wish that I might know as much about you.

In the middle part of last night I awoke in my berth and heard the Old Man, standing by the wheel, grumbling for the benefit of all on the quarterdeck. I listened sleepily to the familiar sound, and then sat up with a start when I realized that this time his subject was *me*.

"Good God!" I thought, with the recent memory of Mr. Almeida's drubbing in mind, "if this gets started, there'll be no holding him for the rest of the voyage."

I had no idea what the matter was, but I climbed on deck, faced him for a few moments while we were both silent, and then said in a voice of the same volume that he had been using, "Captain Cleveland, if you have any complaint of me, I'd like to be the first to hear about it."

His head of steam fortunately lost its pressure. It turned out that his water closet, which only he and I use, had jolly well flooded him, and he chose to assume that I had tossed in something that plugged it. I had done nothing of the sort, which I told him; but I did not add that Johnny frequently took that short cut in the disposal of small lots of garbage!

I remained on deck long enough for the conversation to become casual, and then turned in again.

When I next opened my eyes, it was in the short, pervasive twilight that heralds an equatorial dawn. I found the Old Man seated in a whaleboat on the davits, and joined him

there. The island lay to the southwest, at a distance estimated to be nine miles. It doubtless looked much as it had to
Darwin in 1832 and Moseley in 1874, except that there are
now the lighthouse and several tall wireless towers.

As we drove rapidly toward it before a fair wind, the rim
of the sun peeped up on the port quarter, lighting like a candle
the summit of the famous Pyramid, which is the most arrest-
ing landmark in the whole South Atlantic, and also revealing
the Hole-in-the-Wall at the western tip of the island. Under
the lee a small steamer lay at anchor. When we had approached still nearer, the strip of rough hills, which had first
seemed continuous, gradually broke up to show the straits
that separate several islets off the northeastern end. The
climbing sun disclosed a green lowland, well clothed with
shrubs and small trees and a higher zone of bare, weathered
peaks, among which the Pyramid (1,089 feet) stood nearly
twice as high as any other.

The length of the whole chain is about seven miles.
Within the memory of whalemen still living, the leeward side
of Fernando Noronha was heavily forested, but the larger
trees have all been felled to prevent the exiled convicts, practically the only human beings to share the sea-beaten spot
with countless ocean birds, from building Brazilian catama-
rans or *jangadas* sufficiently seaworthy to carry them to the
mainland. Every now and then a rascal disappears, never to
be heard of more, and the republic is saved his keep. Much
more rarely, one actually succeeds in crossing the two hundred miles to the continent on his frail raft. Then, according
to the Old Man, the authorities conclude that the enterprising
fellow has earned his freedom, and they no longer molest him
so long as he remains inconspicuous. The skipper also tells
me that, while Brazil has neither capital punishment nor life
imprisonment, there is no law to prevent a culprit from

being sentenced to Fernando Noronha for a hundred years!

The skipper reported that the landing at Povoado, the settlement, was very treacherous, usually necessitating a scramble through surf. Since he needed a full boatload of supplies, he said that he could send ashore only Mr. da Lomba and his crew. Accordingly we turned over our letters, and I expected to have to remain all day on board.

However, after breakfast, the weather being docile, Mr. Almeida's boat set forth on a fishing expedition, so I took down my gun and went along. On the way toward land we were surrounded by an enormous flock of noddies, which stretched away into the distance until the birds appeared like swarming insects.

Passing several conical islets on which man-o'-war birds were nesting, we entered a cove of grottoed rock with a crescent of sand at its head. Behind this beach the fissured, yellow wall of a cliff, conforming with the semicircular outline of the cove, rose sheer to a height of three or four hundred feet. Thousands of black noddies were clustering on their scaffold nests along its upper surface, and pairs of snow-white fairy terns, the first I had ever seen alive, sat side by side on twisted boughs at the foot. There was no sign here of the surf predicted by the skipper. The singularly peaceful water had no more than a slumbering swell, and the pale green of the cove was reflected from the satiny white breasts of tropic-birds flying overhead.

Naturally, this emerald pool was not for a moment to be resisted. I soon plunged into the water for the first time since you and I swam together at Dominica, four long months ago. The blurred image of a green turtle glided away before me, and a shoal of porpoises rocked across the inlet. When I came out on the pristine sand, it seemed appropriate to forget my supradermal envelopments and to wander about ungarbed, like wild autochthonous man, while beginning to collect samples of the island birds.

The first report of my gun caused a horde of screaming sea fowl to pour down off the rocks. Other inhabitants may also have been disturbed by the roar and its bewildering echoes, for I arose from picking up a specimen and found myself face to face with a tall, black, muscular fisherman, carrying a tattered fishnet over one shoulder but otherwise wearing just what I wore—namely nothing. Then, out of the shrubbery below the cliff came a fellow of lighter skin, clad in short sailcloth breeches and a blue tam-o'-shanter, and having a wicker basket slung over his back. The pair might have passed for Robinson Crusoe and his man Friday.

I called along the beach for the cooper to come out of the whaleboat, shake a leg, and join me, in order that I might enter into fair converse with the rightful lords of this demesne. At Correia's first words in a familiar tongue, the cap of Crusoe came off obsequiously and both men extended the right hand of welcome. The subsequent exchanges were then carried on through the interpreting of the cooper.

The two men were murderers. The whitish one had been on Fernando Noronha slightly more than fourteen years; the Negro seemed uncertain about the length of his sentence to date. Neither had any particular complaint. They were free to wander until dark each day; the fishing was good, they had gardens, and many edible fruits grew wild. The clothing ration was insufficient, however. There were altogether too few women on the island, and did we have a little tobacco that we might spare? We did.

There was plenty of tobacco on the *Daisy*, I added. How would the light fellow like to come off and ship with us, leaving no trace of his departure?

He shook his head. Any time up to two years before, he

explained, he would have jumped at the chance. But now his durance was to terminate within eight months, after which he could return for the rest of his days to his native Pernambuco. He then informed us that around a small headland to the west there was a bigger beach, with access to the country behind, and he offered to meet our boat there. So we presently pulled offshore, while the islander, after taking a pair of hide sandals from his basket and tying them on his feet, toiled up a stony, winding path across the ridge, leaving his black comrade to cast the net alone.

When our whaleboat had rounded the point, a charming bit of seashore lay before us. The curve of golden sand stretched to another promontory a mile away and sloped gently under the sea, which for a long distance from shore was wondrously transparent. The upper beach was a riot of morning-glories with leaves shaped like a goat's footprint, and mingled with them were many slender-stalked cacti. Beyond, a thicket, alive with small doves, concealed the base of the precipice. The lower face of the latter was covered with vines which clambered up the seams, and its crest was bordered with the pink and orange blossoms of small trees. Sharp slabs of rock projected here and there from the wall, offering perfect nesting sites for the birds that appeared in hosts wherever we turned.

For the sea fowl it is always springtime at Fernando Noronha. The year breaks up into wet and dry periods, the present, according to our guide, being the heart of the rainless season. But the birds, he said, have no fixed or limited time of breeding, and eggs and young for food can be found in every month of the twelve. He grumbled over the fact that while such resources for the inner man could always be seen, they could not always be taken, because of the inaccessibility of many nests. Here's something to be thankful for, thought I!

Crusoe then set about showing us where the birds were, not only the salt water species but also a flycatcher and a vireo that live nowhere on the big round earth except at this tiny island. He chattered glibly to the cooper, stopping only while snaring lizards for us with a noose of grass. Presently we were joined by a number of half-clad or nearly unclad fellow prisoners, as well as by several pitiful boys, the sons of convicts, all of whom seemed to be twisted by rheumatism or as a result of some dietary deficiency. Young and old followed us for the sake of empty cartridge shells which we at first dropped on the ground but later passed to outstretched hands.

The cooper finally went off through a gap in the cliff with the whole native party, in order to visit the penal settlement. Our boat's crew rowed to a reef for fishing, which left me alone at the shore. Later I scrambled up an almost perpendicular footpath into the woods, and then as far as possible up the bare, steep side of the Pyramid. From here I could look down on the picturesque beach, where the fleet-winged birds were crossing and recrossing. Everything seemed as sharp as a diamond in the clear air, from the glittering dragonflies close at hand to a flock of migrant golden plovers on the sand, or even to crabs skittering over the wet rocks and to fishes in the clinkstone tide pools. Here was Prospero's isle, fanned by tireless trade winds. Ariel was no doubt masked as a boatswain bird; the plovers were sprites

> that on the sands with printless foot
> Do chase the ebbing Neptune and do fly him
> When he comes back;

and Caliban?—a black-skinned murderer who might appear at any moment. Here was an island where fruit trees and melons flourish without cultivation, a tropical resort that might be made by the Brazilians into a second Bermuda, yet it was given up to the most miserable of exiles.

When Correia and I were picked up by the fishing party in late afternoon, we found the whaleboat laden down with melons, colorful tropical fishes and several sharks. The latter had been a great nuisance all day, biting many of the smaller victims from the hooks before they could be drawn to the surface, and nipping the larger ones clean in half.

Toward evening we sighted the brig bearing down the coast toward us, and reluctantly we sailed off to join her, leaving doubtless forever the allurements of Fernando Noronha. At dusk we were running swiftly athwart the trade wind, the Pyramid still showing faintly astern through a bluish haze.

OCTOBER 17. Lat. 05° 21' S., long. 32° 44' W. At Fernando Noronha we increased our "navifauna" by four pigs, brought off hog-tied in Mr. da Lomba's boat. They now disport on the main deck, having in a measure acquired sea legs and overcome their suine mal-de-mer. Cadella, however, seems determined that they shall not have a happy voyage and she will probably continue to annoy them until the novelty wears off, or until one of the porkers turns on her.

It has occurred to me that every being on this craft is an islander, which is in keeping with the whaling tradition because boatmen are more important than mere sailors. Consider our origin: not a lubber, nor even a continental, among us! The Old Man, Martha's Vineyard; the "assistant navigator," Long Island; Mr. Vincent, Mindanao; the cooper, Fayal; the others, including Cadella and the cat, Cape Verde or West India islets; the pigs, Fernando Noronha; the rats and cockroaches, islanders and stowaways every one.

Among our other spoil from Fernando Noronha are some bananas, plantains, beans, farina, squashes, and matches, in all "$12 worth of stuff for $34," as the Old Man expresses it. In his own reckoning, he gets the worst of every bargain.

OCTOBER 18. Lat. 07' S., long. 33° 42' W. We are heading about southwestward, with the coast of Brazil only fifty-five miles toward the setting sun. Consistently strong trade winds have been blowing from an unduly southerly quarter ever since we left the island, compelling us to head well to the west.

I have been busy early and late for two days caring for my birds, lizards, fish, mollusks, and less perishable spoils. Eighteen Fernando Noronha bird skins are now labeled, wrapped, and drying.

OCTOBER 19. Lat. 08° 31' S., long. 33° 42' W. Today we celebrated the Old Man's sixty-ninth birthday. I fetched up a small supply of your mincemeat and had the steward make him a pie. He and I also split a pint of Mouton on the quarterdeck.

Just after supper the boats were lowered for what was reported as a pod of sperm whales. The skipper went to the masthead and identified the animals, from their quick, puffy, irregular blowing, and their continuous breaching, as humpbacks. So the boats were recalled. Close to this position, he tells me, he deliberately lowered for humpbacks on a previous voyage. There were hundreds about and, after a vast amount of effort, his men finally killed a twenty-barrel animal, but only after staving one boat and losing the new sail of another. It was somehow torn overboard by a bight of the outrunning whale line. The crew was lucky that a few arms and legs didn't go with it.

OCTOBER 20. Lat. 10° 21' S., long. 34° 04' W. The trade wind has eased off toward its normal course, so that we are able to point S.½ W.

Two parasitic jaegers, or robber gulls, bound southward on migration from their Arctic breeding grounds, tagged after the *Daisy* from nine o'clock in the morning until four in the afternoon. They would fly up our wake with slow wing-beats, hover for a moment above the stern, then glide slowly to the windward side and settle on the water, tucking their long wings into the resting position and floating high and gracefully. When the brig had left them a few hundred yards behind, they would rise, overtake us, and again drop down. All this was monotonously repeated for seven hours, during most of which I was cleaning up bird skeletons from Fernando Noronha.

At noon, fin whales of an unidentified species were reported from the masthead. Two of them, side by side, later passed close to the *Daisy*, one rising at short range and blowing a thin, quick spout.

The Old Man knows a little about the modern steam whaling as a result of his previous visits to South Georgia, where Norwegian stations have now been established for several years. The means of capturing, and the gear for inflating the carcasses of the vast finbacks and blue whales so that they will float, seem almost to fill him with awe. He grew up in the tradition that fin whales are creatures to be let alone, the only exception being the occasional Yankee ventures in "humpbacking."

Sperm whales practically always float after being killed. Right whales usually float, and the skipper believes that excessive puncturing of the lungs and body wall by the lance is responsible for the sinking of some of them. On one voyage he lost five in this way. On another occasion one of his right whales sank in the Japan Sea, where the water was only forty fathoms deep. Knowing that dead whales will rise from such shallow bottoms after a certain stage of decomposition has been reached, he attached a large cask to the harpoon line as a marker and continued cruising for three days. Then he returned to the position and found a floating whale as big as a capsized frigate! By sailing down the wind toward the swollen carcass, he kept his crew from committing suicide or staging a mutiny. They cut-in that whale, they did, and saved the whalebone, which was none the worse for the putrefaction of the carcass. They also tried out thirty-five barrels of oil which, the Old Man euphemistically admits, was "rather dark."

OCTOBER 21. Lat. 12° 15' S., long. 33° 55' W. The southeast trade wind has swung to the east of its normal course and we can head due south with ease.

The cooper has made me a box in which I have packed away forty-six specimens of birds.

OCTOBER 22. Lat. 13° 29' S., long. 33° 37' W. We have had fair and steady winds ever since crossing into the southern hemisphere. The figures on the face of the moon have an unfamiliar orientation down here.

We have seen both humpbacks and finbacks today. This afternoon a humpback leaped clear out of water about half a mile off the lee bow.

Our pigs now seem quite at home on deck. Two are white, one red, and one brown, and all are surprisingly round for tropical swine. The Old Man says that he once took seventy on his little bark *Bertha* from the Isle of Annobon, in the Gulf of Guinea. They, however, were all razor-back hogs, which could not be seen end-on, but only broadside. They ate them every one on the voyage, and picked their bones heighho. That must have been in Captain Cleveland's gustatory, gargantuan prime, when he had his own teeth and a good digestion. Now, I believe, he thinks rather reluctantly of thirty-four men on the *Daisy* devouring even one hog.

However, a mess of Fernando Noronha cabbages tasted excellent today, and we had also an abundance of boiled white potatoes.

OCTOBER 23. Lat. 15° 34' S., long. 33° 17' W. Cool, refreshing weather, with the rare combination of a strong, fair wind and a light sea. We are already a thousand miles south of the equator. This seems a happy, breezy ocean, very different from the one in which we dragged through a long summer. We have just passed the sun on our joint progress toward Capricorn, yet it is delightfully cool and airy—78° F. at noon. Nevertheless, the royal yard was lowered today and is now lashed along the port bulwarks, which is premonitory of severe weather ahead.

OCTOBER 24. Lat. 17° 54' S., long. 30° 10' W. The trade wind is veering around abeam and we are flying southward.

This morning a killer whale crossed our bow, swimming very swiftly and puffing frequently with a low, bushy spout. Later a humpback cow and her calf were playing together within easy range of my glass, and before noon a single finback breached and blew several times, the spout being extremely tall and thin. These be whaley waters, but nothing of a nature to interest the Old Man.

Today I packed up all my cleaned and dried skeletons, and did a lot of reading anent the animals of the cold latitudes ahead of us.

OCTOBER 25. Lat. 20° 11' S., long. 33° 35' W. The wind has now swung north of east. We furled the mainsail, which on this craft is a fore-and-aft canvas, and ran freely under the square sails of the foremast. These, since the royal has been retired, are foresail, lower topsail, upper topsail, and topgallantsail, only the last is pronounced as seven letters (togansl) instead of fourteen. The *Daisy*, being a modest and leisurely whaler, never possessed such clipper-ship wings as skysail, stargazer or studdingsails—pronounced as seven letters (stunsls) instead of thirteen! Sea language would be a very terse and economical speech if the Old Man didn't lose the advantage by padding it with unnecessary expletives.

About four o'clock this afternoon a green hand bawled
out "Grampus!" I rushed on deck and saw not the familiar
grampus, but several of the rare and little known beaked
whales, belonging to a group that the books call "ziphioids."
They were the first I have ever encountered alive and in the
flesh, so this becomes a red-letter day.

Captain Cleveland recognized them, at least to the vague
extent that he had met something like them before. He called
them "algerines." They were perhaps twenty-five feet long,
slender and graceful, and they put on a complete circus as
if for our benefit. I have never seen more frolicsome creatures. They turned their white bellies upward as they passed
our quarter and shot like torpedoes forward and around the
bow, or sometimes dived amidships to reappear on the other beam. They came and went so dizzily that I am not sure
whether there were four, five, or more of them. One turned
a complete backward somersault right alongside. After playing for some minutes before an audience in which I believe
there were several other spellbound members, they darted
sharply away from us, turned astern, and disappeared. But
this was only to tease us, because after a few moments they
came puffing up our wake again from an astonishing distance. Their blowing made an extraordinarily metallic
sound, as though the bottom of a skillet were being banged
with a mallet. Eventually, four of them turned off from us
again, running absolutely abreast at high speed, with their
round backs and little trigger fins all showing together. Then
pouf! They were gone for good, like magic. The whole show
was the most histrionic performance I have ever seen on
the high sea. I believe, also, that it was of a sort that required
good mammalian brains. Whatever dim ideas were in them
were quite unfishlike. These whales undoubtedly saw us,
probably recognized us as another kind of living creature,

and may have believed that they were playing with us instead of merely for us.

What a pity that unwieldy circumstances prevent us from becoming as well acquainted with the personalities of whales, as we have, for example, with those of sea lions that learn to toss balls and ride horseback! I suspect that a whale's predilection for becoming chummy and companionable might astonish the world.

OCTOBER 26. Lat. 21° 40' S., long. 34° 12' W. A dull morning after a stormy night. Variable head winds, making it necessary to tack during the day.

One photograph of the ziphioid whales might have come out well but for the fact that the cursed cockroaches walked all over the plate while it was drying last night, puncturing the gelatin in a hundred places.

Today we saw two sea hens or skuas, the first of the voyage. One flew close to the *Daisy*, and, the wind being light, I shot it from deck and Mr. da Lomba ordered the dory lowered. The dead bird was a half mile astern when I retrieved it, but I was back on board, with the *Grace Emeline* slung on her davits, before the Old Man came from below or knew that anything had happened without his orders.

The skua appears to be the form that breeds at the Falkland Islands. It has never before been reported from so low a latitude, and it will be the first representative of its kind in the collection of the American Museum of Natural History.

The sunset this evening was completely original. Heavy gray clouds in the west were cut into layers by brilliant light-red bands, and the background of all was a pale and bottomless sky of greenish blue. The gray clouds at first had two oval windows that let a scarlet light through, making a pair of pink streaks on the ocean. Then, rather suddenly, the clouds broke into a million fragments as the sun sank. A little later, the full moon climbed over a very high black cloudbank on the other beam. A golden goblet lay on the water and the mackerel sky reflected a mellow light.

Although we are in the latitude of Rio de Janeiro, and still well within the tropics, it is almost cold. We are talking about heavy underwear, the skipper and I.

OCTOBER 27. Lat. 21° 56' S., long. 35° 00' W. Continued head winds. We are beating about with excessive fore-and-aft pitching. Two finback whales were reported and more skuas have passed us.

I have dug out an undershirt, and even a sweater has felt comfortable. For the first time on the voyage, I have slept under a blanket.

The meals have taken a lift of late. Today we had extraordinarily delicious baked beans, made from tiny, sweet, red *feijões* obtained at São Vicente, and also bacon, hot biscuits, cassava, Australian tinned beef, and a can of Danish butter that Johnny magically unearthed in some dark and mouldy corner of the run.

OCTOBER 28. Lat. 22° 45' S., long. 35° 45' W. I now belong to a higher cult of mortals, for I have seen the albatross! Long before I had dared hope, up here on the 23d parallel, I have been watching the wonderful gliding of the grandest of birds during much of the day.

Throughout last night a heavy ground swell, and temperatures that dropped below 70° F., indicated stormy weather to the south. At six this morning the steward came to notify me that a "gony" was about, so I hurried on deck. Near by, in the morning sunlight, flew the long-anticipated bird, even more majestic, more supreme in its element, than my imagination had pictured. It was mature, all white and black, doubtless an adult male, and as it turned and turned, now flashing the bright under side, now showing the black feathering that extended from wrist to tip on the upper surface of the wings, the narrow planes seemed to be neither beating nor scarcely quivering. Lying on the invisible currents of the breeze, the bird appeared merely to follow its pinkish bill at random.

How big was it? What was its spread of wing? To tell you, my love, I'll have to wait until I catch and measure its brother at South Georgia! I don't take any stock in the bosh of the *Encyclopaedia Britannica* that the wing expanse of the species attains seventeen feet, but I would wager that my first bird measured ten.

The albatross remained with us only a few minutes, but at noon the same bird, presumably, was back again, covering tens of miles in the swift wide circles that it traversed astern. When banking, it sometimes tilted to an angle of 90° so that the point of the lower wing cut the water. Twice it dropped into the sea, where it looked as gigantic as the iron birds on the swan boats of my boyhood memories, and allowed the *Daisy* to draw away a great distance before it arose to overtake us. It was a curious sight when the albatross prepared to alight under our stern, and then, changing its purpose, ran heavily on the water for a hundred paces before its wings, beating ponderously, could lift the great body into the air.

I went to my letter bag and found the message from Dr. Lucas marked for the day of the first sighting of an albatross. It told of the same experience in his young life, nearly fifty years agone.

It is gorgeous weather, with an enormous swell from the south. After more than five months in the tropics, nearly all of it directly under the sun, I could swear that the temperature of the air was now diving toward the freezing point. From time to time I can't suppress an involuntary shiver. Yet the thermometer all day has remained within a degree or two of

70° F. At four-hour intervals throughout the past twenty-four hours, the average has been 71.2° F. How relative and untrustworthy are our sensations!

But I have changed to a flannel shirt and everything is pleasant—the weather, the food, and, yes, even the Old Man.

OCTOBER 29. Lat. 24° 42' S., long. 37° 10' W., by dead reckoning.

At three o'clock this morning, a huge flying fish came down on deck, and, through the surreptitious kindness of the watch, I got it into one of my cans of formalin before the steward appropriated it for the table. With your memories of Barbados, you know how I like to eat flying fish, but specimens come before the belly!

At eight o'clock we ran into a large and widely spread shoal of sperm whales. The animals were both to windward and to leeward, traveling rapidly in a southerly direction and breaching a great deal. Never had the brig come so thoroughly into the middle of a school before the first whale was sighted.

I scurried up to the mainmasthead while the boats were being lowered, and had an incomparable view of whales near and far. I saw not one or two, but at least ten or a dozen leap almost or quite out of water. It was hard to tell, because of the great splash, whether or not the creatures actually cleared the surface, but the sight was stirring and awe inspiring.

The fast traveling of the whales, and perhaps the high swell on the ocean, made hunting difficult. One boatsteerer missed what looked like a fair dart, and Mr. da Lomba's boat was the only one that struck. "Long John" and his terrible lance made a corpse of the whale within a very few minutes after the planting of the harpoon. It was a small bull, of about thirty barrels, and during its flurry it vomited fifty or more squids. The mate was thoughtful enough to bring me one that had a body two feet long, and tentacles of three or four. It is now labeled, wrapped in cheesecloth, and snuggling like an imperishable Pharaoh beside this morning's flying fish. We recalled and hoisted the unsuccessful boats about one o'clock.

The Old Man was glum and, for once, silent. Somehow this seemed more ominous than if he had been bellowing. Frank had missed a dart—the unforgivable sin. When the skipper "broke" him and told him to transfer his things from steerage to forecastle, the unfortunate harponeer did so with the air of a man already resigned to the headsman's block. Everybody on board was as solemn as though we were about to witness the demise of Danny Deever, although whispered speculation soon began as to which man forward would be promoted to the vacancy among the boatsteerers.

During the cutting-in of Mr. da Lomba's whale, the afternoon southerly breeze was so chilly that the sloppings of spermaceti from the case solidified on deck. Only a single shark nosed around the floating carcass, and this was a fish with white-tipped fins, a very different species from the blue sharks that besieged us in legions during our equatorial cuttings-in.

The Old Man was as happy and genial as a general who has just ordered the shooting of a sentry for falling asleep. Why not? Frank had missed a dart; the captain had done his duty; fulfillment of duty is an elevating experience. *Quod erat demonstrandum.*

He even sat down beside me while the blubber was peeling off, and gave me the rare opportunity of picking up and stringing the pearls of his whaling wisdom, while Frank was working as a mere lumper at the windlass.

Cow sperm whales, the skipper vouchsafed, rarely run larger than twenty-five or thirty barrels. Twenty-barrel cows are still commoner, though he had once or twice taken cows that yielded as much as forty barrels.

The greatly superior size of the bulls, he went on, is an indication of their polygamy and of the fact that they fight to round up and hold their retinue of ladies. Several times he had seen struggling bulls with jaws locked together. Once he had killed one that had had a foot or more of the tip of its lower jaw completely broken off and healed over, a casualty that could have been caused only by a rival whale. Lone bulls, which are often very large, are sperm whales that have passed their prime, and that have been driven out of the herd by some younger, rising champion.

OCTOBER 30.   Lat. 26° 20' S., long. 38° 04' W. Strong southeast winds and a terrifically rough sea. We boiled during the morning. The smell of hot sperm oil, somewhat suggestive of an infernal hereafter, permeated the whole ship. It is not an unpleasant odor, however, when one becomes used to it, and it should, of course, actually inspire your humble scribe while he is setting down the lore of whaling.

In afternoon we hoisted and reefed the mainsail, and proceeded on our course in the teeth of the wind with an escort of glorious albatrosses. How fast can they fly? Not less than forty miles per hour, air speed, I feel sure. Therefore, when sailing before the wind today, they were attaining a ground speed of at least ninety miles per hour, and possibly more.

Mr. da Lomba and Mr. Vincent were cut short when they started to say a word to Captain Cleveland about Frank. But during the clean-up that follows boiling, while the once proud boatsteerer was swinging a swab on deck, the Old Man called him to the break of the poop, said he might have another chance, and told him to fetch his possessions back to the steerage!

A large, dark pot-roasty looking chunk of sperm whale meat for supper, but not bad.

OCTOBER 31. Lat. 27° 15' S., long. 39° 30' W. Strong southeasterly winds and a rugged sea. Under few sails, we are pitching along toward the Río de la Plata.

Last night was probably the roughest weather yet. We rolled to an incredible angle, so that bubbling, frothing water crept across the main deck from the scuppers. But it all seems natural now, and I calmly developed a dozen photographic plates without even using a ruby light. My back is slightly lame from the constant stress of maintaining equilibrium, but I have no queasiness or other trying effects.

As soon as we have moderate weather, I think that we can hook some of these albatrosses and start my series of specimens, which is going to be the best ever brought back from the southern oceans. Oh how I wish you could see them fly! I stand with mouth open, figuratively at any rate, as they swing through the gale, swaying from side to side and garnering their momentum from nobody knows where. Into the wind or before it, up or down, is all one to them. They continually rock, and sometimes keep their gliders atremble, but an actual wing beat is rare and is usually confined to the hand or last segment. Four little strokes are the most I've seen one make consecutively. One wonders why they don't fall. When the secret of their perfect balance has been learned and applied to man-made planes, then we'll go aflying.

At four o'clock this afternoon a large aggregation of finbacks caused us to lie-to awhile, with sails aback. They were playing in the sunstreak and the mastheads mistook them for sperm whales until the tall spouts could be made out.

About six o'clock a number of humpbacks popped up to windward, three quarters of a mile off. Their spouts were bushy and explosive—all shot forth at once, and as wide as they were high. The sperm whale's spout is also low, but it is blown out much more slowly than that of the humpback, and it slants forward. Only the grampus, which is no bigger than a blackfish, has a spout enough like the sperm whale's to deceive a smart lookout.

We have crossed the Tropic of Capricorn. The days grow longer and the rays of the sun more angular.

4 Cape Horn Weather

NOVEMBER 1.   Lat. 29° 18' S., long. 40° 59' W. Today begins the fifth month of the voyage and of our separation. It is also the beginning of "May" down here in the south temperate zone. So spring succeeds spring in the first period of our wedded life, and when the northern spring follows the southern we'll be together again.

Now that we are out of the tropics, the weather is warmer! That is because a very strong and damp wind is astern, blowing from the hot belt. Last night was so rough that I slid rather wearisomely from end to end of my long berth. This morning one still needs a handhold to move about. We are running straight before the wind toward the River Plate, with sails set only on the foremast.

The first mollymauks, or small species of albatrosses, have appeared. One is the black-browed albatross, and another I am not yet sure of. This morning, just after we had passed a floating timber, I caught a big dolphin and saw others. They never seem to be absent when wreckage is about.

After a dinner of dolphin and boiled potatoes, I felt weary and lonely, perhaps as a result of two nights without good rest. So I reread some of your letters and the Acts of the Apostles, which would tend to restore anybody's courage. Then I fell asleep and knew nothing more until one bell in the afternoon watch.

NOVEMBER 2. Lat. 30° 54' S. Today a haze has obscured the horizon and the Old Man failed to get a good morning sight for longitude. He is not content with yesterday's longitude either, and I suspect that the parallel of this noon is a position of dead reckoning rather than a satisfactorily figured fix. So all day he has been muttering about making a stellar shot this evening in the brief period of twilight during which both horizon and navigational stars may be clearly discernible.

Now in the Navy, or on a modern merchant steamer, shooting the stars at dawn or dusk is a commonplace, taken in one's stride. Not so on the *Daisy*. Here it seems to be a rare and last resort, a bold and esoteric rite. The Old Man has been preparing himself as if for a great ordeal, poring over Bowditch, the *Nautical Ephemeris*, and a star chart. He seems to want the awesome rumor to get around the brig: "The Old Man's going to try a stellar!"

There are at least four favorable pairs of bright stars for our present position and season, namely, Capella and Vega, Hamal and Deneb, Aldebaran and Altair, Fomalhaut and Nunki. Which to choose will depend, of course, upon the fate that scatters the unpredictable clouds across the face of the heavens.

The day has at least been more agreeable than yesterday. The sea is considerate and the wind fair.

The officers have broken out a dozen or more sea-elephant lances and have been sharpening their points and edges on the grindstone, which suggests bloody doings in the near future. They have also been talking about the manufacture for each officer and boatsteerer of a "manduc'"—apparently a Cape Verde Island word for bludgeon. It seems that in this beastly sealing the smaller males and the cows have their skulls bashed with clubs, only the large bulls being dispatched with a bullet in the brain. All are then lanced and bled for the sake of blanching the blubber and the oil that is prepared from it. Something tells me that the "elephanting" at South Georgia is going to shrivel the very marrow of my bones.

One of our four pigs is now much larger than the others and is, moreover, a hog. It gets all its four feet into the feeding tub and fends off its neighbors while it guzzles. Mr. da Lomba has drawn a moral therefrom. "Be a damned hog if you want to," says he, "and you'll be the first one fat enough to knife."

At dusk I saw my first Cape pigeon, which is a checkered, black-and-white petrel, the best known of sea birds of the Southern Hemisphere, mentioned in the account of practically every voyage since the earliest days of exploration. Captain Cleveland calls it Cape Horn pigeon, but this is a misnomer, for in the tradition of the ocean only the Cape of Good Hope is "the Cape," while Cape Horn is "the Horn." The Cape pigeon earned its name long before Cape Horn was first rounded.

The Brave Knight, despite his fasting, vigil and prayer, was left without an adversary for his joust. I mean that the Old Man couldn't find a simultaneous star and horizon. After dark, though, the sky became brilliant. The Pleiades are dropping behind the north. Magellan's Clouds have climbed high overhead. The Southern Cross, now having the rivalry of the brightest field of stars visible from any point on our planet, is much less conspicuous than when you and I watched it, low in the southern sky, on those magical evenings in the Caribbees.

NOVEMBER 3.   Lat. 32° 09' S., long. 42° 15' W. (That's what the Old Man calls the latitude and the longitude, though without too much conviction.)

The wind has been strengthening and the day is gray and dank. "Right whale weather," says the skipper.

We unbent the mainsail, which has been furled for several days, and replaced it with a small loose-foot trisail. Toward evening we took in the foresail. Our course is southwest, with the breeze now astern, and we are covering the miles like the Flying Dutchman. At times we run away from the following waves. We outstrip everything except the albatrosses.

This morning we saw two large loggerhead turtles and a school of blackfish. The memorable event of the day, however, was a trifle pensive, for I ate the final banana from Fernando Noronha, the last fresh fruit I shall see for many and many a moon.

NOVEMBER 4.   Lat. 33° 28' S., long. 45° 42' W. A strong nor'wester, almost a gale, raged throughout the night. At two o'clock this morning we were obliged to luff and head into it, after blowing away the lower foretopsail. I happened to be standing with my head above the after-hatchway, looking at the riotous sky toward the end of the anchor watch, when this sail tore out of the bolt ropes and flew off over the sea like a gossamer web. Its stripping from the spar made a strange sound, pleasant except for its implications, a swift sound halfway between a puff and a handclap, as though the wind were contemptuous in its might, warning us that its mere breath could dismember our refuge.

During the forenoon a large flycatcher with a yellow belly flew aboard, nearly exhausted, collided with the leech of a sail and perched in various parts of the rigging. Later a silver-billed tanager alighted on the foresail yard, followed by a huge moth which, like the two storm-beaten land birds, flew off to leeward and to doom. We were approximately 340 miles from the South American mainland.

Toward noon, the weather cleared and the wind moderated. We restored the mainsail to its boom and gaff, reefed and hoisted it, and then bent on a new foretopsail that came, all clean and white, out of a cask below.

After the ocean had calmed a bit, I saw vast flotillas of salleemen on the surface. Three loggerhead turtles were sighted and one was captured. It was crossing our wake and Mr. da Lomba skillfully jerked the trailing fish line and gigged the unfortunate reptile by the neck. It was then drawn under the counter and harpooned. Its stomach was crammed with salleemen. Its flesh had a rank smell (which I knew of old), but the Portuguese members of the crew welcomed it as a choice addition to the larder. They could hardly have made more fuss over a green turtle, the gastronome's delight.

During the middle part of the day the cooper was persuaded to set up a hand lathe on the carpenter's bench, after which various stout billets of West Indian firewood were fetched up from the hold. It seems that the boys have been quite stirred by the cheerful prospect of braining sea elephants, and each one thinks that he should turn himself out a manduc' that will gratify his pride as well as equip him with a weapon.

So they have been at it in teams for hours, manufacturing policeman's truncheons of dark and heavy wood, each an individual creation with a whimsically ringed handle and a swollen, deadly business end. Each manduc' looks, in fact, like a miniature and fancy baseball bat, and the waste turnings from the lathe have littered the whole maindeck.

But there is a joke on somebody. I don't know what it is, but I recognize it in the sardonic grin on Mr. da Lomba, the irrepressible glee in the expression of Mr. Vincent, and the knowing look on the poker face of Correia, the cooper. These three and the Old Man are the only souls on board who have ever seen a sea elephant or visited the cold south. There seems to be something uproariously funny about the industrious production of a club per man, and in due course I shall doubtless see the point.

Well, turtle guts make the best of bird bait, so in the afternoon I began to troll fishhooks. Presently a giant fulmar seized hold, and in he came, offering so much resistance that I feared my heavy codfish line would snap. This was the first feathered specimen taken by fishing, and I was quite elated.

The giant fulmar, biggest of all the petrels and more generally known to sailors as Nelly, glutton, or stinker, is scarcely more popular as a bird than a shark is as a fish. Its appearance and carrion-eating habits are alike unprepossessing, and in the tender yet prejudiced breasts of seafarers it arouses none of the kindly sentiments of which albatrosses and Mother Carey's chickens are often the beneficiaries. A bird of prey, it is, nevertheless, ungainly and uncouth, lacking the beauty and dash that win admiration for even the most bloodthirsty of falcons. More appropriately, of course, it should be compared with a vulture rather than a hawk.

But, catching my stinker was only the beginning of a Roman holiday. As the sea became rougher, various other petrels and albatrosses gathered astern to fight over the fragments of turtle intestines. The Old Man and others joined in the sport, and we were soon hauling examples of the smaller seabirds down from the air as animated kites, after they had pounced upon the trailing baits and had started to fly off with them. After seeing captives pulled on board the *Daisy*, the free birds were just as eager to bite as before. Even those that shook out one hook, while being pulled in, promptly snapped up another.

We caught five kinds, four of them new to my collection. One was the Manx shearwater, which nests in Europe. I identified thirteen species, comprising four of albatrosses, six of petrels and shearwaters, and two of Mother Carey's chickens.

The day is closing with a howling head wind that has shifted by way of west to south. It is now very rapidly kicking up a tremendous sea.

NOVEMBER 5. Lat. 35° 00' S., long. 46° 55' W. Election day! Dare I venture three cheers for President Woodrow Wilson? To you, perhaps, even though you are a dyed-in-the-wool Rhode Islander, but hardly to the crabbed Old Man. After five months of close association with him, I have been well schooled in a set of Down East sea dogs' tenets, such as (1) fish is good food on any day except Friday; (2) virtue and honesty do not exist west of the Rocky Mountains; (3) respectability and statesmanship are exclusive attributes of the Republican party!

It is too uncomfortable to sit still and write. The ocean is horribly rough, so that there is constant danger of being battered against something. Whatever is not lashed down, slides. The chairs in the after-cabin fall over and bang, and I slithered the length of my berth through the night. Yet I've been skinning birds all day, with my knives and scissors rolling around 'tween decks, below the main hatch. We are plying to windward under only a dishrag and a napkin. It hurts to sit down and my back is lame from balancing. I'll tell you more when we get on an even keel.

I took from your letter bag today a most winning epistle from John Francis Green, Professor of Roman Literature and History at Brown. It is dated May 5th, exactly half a year ago. He writes, among other things:

"Naturally, when I think of a former pupil like yourself, I often recall the subjects we thrashed out together—Horace, for example. You certainly are going to have a chance to prove the philosophy of the 'Integer vitae.' Sing of your Lalage and the brutes will flee from you, though perhaps you would rather catch 'em. At any rate, you will have the scenic background . . . either the sunscorched tropics or the polar fields where there are no trees refreshed by summer's breeze."

I realize that the day of the classical languages is waning, and that there are new humanities which will make it impracticable for the average educated man of the future to dig into Greek or Latin, or both, for from four to six long years. But I'm glad that I lived before the end of the transition, because the apogee of my college course, for sheer fun, came when I faced the inspired countenance of Johnny Green and read Horace, Catullus, Tibullus, and Propertius. I have Horace with me but, in any case, I know by heart many of the lyrics. Now that we have left the region of the "too near sun" and are drawing nigh one "o'er which brood mists and a gloomy sky," I can still walk the quarterdeck with my Lalage and sing, under my breath, to her alone,

> pone sub curru nimium propinqui
> solis, in terra domibus negata:
> dulce ridentem Lalagen amabo,
>   dulce loquentem.

NOVEMBER 6.   Position undetermined.

It is evening and a cold one, with a gimlet of a south wind. It is just such an evening, in fact, as we have in November at Old Man's Harbor, and against just such an orange sky I used to shoot ducks. I wish that I were there with you now, my Grace. What a pity that we can't celebrate together the result of the election! It is queer to think that I may not learn what transpired yesterday in mine own country until some Britisher tells me next spring! I suppose it is hardly likely that we shall see a human being at South Georgia, even though whalemen are established in one or more of the fiords. On the last voyage, the cooper tells me, only two whale-chasing steamers were sighted at long range during several months in which the *Daisy* lay embayed.

It has taken me most of the day to make up the last of my bird skins, including two wandering albatrosses, the largest fowls that fly. The weather has been rough, rainy, impenetrable, and uncomfortable, but the afterglow holds a promise. *"Tempo vae, tempo vem,"* remarks Mr. Almeida, which I take to mean that time comes as fast as it goes. More than a third of my exile is over.

NOVEMBER 7. Lat. 35° 40' S., long. 46° 35' W. A clear day with brisk westerly winds.

I now wear plenty of woolens. Reading is a thing of the past, because it is too cold to sit on deck, and too dark below.

We are on the River Whaling Grounds, named for the Río de la Plata, and at the moment you would think that the Old Man had no aim to get anywhere. He has ordered sail shortened for the night and has pointed us on a northwesterly tack. Evidently he wants to hang around here for sperm whales, which leaves the officers disgruntled because they say the best of the sea elephant season will pass before we make South Georgia.

One displeasing step starts the contagion of discontent. The men are now reminded that the quality of the food is falling off again. The Old Man has not issued sufficient warm clothing. He probably won't get half a cargo of "elephant" oil. They are going to demand discharge, or desert if necessary, at the first port, by God!

Blackfish, porpoises jumping in lines as far as the eye could reach, a finback, an ocean sunfish—all these we have seen today, but nary a sign of a sperm whale.

The Old Man eyes his crew like a hawk. In the mate's

watch today he suddenly asked, "Where's Frank?"

The slow response of the third officer indicated embarrassment, but he finally replied, "Sick."

"Sick! Why hasn't he reported? What's the matter with him?" snapped the skipper, evidently recalling that the boat-steerer had been missing for two days or longer.

"Blue-balls" (meaning buboes or swellings in the groin), went on Mr. Almeida, ignoring the first question.

The Old Man's visage screwed up into the expression we dread to see. "Bring him up," he roared; "blue-balls, clap, pox, strangury, good God, what next? He'll die on deck, he will, not down in that steerage. What kind of officers have I got, to let a man on my ship cuddle his guts without reporting for medicine?"

He then strode aft and went below. Frank was assisted up the vertical ladder, clad in underclothes and wrapped in a blanket. He was sick, all right. He lay down on the booby hatch because he couldn't stand, and his shipmates tucked him up.

A while later the Old Man came back and grimly worked him over in silence, examining the glandular swelling, gingerly testing the area of sensitiveness, and looking at the man's gums, throat, eyelids, and the skin of his legs. He ordered him back to his bunk, and afterwards sent a concoction to be administered four times a day by Mr. da Lomba.

In such emergencies, the captain does his best, but I fear he'll never save young Francisco Nicolau from an early grave.

NOVEMBER 8.   Lat. 36° 16' S., long. 46° 35' W. A northwest wind is again piling up the waves. At least it makes the air warmer than last evening.

I did some further fishing for birds and then shaved off my beard, retaining the moustache that Johnny, the cabin boy, regards with frank envy.

There was a strangely beautiful, vermilion sunset toward

the estuary of the Río de la Plata. Once more the skipper has had the courses furled, and we are to lie-to for the night under trisail and staysails. I believe that he smells whales.

NOVEMBER 9. Lat. 36° 46' S., long. 46° 29' W. Reasonably calm, after several days of rugged weather. About five o'clock in the afternoon, when the brig was yawing for want of a breeze, I obtained the Old Man's permission to lower the *Grace Emeline* and I took the cooper with me.

It was quiet on the great gray swells. Birds were moving about without either avoiding the dory or being attracted by it. They were simply indifferent. I began the slaughter when the first petrel flew within range, and soon Correia and I were banging away together, endeavoring to collect the greatest variety of specimens from among the bewildering thousands of waterfowl. We presently rowed back to the *Daisy* to discharge our catch before it became too bloody or messy, but, after staying on board for supper, we set forth again. No birds seemed in the least disturbed by the roar of the guns.

Altogether we acquired thirty-six specimens, of which thirty-five were petrels and albatrosses, and one an Arctic tern on its winter migration into the southern oceans. Many of the ten species were first captures for the voyage. They included examples of a rare gadfly petrel which the Old Man and the officers know as the Tristan mutton bird, because it nests at the islands of Tristan da Cunha.

The captain either felt or feigned a certain consternation over the fact that I had shot several albatrosses. It appears that this is still taboo, whether the weapon be a crossbow or a shotgun. Of course, it is perfectly good form to catch an albatross on a bent nail or a fishhook, hit it on the head with a belaying pin, consign its carcass to a stew, use its snowy plumage as a swab, make pipestems and needle cases from its wing bones and tobacco pouches out of its big webbed feet. No curse attaches to all that. But shooting one is different.

NOVEMBER 10.   Lat. 37° 33' S., long. 46° 48' W. Calm
and fog. I am in fear that the charge of "diomedeicide," or
albatross murder, will be raised against me at any moment.
Perhaps, however, my standing as a provider of an abundant
and truly delectable mutton bird fricassee—enough for all
hands—may keep the indictment in abeyance.

You may believe that I labored hard all day, but I at
least had a capacious table that the cooper recently built for
my operations of skinning, skeletonizing, injecting and pick-
ling specimens. Twenty-one cleaned and poisoned skins are
ready for making up tomorrow.

NOVEMBER 11.   No sights obtainable.

> And now there came both mist and snow,
> And it grew wondrous cold;
> And ice, mast-high, came floating by,
> As green as emerald.

We have not yet seen the ice, but we begin to feel its
breath. From where I stand by the wheel, a man on the topgallant forecastle is only a gray wraith.

Many huge finbacks, and possibly blue whales, passed
very close to us this morning. They, too, looked dim and
veiled, but their spoutings made a startling racket. We lowered the dory to pick up a stick of lumber which, the Old Man
says, is worth $20. It has a fuzz of goose barnacles and it was
accompanied by fish, but we caught none. Furthermore, four
skuas were resting on it when it first loomed up through the
cold mist.

The twilights are lengthening now. Last evening we saw
the new moon, but tonight visible space ends just beyond the
rigging.

NOVEMBER 12.   Lat. 39° 41' S., longitude undetermined. Fresh northerly to easterly winds.

Large masses of floating kelp were sighted. Small blue
petrels, known as broad-billed prions or right whalebirds (the

captain's name), became abundant, dancing around like snow flakes in the wind.

NOVEMBER 13.   Lat. 41° 00' S., long. 44° 48' W. Course southeast.

After breakfast, a school of blackfish approached and many of the animals practically rubbed the weed off the *Daisy*'s waterline as they passed. They came, obligingly, while I had the Graflex in my hand, and I snapped one photograph that should fill the plate. My file of negatives has already grown to be a great treasure.

We stuck the pig which had made the greatest strides toward becoming a swine, and then enjoyed fresh pork and deepdish blueberry pie. I happened to be seated on the leeward side of the table, so my wedge of pie contained more blueberries and juice than the portions of the first officer and the cooper, both of whom sat up to windward!

Johnny sheared off my long brown locks on deck in the bright and dazzling afternoon. The weather reminded me of Indian summer up home, for the sunny air had a bite, the horizon was misty and the sky full of mackerel scales.

NOVEMBER 14.   Lat. 42° 24' S., long. 42° 28' W. Wind moderate and fair, weather cool, sky mostly overcast.

Early this morning a group of finbacks was mistaken at long range for right whales, but a single glance by the Old Man settled the question. Later, other finbacks came up to blow close alongside. Moreover, porpoises of a new kind played across the cutwater. They were stunning creatures, marked with broad longitudinal bands of white, and had high and graceful back fins. Most porpoises are not known well enough to possess common names. These matched the picture, in True's book, of a species called *Lagenorhynchus cruciger*.

I am writing this entry today with a pen made from an albatross quill. When I was a small tot, my Great Uncle Herbert taught me how to cut a pen from a goose quill, and his method still serves.

Sea birds are becoming more abundant daily, or even by the hour, as we penetrate the Roaring Forties. Nearly every record in my table of observations now lists new species of ocean birds. I have seen twenty-four between the equator and the latitude of this noon.

NOVEMBER 15.   Lat. 45° 18' S., long. 41° 10' W. It has been, or rather has seemed, cold, with strong westerlies and a very long Cape Horn swell. The poor West Indians think that we have reached the limit of terrestrial frigidity, yet the mercury has not descended far into the forties. Mittens and heavy coats are beginning to appear, and more blankets have been broken out.

At sunset birds of a dozen kinds were about in tremendous numbers, rioting in the wind and frequently poising over the *Daisy's* quarterdeck as though interested in affairs on board. Just as the sun was sinking, I heard a curious braying call from the waves. Then, half a ship's length to windward, I saw the first penguin. Soon small bands were passing, all heading northward. The birds dived like porpoises and remained under water most of the time, but their braying occasionally attracted attention toward sleek heads and upright tails, the only parts above the surface. From the white markings over their eyes, they were readily identifiable as gentoo or "Johnny" penguins, a kind with which I hope soon to become well acquainted at South Georgia.

NOVEMBER 16.   Lat. 44° 57' S, long. 39° 51' W. It is cold now, beyond mistake, and the wintry southwest wind howls dolefully. Why the Old Man keeps the mastheads up there through the penetrating squalls is a mystery to me, because it is too rough to lower a boat even if whales were raised. The boys, still fresh from the tropics where most of them have spent their lives, are livid and utterly miserable.

Perhaps the captain thinks that this is the way to begin acclimating for the ice fields. He allows the wind to sweep through the cabin too, and has ordered Johnny to build no fire in the wood stove.

The Old Man has taken from his rack two high-latitude charts of the South Atlantic, and is following on one of them the pencilled track of his former approach to South Georgia. They are grimy old charts, but gay too, because one is backed with light blue calico and the other with a textile of red and white checks.

I have been entranced by the antics of the mollymauks, or smaller albatrosses of three or more kinds, that are following us in ever-increasing numbers. The black-browed albatross is the most abundant, the gray-headed the rarest, and the sooty (an all-black species) the most graceful and exquisite.

The black-brows sail again and again across the quarterdeck, jerking up their heads like spirited steeds and showing curiosity in every action. Sometimes they wiggle their feet with a running motion, even though high in air; sometimes they tip up and halt as abruptly as though they had struck an invisible barrier. They sweep across the stern so close that I can see the recognition in their brown eyes and hear the humming swish of their stiff quills. I can watch the action of elevators and depressors (in the form of tail and broad-webbed feet), and the perpetual adjustments of slender, quivering planes.

As their numbers increase, competition for food becomes keener. They now show more excitement than formerly when I trail bait on fishlines. They drop like pillows, spreading wide their legs, throwing their bulging breasts forward and their heads far back, thus assuming awkward and ridiculous attitudes on their way toward the water. Before alighting, they stretch down the legs and turn the toes upward. Then the huge webs strike the surface obliquely and the birds glide forward several yards, like boys on an ice slide, before they slowly settle into the buoyant swimming position, with angels' wings held high above their backs. But then they are apt to waste time by quarreling in a laughable, solemn way, sidling around each other and croaking loudly while the bait is relentlessly towed out of their reach.

Evidence is convincing that some of the same individual mollymauks follow the *Daisy* day after day. Birds with distinguishing marks, such as a missing wing quill or a patch of immature or faded plumage on some part of the body, have come to be well-known to us. One group of four sooty albatrosses, in particular, has convoyed us for a week. The birds appear shortly after noon each day and accompany us majestically until darkness hides them.

NOVEMBER 17. No observations with the sextant. For the first time I spent the night in the inner container of my sleeping bag.

It is very cold. A gale, marked by spittings of sleet, blows from the southwest and the sea is enormous. Two or three times the deck has been bouncing hailstones. It is unsafe to sit, stand, or lie down without a good grip on something, and at meals the food and dishes show an aversion toward the table and an affinity for the deck underfoot.

The temperature in the cabin, during midday mess, was 44° F. Needless to say, we are all bundled up in winter clothes. Above I have recorded that the wind was southwest, but actually it made a complete circuit of the compass before nightfall. At one time it was roaring from due east.

At least the Old Man sent up no mastheads—the sissy!

NOVEMBER 18. Lat. 48° 39' S., long. 36° 40' W. Southwesterly gale, with sharp hailstorms, all day. Temperature 40° F. Barometer 29.24 inches at noon, rising at sunset.

The time is now six bells of the afternoon (three o'clock, if it's too much trouble to figure). You may cross out every previous statement I have made about rough seas since we left Dominica. It has never been rough until today. We are in the heart of the trackless south Atlantic, far from the trade routes, with South Georgia only 325 miles away, and we've been lying-to under staysail and trisail since dawn. The lee whale boats are hoisted to the davit tackle blocks, the seas break over the maindeck, and the whole ocean is seething and covered with white froth. A sou'west gale tears the surface to shreds and rolls the old *Daisy* on her beam ends. It is glorious, even if uncomfortable. Dark hailstorms have alternated with furious puffs of wind, but frequently the sun breaks through the massive round clouds, and then the light on the cavorting waves and the little silvery whalebirds is exquisite. What though we have to cling to a rope, and what though one dives from dining room stool to the northeast corner of the ceiling!

"Cape Horn dirty weather," the Old Man calls it, too cold to do anything sedentary and too rough to do anything vigorous—beyond what is necessary. This morning, braced in the spare whaleboat across the stern, I photographed albatrosses and other birds until my hands, arms, and neck practically froze in the "Graflex posture." Then I came down to thaw out in the cabin, where the temperature is 40° F.

NOVEMBER 19.   Lat. 49° 40' S., long. 35° 51' W. Continuation of the "pampero"; westerly gales and snowstorms.

If you want to imagine my situation, here in a latitude corresponding to that of Labrador, just think of spending a few February days and nights on Angell Street, Providence. You are allowed plenty of clothing, but cannot walk more than twenty feet in any direction. At mealtimes you sit on the curbstone to eat, and at night you crawl into a nice warm

sleeping bag on the flower bed. But on no account are you to
step out of the open air.

Even such a conception falls short, because it is at least
safe to stand up on Angell Street, but here it is a struggle to
maintain any position whatsoever, not excluding a horizontal
one! I am bulging with heavy clothes, yet my feet are congeal-
ing while I huddle in the corner of my berth and write this.
Whenever the sun shows its face for a few minutes, I pull on
mittens and dance on the quarterdeck, hanging onto a rope's
end to keep from being pitched into the sea.

I hope that it will soon let up enough so that we can proceed. I am eager to feel terra firma, to sleep outside a churn,
to walk a straight mile, and to gloat in the shelter of the hills.

Just before five o'clock this afternoon, while a snow
flurry came up with an extremely violent southwest puff, the
Daisy was suddenly surrounded by blue petrels or whalebirds.
Several hundred of them settled on the water near the stern,
and for a quarter of an hour I had an opportunity of watching
them feed at very close range.

The small, pale blue-gray, white-breasted creatures
worked along with an odd creeping motion, resting their
bodies lightly upon the surface but holding their spread wings
just above it, the feet apparently furnishing their motive
power. Then, as they scurried rapidly forward in droves, their
heads would be thrust under water and their wide bills would
scoop for food. The Old Man, who was watching with me, said
that Yankee whalemen sometimes call these birds scoopers.

It was impossible for me to tell what they were feeding
on. Groups of the birds reminded me of a human swimming
race, for the bodies were stretched out along the water in the
attitude of the crawl. But frequently each one would dive out
of sight, to emerge a yard or less ahead. Each stayed below
not more than a fraction of a second except, perhaps, when it
shot through the crest of a wave, but in a particular field on

the water the birds disappeared and reappeared with such rapidity that the area fairly twinkled. About as many were below as above, most of the time. There were wide troughs between the waves, and whenever a mighty roller with a white and broken crest hurtled along, the whalebirds would not attempt to dive through it but would lift themselves daintily at the last moment, fly through the spume of the comber, and settle immediately on the downward slope beyond. Ultimately, they all arose like a school of flying fish and darted off over the ocean on a quest elsewhere.

NOVEMBER 20. Lat. 50° 12' S., long. 34° 47' W. The storm still stews. We toss about, helpless to do anything more than keep pointing into the wind. Last night a heavy sea broke over the whole cabin, and the chilly brine came pouring down via companionway and skylight. My corner remained dry, but the air below has since been more damp and frigid than ever.

At noon the Cape pigeons were flying close about the stern. Finally one actually dropped into the spare whaleboat and I caught it in my hands.

In the early evening, the quartet of sooty albatrosses that convoys us each afternoon was swinging repeatedly across the quarterdeck. I therefore watched my chance and shot one so that it came hurtling down into the Old Man's open arms.

"My soul and body!" he grunted, with the breath nearly knocked out of him!

The specimen was my first of its kind, and a magnificent bird, its plumage varying from black on the head and wings to pale ashy gray on the back. Around each eye was an incomplete ring of white feathers, and along the length of its lower bill a fleshy, bright blue stripe. Its tail was long and wedge-shaped, quite unlike the stumpy tail of the wandering albatross. Its extraordinarily slender and graceful wings measured, when stretched out, six feet, nine inches from tip to tip.

NOVEMBER 21.   Lat. 51° 37' S., long. 34° 56' W. South-westerly winds of diminishing strength, and prevailingly overcast skies. The great storm has run its course, though the ocean is still riotous.

Shortly after noon, three sooty albatrosses overtook and accompanied us, which is indication enough that our familiar four of the past week or so have represented the same individual birds each day.

NOVEMBER 22.   Lat. 53° 00' S., long. 35° 25' W., by dead reckoning. Heavy fog, and cold, wet air that fairly burns the nostrils. The storm is spent, the ocean relatively quiet, the breeze light, swinging during the day from northwest through north to east.

At midday the mist lifted, and there on the weather bow lay a noble, two-hilled iceberg with a hoary top and emerald walls, just as Coleridge testifies. Its highest elevation seemed about level with our topmasthead. Two right whales, showing a double spout when seen end-on, were blowing half a mile to the west of us, in the direction of the iceberg. The Old Man could not suppress a certain itch to go after them, but the greater part of our whalecraft, including the line tubs and boat equipment, has been stowed away below during the past forty-eight hours.

A large dead whale, much distended—but, happily, to leeward—also lay afloat, telling us of our proximity to the Norwegian whalemen of South Georgia. Six months from home, but at last we are nearing our long-sought destination! I can hear loops of the anchor chain being hauled up from the locker.

We saw no sun today, although its presence above the fog was told by curious fields of pink light on the ocean. At nine o'clock this evening it is still daylight. We are passing innumerable masses and tangles of floating kelp.

NOVEMBER 23. A brief squall from the southeast blew up during the night. Doubled lookouts for bergs and growlers were stationed at the bow, but we have thus far met only small rafts of floe ice. It has been rough all morning, and a mixture or alternation of rain and sticky snow has cut down our vision. One small whale-chasing steamer was reported, but it paid no attention to our old black windjammer.

It was a strain through the long hours of the morning and the middle of the day to look ahead and look ahead into the tenebrous mist, while the *Daisy* rolled jerkily. There was hardly enough wind to fill our canvas, but the dull waters were still troubled by the memory of the four-days' storm. Masses of brown kelp and scattered chunks of worn ice heaved with us on the surface of the sea and slowly fell astern. A gleaming-white snow petrel (the first I had ever seen) brushed the rigging in its flight, and our familiar trio of sooty albatrosses circled round and round the brig, poising successively above the truck on the foretopgallantmast.

The Old Man, close-mouthed as always, passed out no overt word of his noon reckoning, but the signs, both seen and felt, told of the proximity of a landfall, and we were all in a fever of expectancy after five months on the Atlantic. When the grayness of the antarctic spring day began to deepen, shortly after three o'clock in the afternoon, I fancied that I saw a flicker of anxiety even on the set face of the skipper himself, as he stood by the helmsman, peering ahead and ahead and ahead.

"Land-ho!"

I rushed to the bow, when the welcome cry from the masthead snapped the tension, and gazed into an unbroken monochrome of gray. But dimly, gradually, a long, dark line loomed out, and above it an area of intangible whiteness blending with the soft sky. Before we could see as distinctly as the men at masthead level, evening closed in with a wet snow squall, so we wore ship and stood offshore. We knew, however, with a thrill of exultation, that our outward voyage was about to end, for through the darkening haze we had caught a glimpse of the coast hills and illimitable snowfields of South Georgia. The sagacious Old Man had done even better than that, for, when I joined him at his chart table below, he informed me that we had made the land at a promontory just east of Possession Bay. He said that we had sighted it at a distance of between six and seven miles—and just in time before the curtain fell.

The Old Man celebrated in a way that nobody else could ever have thought of. For the first time, he permitted, and ordered, a fire in the wood-burning cabin stove. It is now yielding considerable smoke, and some heat; at least the temperature is climbing into the high forties!

It is night, and we are lumbering slowly eastward toward Cumberland Bay, and also slightly offshore. Before dark there was another lift of the pervading mists and a short view of towering mountains. The cabin is almost warm, or seems so, albeit somewhat choking. In the miserable light of the lamp I have been running over my typewritten summaries of the historical and scientific literature relating to South Georgia.

"We are here!" I keep thinking over and over, even though one previous explorer, Szielasko, lost his ship on a sunken rock when he was within a mile of landing! Tomorrow marks the attainment of what you and I have aimed at for nearly a year, beloved. From this point forward it is proper to consider that I am on the homeward stretch.

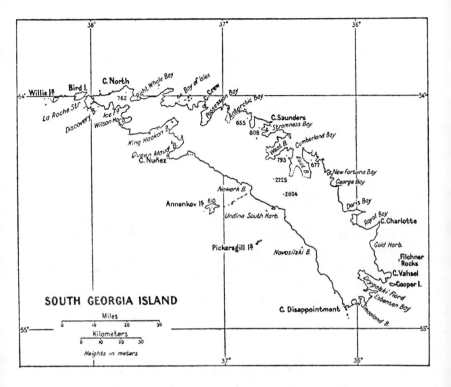

SOUTH GEORGIA ISLAND

Miles

Kilometers

Heights in meters

5 Outpost
of the Antarctic

NOVEMBER 24.   A small speck near the bottom of an
unfamiliar map may be all that South Georgia means to most
Americans, and yet for more than a hundred years Yankee
mariners have voyaged to this faraway isle, and some of them
have grown wealthy on its spoils. About the size of Long Island, lying in a blustery ocean twelve hundred miles east of
Cape Horn, South Georgia is one of the broken ring of mountainous, bleak, and treeless islands around the southern end
of the earth. These islands have an almost antarctic climate

in spite of their relatively low latitude. They are the homes of
albatrosses and many other sea birds that do not nest on the
Antarctic Continent, as well as the breeding grounds of fur
seals and sea elephants, and the range of the southernmost
flowering plants.

Some believe that Amerigo Vespucci, while serving as
navigator of a Portuguese fleet on his third voyage to the New
World, sighted South Georgia in April, 1502. There is more
reason to credit its discovery by Antoine de la Roche, an English merchant, although the son of a French father, in April,
1675. Still more likely is the tale that it was seen by the crew
of the Spanish ship *Leon*, en route from Lima to Cadiz, in
June, 1756. A Frenchman of St. Malo, Ducloz Guyot, wrote a
journal of the voyage, and stated that the island was named
San Pedro, after July 1st, the saint's day on which the *Leon*
sailed south of it.

But all of the foregoing sightings are unimportant and
half legendary. South Georgia was discovered, in the true
sense of the word, and likewise named, in January, 1775, by
Captain James Cook in H.M.S. *Resolution*, while on his second great voyage around the world. It was Cook and the naturalists with him—the German Forsters, father and son, and
the Swede, Anders Sparrman—who first explored and charted
the forbidding coast of the new land. I have before me, in the
cabin of the *Daisy*—which is probably far less luxurious than
that of the *Resolution*, our predecessor by 137 years!—copies
or translations of every word that Cook, the Forsters, and
Sparrman wrote about the island. It makes me feel almost
mystically close, in this icy and silent setting, to the heroes
who cruised in the Golden Age of exploration.

Captain Cook believed at first that he had reached the
Terra Incognita Australis which he was seeking, but on finding the ice-capped, lofty region to be merely an island of seventy leagues in circuit, by which, he observed, no one would

ever be benefited, and which was eminently "not worth the discovery," he naively entered in his journal: "I called this land the Isle of Georgia in honor of his Majesty."

Today opened as a clear and sparkling morning—what a happy change after the pea-soup atmosphere through which we have been groping! A thin fog half veiled the valley glaciers and the bases of the steep, bare coastal ranges, reddish-brown in the sunshine, but the white mountain ridges and ice-sheathed pinnacles beyond gleamed in sharp detail against the bluest of skies. South Georgia can smile, even if it rarely does.

As we cruised all morning before a gentle breeze along-shore, we passed close by several dazzling, water-worn icebergs, in the crevices of which the swelling seas made mushrooms of spray as tall as our masts. All about us were great numbers of sea fowl, of the very kinds reported by Captain Cook so long before. There were blue-eyed shags with pure white throats and breasts, albatrosses and petrels wheeling over the sea, and flocks of terns and screaming kelp gulls on the shore rocks.

On our eastward course, which was also somewhat southward or slanting toward the coast, we saw four of the little whale-chasers chugging out of fiords on their way to sea. As we passed the light on Cape Saunders, two large steamers showed up inside Stromness Bay. All these signs of human activity and occupation seemed to puzzle and trouble the Old Man, who recalls the South Georgia of former years as quite outside the human and lawful world. However, when we drew close to the land, it was exciting to discern the manlike forms of king penguins standing on lonely beaches and to pick out through field glasses an occasional brown mound that was a slumbering sea elephant.

We finally made out the entrance to Cumberland Bay, our destination and a very extensive body of water. The skipper was, however, disturbed by the apparently incorrect plotting of a light and a beacon on his chart. Furthermore, the wind had died and the brig could make no headway. So Mr. da Lomba was ordered ashore with a boat's crew, I to accompany him as a supernumerary, with the added privilege of being the first to set foot on the soil of South Georgia.

It was a pull of many miles, despite the deceptive appearance of nearness of the mighty hills. As we gradually approached them, they were seen to be covered with a mossy carpet, and, on their lower slopes from which the snow had all melted, with patches of rank, green tussock grass. Beyond these coastal ridges, the great range of perpetual whiteness rose far into the pale blue vault and a few streaming wisps of cloud trailed from the peak of Mt. Paget.

The sea birds, too, were putting on a stunning show, and for the first time in my life I saw many petrels and their relatives flying extremely high. Among those that spiralled far up toward the zenith, until they became indistinguishable specks against the thin cirrus clouds, were hundreds of wandering albatrosses. Since some of these approached, or probably surpassed, the limit of our vision, it is likely that they soared to an altitude of a mile above the bay and the surrounding land. Two smaller species of albatrosses, as well as numerous giant fulmars, Cape pigeons and whalebirds were sharing in the performance. Especially notable is the fact that the greater part of the upward circling was taking place over water, because similar flight by vultures has usually been interpreted as the result of vertical convection from the easily heated surface of bare land.

The whole shoreline of Cumberland Bay proved to be lined for miles with the bones of whales, mostly humpbacks. Spinal columns, loose vertebrae, ribs, and jaws were piled in heaps and bulwarks along the waterline and it was easy to count a hundred huge skulls within a stone's throw. The district is an enormous sepulcher of whales, yet no one can guess how many thousands of flensed carcasses have been borne out to sea by the tide, and so have sunk their skeletons in the deep.

The tiny, land-locked haven of Grytviken, or King Edward Cove, finally greeted us through the sense of smell even before we had rounded the point that hides its entrance. The odor of very stale whale then increased amain as we entered the cove, which might be likened to a great cauldron so filled with the rotting flesh and macerated bones of whales that they not only bestrew its bottom but also thickly encrust its rim to the farthest highwater mark. At the head of the cove, below a pointed mountain, we could see the whaling station, its belching smoke, several good-sized steamers, and a raft of whale carcasses. Fragments of entrails and other orts of whales were floating out to sea.

Near the entrance of the cove was a substantial frame building flying the Union Jack. Toward this we headed and, upon landing (I first), we were courteously greeted by a gentleman in tweeds who introduced himself as Mr. James Innes Wilson, His Majesty's Stipendiary Magistrate, representing the Government of the Falkland Islands in the Dependency of South Georgia.

And the Old Man had believed, and told me, that there was no government at all at this God-forsaken but profitable island!

Mr. Wilson, a Scot, was attended by a Guernseyman, Hardy, presented to us as Customs Inspector. These two were the sole officials of the Crown. Jointly or severally, they served as governor, postmaster, port captain, health officer, police force, judge, jailer—I mean gaoler—the cook and the captain bold and the mate of the *Nancy* brig, etc.

The magistrate hardly waited for my first question. Post? Of course; it arrived at and left the island about once a month. Registry? Certainly; one room of his residence was a full-fledged Empire Post Office. It was all quite bewildering, after my expectations. The southernmost post office in the world; and across the cove, in the Grytviken community, a Lutheran chapel which was the southernmost church in the world!

The *Daisy*, it appeared, would have to be "received" (I could hear the Old Man's groans). Officer Hardy entered our whaleboat to row off with us for the necessary formalities, and to pilot the brig to an anchorage. But at that moment our weather-beaten craft rounded the point in tow of the whale-chaser *Fortuna*, which had picked her up in the outer bay. She dropped anchor in the very center of King Edward Cove. We went aboard and found the skipper in a funk and a highly apprehensive state of mind. He had no liking for the civilized look of things.

Later, Hardy came out in his own pram, examined the *Daisy*'s papers, and brought invitations for Captain Cleveland to confer with Mr. Wilson at his convenience and to take dinner with Captain Larsen, head of the whaling station, tomorrow.

It is an infinitely sheltered and soft and peaceful evening here, despite the acrid whaley smell. In the morning, my darling, some heavy registered mail, addressed to you, will receive the postmark of South Georgia. The stamped covers should be a philatelist's delight. Sell 'em!

NOVEMBER 25.   What a night for sleeping, once the Old Man's grumblings had died away!

He had called on His Majesty's Magistrate, and his worst fears were confirmed. Sovereign government functions at South Georgia; law and regulation have reached an island that was formerly the Old Man's personal property; King George is being nasty to him. There are rules about what size and sex of sea elephants he may kill. There are port charges in

Cumberland Bay and a fee for his sealing permit. Worst of all, in accordance with a statute in force only since last month, an export license is required for the sea elephant oil that he will take away with him. What is the world coming to, when a peaceful whaler and sealer can't go about its business without being pestered and bled white by a gang of ———, ———, ——— limejuicers!

Much else the skipper also learned during his late session ashore. The reckless waste of whales, such as the beaches of this bay attest, has likewise been stopped by British law. Formerly the exceeding abundance of humpbacks in the waters off South Georgia led to the neglect of all products of secondary importance to the blubber oil. Latterly, however, the operating companies have been required to utilize the entire carcass of each whale, and they have either installed bone- and flesh-boiling guano plants at their shore stations or have sublet this branch of the work to floating factories. The fertilizer now manufactured is worth almost as much as the whale oil.

Today the Old Man very generously took me with him for his official call on the great Captain C. A. Larsen, founder of the Grytviken whaling station (properly the "Compañia Argentina de Pesca," because it was financed in Buenos Aires). Captain Larsen is the king of modern whaling and the first to establish the industry or, as I prefer to say, "exploitation," in the oceans of the far south.

He was once captain for both Nansen and Nordenski-öld, and leader of the *Jason* Antarctic Expedition. Noting the amazing numbers of whales in these southern latitudes, Captain Larsen organized the first station at South Georgia several years ago, and the success of his venture soon led to the establishment of other stations, both Norwegian and British, in various fiords along the northern coast of the island.

Captain Cleveland and I were put ashore at the Gryt-

viken whale-slip, near which we saw the oil factory, docks, a
marine railway, dwellings, dormitories for two hundred men,
carpentry and cooperage shops, metal workers' forges and
machine shops, cattle and poultry shelters, a powerhouse for
electric lights and telephone system, a library, chapel, in-
firmary, and other amenities of civilization.

When we entered the residence of Captain Larsen and
his staff, our illusions of the rude Antarctic were shattered for
the moment by luxuriant palms and blossoming plants that
banked walls and casements. A glance through the window of
the billiard room showed that "the maid was in the garden,
hanging up the clothes," but we afterwards learned that she
was the only woman in all South Georgia. Still farther within
this crude abode, or igloo, we were shown into a salon containing a piano, a conservatory of plants, singing canaries,
and several portraits, including one of King Haakon, of Norway. Every evidence of hardship, what?

I kept in mind that the Old Man is always rather proprie-
tary about me on such occasions. He swells up with pride, and
fairly bursts with modesty, over the fact that he is charged
with a mission for the American Museum of Natural History
—over and above his blubber hunting—and he likes to keep
his young "scientist" under his thumb so that the boy won't get
out of hand and act in too froward a manner. In particular, he
is quick to answer questions addressed to me, as he did to the
United States Consul at Barbados and the Consular Agent at
São Vicente. But I beat him to it today!

We were greeted warmly by Captain Larsen, and
ushered into a snug room where we met the physician and the
clergyman of the station (German and Norwegian, respectively), the local meteorologist of the Argentine Government
(a Swede), two superintendents, one of whom was Captain
Larsen's son-in-law, and two secretaries. After chatting with
the Old Man—the pair sounding like mellow sea dogs thor-

oughly in cahoots—Captain Larsen beamed on me and asked, "Professor, how long have you been going to sea?"

It was a shame to forestall Captain Cleveland's ready reply, but I did so, all in one breath, as follows:

"All me bloomin' life, Sor. Me mother was a mermaid; me natural father was King Neptune. I was born on the crest of a wave, and rocked in the cradle of the deep. Seaweed and barnacles be me clothes. Every tooth in me head is a marling spike; the hair of me head is Eyetalian hemp. Every bone in me body is a spar, and when I spits I spits Stockholm tar. I'm hard, I is, I am, I are!"

"My soul and body!" muttered Captain Cleveland, with a shocked gasp. But the eight other men in the room were giving vent to loud Norse guffaws. Nobody knew that my outburst was merely the required reply of the plebes at Annapolis, whenever an upper classman asks them how long they have been in the Navy!

Well, to go on with my tale of hardship, the meal was served by only one butler and it comprised not more than eight courses, with beer. An excellent brand of Havana cigars was passed at the end, and I was almost sorry that I do not smoke. It calls for a good constitution to endure this antarctic fare—otherwise a man could die of gout.

All the Vikings and the German physician spoke English as well as we do, although it took me a few minutes to understand that questions they asked about the "Dicy" referred to our good old brig! I explained to Dr. Lampert that daisy meant *Massliebchen*, which they all told me was *prestekrave* in Norwegian. So they agreed that our craft had a beautiful and nostalgic name, and learned how to pronounce it.

After the meal, we sang from a book of English university songs until the station whistle blew. Then Pastor Löker, the clergyman, together with the physician, and the secretary who had been playing the piano, said that they had

arranged to guide me on an afternoon walk through the surrounding country. So off went the four of us, leaving Captain
Cleveland to recover as best he might from the most sump-
tuous repast he had guzzled for at least six months.

We hiked along miles of shores white with myriad whale
skeletons. Here and there we would stop to poke a dozing sea
elephant in the ribs so that I might enjoy and photograph its
enraged expression. We also captured a number of gentoo
penguins, an easy feat because the silly creatures always ran
up the beach, whereas if they had taken to the water they
would have circumvented us with no trouble at all. They tried
to bite until we scratched their backs; after that they were
pleased, and would even mutter their thanks as they waddled
away.

I was surprised at the extraordinary number of dead animals, in addition to whales, strewn along the shore. We
passed dozens of sea elephants whose skeletons were broken
through the skin, the carcasses quite unutilized except that
the Norwegian workmen had sawed off their dentary bones
and the tip of the lower jaw in order to acquire the huge ivory
teeth. Every few score yards we would find dead skuas, gulls,
terns, Cape pigeons, or rats. Two dead penguins, one horse,
and one sheep completed the list!

We came by and by to a deep and wide meadow, overgrown with magnificent pasture in the form of shoulder-high
clumps of tussock grass. And here we found a small herd of
wild horses, at least in the sense that they had been unshel-
tered, unbroken, and fed by no man, since the German
Antarctic Expedition, under command of Dr. Filchner, had
left them in the valley about two years ago. Colts had been
born in the interim and all the animals were sleek and sound.
They were not shy, and one handsome young stallion with a
shaggy mane and fetlocks walked up, nibbled my jacket, and
allowed me to warm my hands by whacking his neck.

Pastor Löker informed me that horses and reindeer both thrive at South Georgia, but that sheep and rabbits have always failed to survive the blizzards. The only other land mammal that has become established is the rat.

After arriving at an arm of Cumberland Bay called the Moränen Fjord, we removed our boots and stockings and waded across a brook known as the Hamberg, below a shining glacier. Then, reshoeing ourselves, we followed a torrent through a gorge to Gull Lake, ascended a ridge of the foothills, and were soon in pristine snow. Over all were the pinnacle of Mt. Paget and the white mound of Sugartop, both in the main range of the island.

We returned to Grytviken over a terrific scarp and slope. My sea legs are not yet quite ready to go mountaineering with these Norsemen, but within a few days I shall be fit again.

Before and after our lunch and walk, incidentally, I watched at least fifteen humpback whales being drawn up the slip and flensed with incredible dispatch. The Old Man is nothing short of goggle-eyed over the big-scale butchery of modern whaling.

Before turning into my bunk, I took from your letter bag

Our hero's first introduction to the penguin

the envelope marked "For Bob's first visit to the penguins." It contained this sketch by Dwight Franklin.

NOVEMBER 26.   At the invitation of Captain Larsen I went to sea this morning on the whale-chaser *Fortuna*, which was the first steamer that ever hunted whales commercially in the waters of the far south. The banks where the whales feed in greatest concentration lie thirty-five or forty miles off the northeastern coast of South Georgia. This is supposed to be because the cold currents from the southwest, which swing around both ends of the island, form a great eddy in what might be called its watery "lee," and this area is filled with an incredible profusion of the small antarctic opossum shrimp known to the Norse whalemen as krill. The krill is the principal food of the humpback, finback, blue, and smaller whales found in these waters, as well as of the enormous flocks of petrels and other flying birds, and of the penguins which feed mostly beneath the surface but which leap out of water, like jumping fish or porpoises, to obtain their necessary gasp of air.

We were four hours steaming from Grytviken to the field in which we began to see whales in all directions. The commonest were humpbacks and finbacks, which can be very easily distinguished even at a great distance by their spouts, because the finback has the tallest spout of any whale, whereas that of the humpback, as I have noted before, is short, bushy, and explosive. Humpbacks are preferred game. They are fat, easily approached, and small enough to handle with relatively little effort. I have already observed that most of the countless skeletons lining the beaches of Cumberland Bay are of humpbacks that have been slaughtered during the past six years, although the remains of other fin whales, and a few of right whales, can be identified here and there.

The captain and gunner of the *Fortuna* is a younger man than I, by name Lars Andersen. The jolly old Santa Claus of a mate is Johann Johansen. He speaks good seafaring vernacular English as well as I do, but says that he can't read a sentence of the language. The steward is Gerlick Gerlicksen. I have seen practically nothing of seven or eight other members of the crew, most of whom are down in the bowels of the *Fortuna*, although one is now standing in a barrel at the masthead, with his eagle beak projecting just over the rim. It at least offers a hundred per cent more protection to the lookout than the wide-open perch and iron spectacles to which we on the *Daisy* have to cling like spider monkeys.

This steamer rolls so that all the while it is tossing an avalanche of water back and forth across its maindeck. Fortunately it was designed and built for semisubmarine operations. High combings keep the brine from pouring into the hold, and the cannon platform at the bow is reached by a catwalk well above the wet deck. Every now and then it still looks as though the prow and gunner were about to plunge into the arched trough of a wave, from which only an empty platform could rise again. Each time, however, the *Fortuna* thrusts up her snout, and remains in air. I have been spending most of my time on the bridge, where I get wet only with spray.

The whale gun was loaded through the muzzle by three men, under the supervision of the mate, about two hours after we had left port. It is a short, thick cannon, balanced so delicately on hinges and a turnstile that the gunner can point it in almost any direction as easily as though it were a pistol. The mate rammed home the charge, which consisted of a muslin bag containing about a pound of large-grained black powder. Over this he placed a handful of hemp oakum, a rubber wad shaped like the bung of a cask, and then a mass of cotton fiber. All this pillowing is to prevent the harpoon from being broken by the discharge. The harpoon weighs about one hundred pounds. Its shank fills the whole barrel of the cannon, and it is held in place by marline seizings, hitched around iron buttons on the muzzle. The part of the harpoon projecting from the gun has four hinged steel barbs, which are also lashed down tightly with marline. The lashings break when the harpooned whale tugs the line, and then the barbs open out like the ribs of an umbrella inside the body of the whale.

The last step in preparation is screwing the bomb point onto the tip of the harpoon. The bomb is a cast iron container of a charge of powder and a three-second time fuse. It is, of course, blown to fragments by explosion inside the whale, but the harpoon itself, which is forged from the finest Swedish steel, is usually undamaged or, at any rate, needs only a little subsequent straightening on the anvils of the smithy. It can thus be used over and over again, requiring only a new grenade for each discharge.

At one time during the morning, eleven steamers from Captain Larsen's company, or from those in other fiords, were within sight of the *Fortuna,* and the banging of harpoon guns was almost continuous. Humpbacks seem usually to travel in pairs. When we sighted the first two spouts, another steamer was heading toward these same animals, but we were closer and consequently beat our rival to their vicinity. After we had maneuvered for some time, one came to the surface just off the port bow. Captain Andersen swung the cannon, the prelude to a great roar and a dense cloud of smoke. Then I heard the muffled crack of the bomb and, as soon as I could see anything, a whale, already dead, was slowly sinking, belly up, at the end of our heavy hemp foreganger. The latter is the part of the harpoon line that lies in a coil on a platform just under the gun. It is held in place with ties of marline, which part like cobwebs when the line goes out. Only the best of Italian hemp is sufficiently strong, supple, and elastic to follow the projectile without breaking. Forty fathoms of this hemp, representing a greater length than the range of the harpoon gun, are attached in turn to five hundred fathoms of Manila line. The latter rides over a snatch block connected with strong steel springs in the hold, and these prevent sudden and strong jerks from breaking the gear. The whole outfit represents a sort of gigantic counterpart of the rod, reel, and sensitive hands of a trout fisherman.

The winch quickly hoisted our sinking humpback to the surface, after which a sharp pipe was jabbed into its body cavity and it was pumped full of air until it floated like a balloon. After the pipe was withdrawn, the hole was stopped with a wooden plug. The carcass was made fast by a chain passed through a hawse pipe and around the small. The flukes were then sliced off with a cutting spade. This was because the whale's "propeller" has a certain tort, one stiff fluke bending slightly downward and the other upward. It has been found that when whale carcasses are towed rapidly tailforemost, the tort of the flukes is sufficient to start the whole body spinning around its long axis, with momentum enough to break any chain or cable.

All these operations took only twelve or fifteen minutes, and I felt cheated because the kill had been so unexciting. We then resumed hunting, with our catch floating limberly along the port side of the *Fortuna,* and within half an hour Captain Andersen killed a second humpback. The process looked more than ever like murder with ease and no trace of uncertainty, but the officers assured me that it is not always so simple. They say that two harpoons are frequently needed, and that three, four, or even five are not highly exceptional. The bomb must blow up in the thoracic viscera to cause practically instantaneous death, and in the after part of a whale there are large masses of muscle and other tissue not easily shattered. This hinder end of the body may present the only target unless the gun is well within range before the whale starts its downswing after spouting and inhaling.

I noted that a neat little white notch was cut in the front edge of a fluke stump on each of our chained carcasses. The purpose of this was to inform the flensers at the shore station that they were to recover only a single harpoon from the body of each victim. The first thing that the men with the long-handled knives look for is the harpoon count, as shown in this way.

Well, livelier times were in store, for presently the man in the barrel uttered some guttural croaks which were translated for me as

"Blue whale, dead ahead!"

We were all agog to outguess this leviathan, which was engulfing krill with the joy of Eden, unconscious of a foe armed with devices worse than those of the serpent. Whispered messages passed down the speaking tube.

"Half speed."

The gunner ran forward to his platform, where the harpoon was then being rammed into the weapon and seized in place. Its bomb point began to sway back and forth over water that would soon run red. The whale slick was closer. Engines at quarter speed—it might breach within range at any instant.

"Under the bow!"

Up swung the butt of the swivel gun. A flash and a deafening detonation split the frosty air, and this time I actually saw the iron, flinging its wild tail of line, crash into the gray hulk. Three seconds later—a long while it seemed—came the strange, faraway crack of the bomb. Had it reached his lungs?

No, the shot was too far aft for an instant kill. The wounded whale summoned his final energy and towed us, against the drag of the winch, against the whirl of propellers that had responded to full speed astern.

No being can reveal more marvelous grace than a whale.

Do not think of them as shapeless, as I once did, because of seeing only bloated carcasses washed ashore on Long Island beaches, with all the firmness and streamline of the body gone. Envision, rather, this magnificent blue whale, as shapely as a mackerel, spending his last ounce of strength and life in a hopeless contest against cool, unmoved, insensate man. Sheer beauty, symmetry, utter perfection of form and movement, were more impressive than even the whale's incomparable bulk, which dwarfed the hull of *Fortuna*.

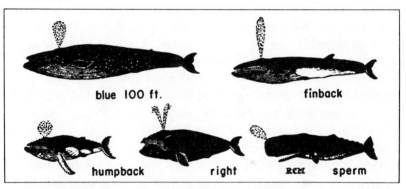

blue 100 ft.   finback

humpback   right   RGM   sperm

By their spouts shall ye know them.

Our next experience was a dud, because the gunner missed his shot altogether, and the humpback waved a hurried goodbye, with flukes brandished high in air. The bomb explosion, far below the surface, whacked the steel bottom of the steamer.

This marked the end of our effective cruise, because a fog then rolled down upon us with the speed of a falling theater curtain. We cut closely across the bow of the chaser *Edda*, which was winching a dead whale to the surface. I snapped a photograph through my Graflex and then, even as I was watching, the whole scene was blotted out. Horns began to moan through the white atmosphere, from port, starboard,

ahead and astern, both near and far off, and I realized that
collisions were no small hazard on such an overpopulated
hunting ground.

Before the pea soup rolled over us, the white mountains
of South Georgia were a glorious sight from our position
thirty-five miles off the coast. Rising directly from the sea,
they looked supremely lofty, and yet Mt. Paget and Sugartop
seemed almost near enough to hit with a stone. The range re-
sembled the upper 8,000 or 9,000 feet of the Alps.

While the sun was shining, I was so busy watching
whales and steamers that I paid only incidental attention
to waterfowl. I could not fail to notice, however, that six or
eight whalebirds were knocked into the ocean by the last discharge of our cannon. After the smoke had cleared away,
these lay dead or struggling on the surface, snuffed out by
powder grains, fragments of the wadding, or perhaps just by
the blast of gas. But after the fog had enveloped us, I saw
more birds than one could believe existed on earth. There
were millions and millions of petrels and albatrosses, filling
the air like snowflakes, or afloat. The albatrosses were mostly
grouped in gams, in some instances with giant fulmars mingled peaceably among them. From six to twenty of the big
birds might be together in such companies, and now and then
the huddled albatrosses would suddenly become interested in
others around them and would begin to bill and bow, spread
their wings, bob their heads, and caress each other by nib-
bling. The reaction worked rhythmically, for the initial movements of one bird would spread rapidly through a group, and
within a few moments all of them would be spinning on the
water, each paying attention first to one neighbor and then to
another.

The wind died away with the coming of the fog, and the
wandering albatrosses became too lazy to run across the
water and launch into flight when *Fortuna* bore down upon

them. Several of the huge birds were actually bumped out of the way by the bow of our steamer, but the experience only made them whirl around and look indignant instead of trying to get into the air.

NOVEMBER 27. At half or quarter speed it took us all afternoon and a good part of the night to navigate through the impenetrable gray to the snug haven of Grytviken. On *Fortuna* we could at least eat well, which made a painful contrast with life on the *Daisy*. At half past six yesterday morning, coffee was served to everybody, followed shortly by a good breakfast. At noon we had barley soup with greens in it, a pot roast of beef and potatoes, and an abundance of loaf sugar and condensed milk for our coffee. Coffee was served again at 3:30 P.M. along with white, whole wheat, and rye bread, liverwurst, cold ham and beef, butter and maple syrup. For supper at nightfall we had our choice of boiled or fried penguin eggs, with fried potatoes, pickles and various other good things.

At eight o'clock last evening I went to sleep on the cabin lounge of *Fortuna* and I knew nothing more until we chugged past the anchorage of the *Daisy* at half past one this morning. Then I hallooed for the watch to come pick me up in the dory. So by two o'clock I had turned into my own berth, where I finished the night.

All my records up to date will be leaving here by registered mail on Thanksgiving Day. You must be careful not to repeat all I tell you about the luxury of Cumberland Bay because, after all, a voyage to the Antarctic is supposed to be a hardship rather than a garden party!

I have just been ashore, again looking over the flensing and processing of whale carcasses, while domestic pigeons flitted in the sunshine around the slips. Men carrying sharp curved knives, which have handles four or five feet long, make longitudinal slits in the whales, and the blubber is then peeled off from end to end by steel cables wound on the drums of winches. Nearly all the men are young, strapping fellows, strong and graceful. They wear suits of soft thin leather, and boots with spiked soles that enable them to walk all over a whale carcass. So far as appearances go, they put our non-descript crew of the *Daisy* to shame. Furthermore, they regard black men as rare curiosities, and many of them have told me that the Negroes on the *Daisy* are the first that they have ever seen. Those who have cameras bring them off to our brig in their free time in order to obtain photographs of live men with black skins. In spite of their curiosity, and in spite of the fact that these Norwegian boys are better born, better fed, better clothed and better treated, they appear to have no race prejudice. They greet and entertain our dark fellows ex-actly as Captain Larsen treats the Old Man and me. They even raise their hats to Cape Verders and West Indians, just as they do to one another. It interests me to see for the first time as a manly custom the gesture which we Americans re-serve for ladies.

Day before yesterday sixty whales were received at Grytviken slip. A pod of carcasses lay afloat, in addition to those lying side by side on the incline. Now they are all gone, except for two or three still in the works; the rest are already oil and fertilizer. Last year 51,000 fifty-gallon barrels of whale oil were made at this plant alone, and the prospects of the current season, which will end next March, are still better. Since six additional whaling stations are already operating in other fiords of South Georgia, you can imagine what the slaughter amounts to.

NOVEMBER 28. Thanksgiving Day would probably have gone unnoticed at sea, but where we are surrounded by Norwegians and other Europeans, including the British mag-istrate and his Guernseyman, the Old Man made a point of hoisting the flag and of ordering something that had to pass as

a Thanksgiving dinner. We even had roast turkey, except
that it was penguin instead of turkey, and it wasn't roasted.
Worse than that, it was not very palatable. Penguin flesh is to
be chosen only to save one from starvation. The single objection to the eggs relates to sightliness rather than to taste, because it is difficult to make the whites fully coagulate, with
the result that when boiled they still look slightly like a jellyfish. The *chef d'oeuvre* of the Thanksgiving meal was the
steward's plum duff, which was really a very fine puddin'. If
the Old Man had loosened up enough to pour some of his rum
over it, and to set it afire, the illusion of a Thanksgiving banquet would have been still better.

I made an advance draught on my Christmas box and
drew out a package of figs, which was shared with the skipper,
officers, boatsteerers, and cooper.

I don't know why Captain Cleveland is remaining here in
Cumberland Bay, now that he has completed his acrimonious
but inescapable agreements with the British magistrate. We
are apparently to lie at anchor in King Edward Cove for several days more, which will give me an opportunity to see the
local country and perhaps also to receive a first letter from
you—although I hardly dare breathe such a hope as the last.

When we leave here, it will be for a lonely destination in
the Bay of Isles, many a mile from the nearest whaling station. My subsequent letters are thus likely to be rather infre-
quent, but if you do not hear for what seems like a long while,
just assume that the *Daisy*'s whaleboats have not fallen in
with one of the Norwegian or British hunting steamers which
could carry my letter from the Bay of Isles to King Edward
Cove, and thence pass it to the outside world by way of
Buenos Aires. It is at least a cause for rejoicing that I am able
to communicate at all, because no such anticipation figured in
our plans. Another bit of pure velvet is that I shall always be
within one or two days' voyage of a competent German physi-

cian and surgeon. This is something upon which we did not count during my stay in the empty Antarctic. Another matter for thankfulness is that the British magistrate has promised to make every effort to send to the Bay of Isles any letter that comes from you, or in fact anything addressed to the *Daisy*. One or more whaling steamers and crews are soon to be assigned to sea elephant hunting around the beaches of South Georgia, and it is taken as a matter of course that seamen in this part of the world are willing to change their plans, and even to go to considerable inconvenience, for the purpose of delivering letters to their lonely confreres.

Some of our forecastle and steerage boys, who have been wandering in the hills and getting their feet in snow for the first time in their lives, have brought back an extraordinary story of South Georgian wild goats. I knew that there are no native land mammals in the far south, and I knew also that neither goats nor sheep can survive in the South Georgian climate, but the tale brought back by our sailors was too circumstantial to be doubted. They had seen the animals only at long range, but they said that they were much bigger, and had immensely longer horns, than the goats of the Cape Verde Islands.

The mystery has now been cleared up by my friends at the whaling station. The animals are reindeer. A small herd was brought from Lapland two years ago and turned loose on the tundra of the hills. The reindeer have waxed fat, bred, borne fawns, and are now rapidly increasing. They have the richest imaginable pasture and no wolves or other predators to worry about. If the herd ever grows too large for the borders of this great fiord, some of them will be corralled and transported to other green bays along the coast. They have many square miles in their Cumberland Bay range, but it is believed that they could never surmount the icy stockade of mountains so as to get into fields beyond. Their only means of spreading naturally would be by a swim around great headlands to a new landing place.

NOVEMBER 30. All my records to date have gone to you by registered mail yesterday. It was a wistful sight to see the steamer pull out, carrying the hearts and longings of so many exiles.

The handwriting in my little books is dreadful, mostly because of the circumstances under which I set it down—a rolling ship, a roaring, rainy out-of-doors, a dim and smelly cabin. Take it in easy stages. Anything you can't understand, guess at for the moment, and trust me to enlarge upon it at some future time when I shall talk from nightfall until the sun rises.

I have begun exploring and collecting in the country around Cumberland Bay. Also I have created a sensation by carrying Indian snowshoes into the hills and using them for crossing the valleys filled with unplumbed snow. Nobody here has ever before seen such contraptions, although every man has his skis.

Today the cooper and I walked through what is called the Bore Valley to a stone cairn at the divide, and thence down the bed of a long-vanished glacier to May Cove in West Fiord. The pass is at an altitude of a thousand feet, and this is the route taken by the terns and skuas when they fly between Grytviken and the picturesque grassy lakes that lie behind the beach of West Fiord. It is odd to find sea birds among the snow-covered inland hills at altitudes up to 1,800 feet.

The lakes at West Fiord are fed by clear, cold torrents that tumble from all directions down the rocks and flow through meadows of green and spongy moss. There are five lakes, no two of which lie at the same level. They are surrounded by drumlins overgrown with rich tussock grass. Toward the rim of the bay, the land rises again, ending in bluffs against which ice-filled waves dash. Offshore in May

Cove are masses of rock as large as cathedrals, which have fall-
en on their sides from the coastal hills so that their strata,
marked by streaks of white quartz, are now perpendicular. All
about their bases the green sea ice sparkles like a field of dia-
monds, and among the fragments, as well as in the air above,
are countless thousands of speckled Cape pigeons and of the
larger black petrels which the Norwegians call shoemakers
"because they sit at the door of their shops and sing."
(Cobblers may have this habit in Norway, but in New York I
have never observed it except on the stage of the Metropolitan Opera House.) At any rate, the shoemakers here have
their shops everywhere in the thick, black humus under the
tussock grass. In some areas I have found a burrow beneath
practically every hummock, and from underground I can hear
the trilling of the owners.

All of this setting seems at first sight like primeval happi-
ness, but, alas, there is a canker in the Garden of Eden.
Everywhere I have found the holes of the brown, or so-called
Norway, rat, a scourge introduced at South Georgia from the
ships of the early Yankee sealers a century ago. Wherever I
have rooted up the earth and vegetation over the subterranean runways of the rats, I have found vast graveyards of
the clean-picked bones of terns and petrels, many thousands
of bones in some of the single heaps.

A German, named Klutschak, who visited South Georgia
in 1877, transcribed and published an American sealer's chart
of the island. On this a bay near the western end is called Rat
Harbor. About 1872, rabbits were introduced by a sealer coming from Tristan da Cunha. They never gained a foothold, because if the snow didn't kill them, the rats ate them.

In 1906, the Swedish zoologist, Dr. Einar Lönnberg,
whose publication I have with me, described the rat of South
Georgia as a newly evolved subspecies, alleging that in the
course of the century since the introduction of the rodents

they had acquired a thicker skin, denser and longer fur, and a more rusty color. The describer is a bold zoologist, though the future may prove him to be correct!

I have fully reacquired my land legs, and am as tough as John L. Sullivan. On the walk back from May Cove, the cooper and I were laden down like coolies. I had on my back bird specimens weighing forty pounds, besides an eight-pound photographic outfit and a shotgun. We took it all in our stride, resting briefly during the higher part of the climb, and arrived at Grytviken unblown.

DECEMBER 1. The Old Man evidently intends to lie here until the steamer *Harpon* arrives from Buenos Aires with mail and news of the world. He has little to do, because there are extremely few sea elephants in Cumberland Bay. He has been replenishing his supply of ship's clothing from the slop chest of Captain Larsen's station, and I also have expended $5 on an exceedingly well-tailored dogskin jacket, lined throughout with red flannel.

Captain Cleveland has made a discovery which surprises him greatly—because nobody in New Bedford has learned it between 1755 and the present date. It is merely that oilskins can be prevented from sticking together by sifting a little ordinary wheat flour over them as they are stowed in layers. After our passage through the tropics, the *Daisy*'s oilskins come out of the casks in a solid block, and the garments have to be pulled one from another by the strength of wild horses. The Norwegian supply at Grytviken is dusty with flour, but each coat, pantaloon, or sou'wester comes off the top stratum loose and dry.

The Old Man has issued two or three shotguns and a few shells to his shore parties, and the whaleboats have been coming back with ducks and other birds, in addition to a great supply of fresh penguin eggs and a small quantity of sea elephant meat and blubber. Boiled tongues of the sea elephants are excellent; the rest of the flesh belongs in the category with that of penguins. It grieves me to see the ducks killed because the little native teal, a relative of the South American pintail, is found nowhere in the world except at South Georgia. I doubt, too, whether it is legal to shoot the teal for food, because Mr. Wilson, the magistrate, has given me a special permit to collect birds for scientific specimens, the only excluded species being the upland goose. All mariners are entitled to gather penguin eggs for food, and also to eat the penguins themselves—if they can stand it!

The upland goose is not a native bird, but is a species of the Falkland Islands, introduced here in 1910 by the British magistrate. It had become persona non grata at the Falklands, because nature designed it to graze upon grass, and hence it was considered a rival by the sheep ranchers. So the muttonheads outlawed the fine bird, placing a bounty on its life. There are now six or eight pairs of adults in West Fiord, Cumberland Bay. It is hoped that the geese may become thoroughly established here in a land from which sheep will never oust them.

Aside from penguin eggs, the best native provender we have found at South Georgia is fish that our men catch on hooks in the kelp beds, and fresh whale meat from Captain Larsen's station. The fish are rather weird in appearance, being dragon-headed creatures belonging to a family distributed all around the world in the far south, but their flesh resembles fresh cod and is a welcome addition to our fare. Humpback whale meat is surprisingly palatable and much superior to sperm whale. The skipper has also instructed the steward in the preparation of a supply of *muctuc*. This is a delicacy that originated with the whalemen of Bering Strait, and the word is presumably Eskimo or Aleut. It is a pickle, and, according to Captain Cleveland, would be prized by the gods on Mount Olympus. This is the way it is made:

Obtain a chunk of blubber from a freshly killed whale. Slice it neatly crisscross, from the outer side, using a sharp knife. You should then have black squares measuring an inch on a side. The blackskin of the whale is about a half inch thick, and under this the firm, white blubber begins. So you cut through a half inch of this blubber, producing several quarts of one-inch cubes, each of which is half ebony and half ivory. They look like big, bicolored dice without the dots.

Next you boil your cubes in a large pot of sea water, until a fork will slip easily into the black or the white halves. They are then sufficiently tender, but are still firm enough to keep their cubic shape. The cubes are drained and packed into Mason jars, which are filled with vinegar and capped. They look very pretty, but the Old Man says they will not be ready to eat for a month. Nevertheless, he is already licking his chops. In one of our subsequent numbers, I shall duly report upon the gastronomic delectability of blubber-rubber *muctuc*.

DECEMBER 2.   We are still waiting for the mail steamer. I am wild to get away toward the lonely end of this island, and yet I also dread the thought of departing, even though it is hardly possible that the *Harpon* will bring a letter from you. If I had only known at the Cape Verde Islands, or at Fernando Noronha, that there is a post office at South Georgia, we might never have been more than six weeks out of touch.

My days are busy enough through long hours. At the Bay of Isles, however, there will be no one to interrupt my work, while here a certain amount of visiting is a polite necessity. This afternoon I had coffee with Eric Nordenhaag, the Swede, who is the representative at South Georgia of the Argentine Meteorological Service. Later I dined with the British magistrate, Mr. Wilson, who put on a dinner jacket in honor of the birthday of some member of the royal family, and who also opened a bottle of port. Afterwards we sat before his com-

fortable fire and chatted. He is a jolly Scot when separated
from the company of Captain Cleveland, and in the course of
the evening he produced an excellent bottle of his native dew
or nectar, so that before I knew it, it was one o'clock in the
morning of the next day. That makes it an unseemly hour in
the cabin of the *Daisy* for a naturalist who is planning an
early trip to the Nordenskjöld Glacier on the same
morning.

DECEMBER 3 (NIGHT).   I have been off all day long on a
two-whaleboat trip with Mr. da Lomba and the second mate.
The Nordenskjöld Glacier is the largest in Cumberland
Bay, and a glorious sight it was when we approached the wall
of its front and watched the spray dancing from the foot of the
ice. The séracs on top gleamed like rock crystal. South Georgia is a gorgeous place in the sunshine, though grim in stormy
weather.

The men killed a huge sea elephant, and while they were
working on it, I climbed the hills along the edge of the glacier,
collected several nestling giant fulmars and other birds, and
put numbered aluminum bands on the legs of many others. I
also made thirty-six photographs of birds and landscapes.

We reached the brig just before dark with a load of elephant blubber in the bottom of our whaleboat and approximately a bushel of eggs, all freshly laid, we hope. The Old
Man had some hot ginger tea ready for me. He and the cooper
kindly had built a rack containing several shelves, on which
my bird skins may lie while drying. Under the influence of the
luxurious life at the Grytviken plant, the Old Man seems to
have grown positively maternal. I am healthily tired and
about to turn in.

DECEMBER 4.   The *Fortuna* puffed into port at noon
towing nine dead whales. Except for her superstructure, she
was practically concealed by the bloated carcasses. The blubber of a whale gives such complete insulation that the bodies

do not quickly become cold, even in this icy ocean. Consequently the gases of decomposition rapidly develop and more than compensate for leakage of the air that is pumped into the animal immediately after it has been killed. The usual result is that the dead whales look more or less like inflated bladders by the time the chasers bring them into port. A steamer preceding the *Fortuna* brought in six whales this morning, and the water off the flensing slip is now covered with a huge raft of carcasses.

Today I helped Nordenhaag, the meteorologist, to skin a king penguin which he wishes to send home to Sweden. I also gave him a mug of my best Formosa tea, served with biscuits and candied ginger. He liked it, although his usual afternoon drink is coffee, which he brews in the watertight hut and meteorological observatory where he lives alone with his dog. Nordenhaag has given me some very enlightening tables of meteorological data obtained at his little observatory since 1907. These show that South Georgia does, indeed, lie in a stormy area of low barometric pressure. It is interesting and curious, however, that the lowest readings of the barometer are never attended by violent storms. The annual mean here is 745 mm., as against 763 mm. in New York City. Great changes of pressure within a few hours are common, resembling conditions at Iceland in the northern oceans.

The mean annual temperature for the past three years has been 34.4° F.—not very far above the freezing point. This, of course, refers to sea level; in parts of the mountains only the full rays of the sun can produce thawing at any season. February, the warmest month, has a mean temperature of 41° F.; June and July, the coldest months, a mean of about 28° F. The limitations imposed upon the island by its purely oceanic climate are illustrated by the records of absolute maxima and minima of air temperature, which are 69.3° F. (in February), and 10° F. (in July). Thus, while it never becomes warm at South Georgia, neither does the mercury fall as low as it frequently does in New York City.

The gray canopy is indicated by the average annual amount of cloudiness, which is seven in a scale of ten! It is most cloudy in summer (December and January) and clearest in late winter (August and September). Precipitation is not much heavier (in millimeters of water) than that in New York, but here snow mingles with rain all through the year. And, as for the winds, you already have a good idea of what they are like.

Nordenhaag informed me that the *Fortuna* had not brought in her whole day's catch today. She had killed also a tenth whale, but being unable to find room to make it fast, had left it waifed and afloat to be picked up by one of the company's other steamers! These humpbacks are now worth about $500 apiece. A $5,000 catch is not bad work for one chaser in one day! Two other steamers have now brought in eight additional whales, and it is anticipated that others will arrive during the night.

The gossip at Grytviken is that Captain Larsen's company has paid annual dividends to the stockholders of from 40 to 130 per cent ever since the station was founded. I don't know what the machinery cost, but it is said that it was transported and erected here in King Edward Cove for only $10,000. Twenty-five thousand dollars bought the first chaser with which the company started, and at the end of the six months' summer season the first shipment of oil was sent to market. The first year's dividends were regarded as low, being only about 40 per cent on the invested capital, but at the end of the second year, the stockholders received a dividend of 100 per cent.

DECEMBER 5. Last night the weather was clear, cold and crackly, and on this brilliant sunny morning I find King Edward Cove partly frozen over. It would be almost safe to walk ashore from the edge of the thin ice within a length of where the *Daisy* swings at anchor.

In the next outgoing mail, which will leave South Georgia shortly after the arrival of the *Harpon*, I am sending you prints of a few very choice South Georgian photographs, kindly supplied by Mr. Wilson, the magistrate. I have equally good negatives of my own, but no prints. Those from Mr. Wilson will give you a fair idea of the country, and I have written brief descriptions on the back.

DECEMBER 6. I hope that you are properly puzzled about the source of the flowers that should have been delivered to you early on this glorious, if secret, anniversary.

Here at South Georgia we have had a tragedy in a fatal accident to Captain Beckman, who had the reputation of being the best whaling gunner in the world. He was a pioneer here with Captain Larsen, and was idolized by the members of his crew. This afternoon, while returning from a trip in the mountains, I was alarmed by seeing the *Daisy*, on the cove far below, with the Stars and Stripes flying at half-mast. Hurrying down to the station, I learned that the recoil of the whaling gun on the *Don Ernesto*, the newest of the hunting steamers, had broken its mountings, instantly killing Beckman. He was only twenty-seven years old and leaves a wife and four children. His body is being prepared for shipment back to Norway, instead of being interred in the lonely little graveyard of Cumberland Bay.

DECEMBER 7. Still waiting for the mail steamer. I am now regarded as a regular member of Captain Larsen's family, which comprises Dr. Lampert, Secretary Willberg, the British Magistrate, the Swedish meteorologist, and half a dozen other good fellows who come in at least casually for afternoon coffee. I have had the group for tea on the *Daisy*, and after my callers saw that I had nothing but West Indian yellow sugar crystals to serve, they sent me a two-kilogram box of beautiful loaf sugar from the whaling station. Against the possibility of future famine, I have bought and secreted a case of excellent Norwegian condensed milk. They seem to be willing to let us have whatever we wish to purchase from the storeroom, remarking that the company makes a profit on everything sold.

Today Captain Cleveland and I paid a call on the Captain of the whaling factory ship *Nor*, which is cooking carcasses for fertilizer in the harbor, thus supplementing the work of the overloaded shore factory. This skipper was a rough-and-ready Norwegian, whose manner gave no indication of any particular esthetic sensitiveness. Yet when we entered his commodious cabin, we found that it was a conservatory of potted and blossoming plants. The whole upper half was covered with racks, from some of which vines had extended to the skylight. A flowery taste seems to be characteristic of Norsemen, for Nordenhaag's hut is full of roses, separated only by window panes from the blizzards that howl outside.

DECEMBER 9.   It was snowing very heavily this morning so that along the Bore Valley, on another trip to May Cove, Correia and I could see not a hundred yards in any direction. About half past nine o'clock, however, a soft mist began to roll up the rocks out of the gulches. Then the snow turned to rain and presently ceased, and dazzling sun burst through the clouds. Within a few moments many small flies and other insects could be seen flitting about the snow-sprinkled tussock grass.

In the May Cove I found a natural arch through fifty feet of rock. The brook flows under it to enter the bay, and here we came upon a dozen sea elephants, mostly cows and large pups, which were heaped one upon another like a mound of sausages. It was my first opportunity to see the brutes at a time when my bloodthirsty shipmates were not standing around with lances, aiming to murder them. I found also beautiful growths of small ferns growing in the rocky ledges of the coastal hills. Before we had returned to Grytviken, the snow had almost entirely melted, and the remainder of the day was mild and clear.

DECEMBER 10. Hurrah!, and praise be to God! Your letter has reached me. An original and a carbon arrived together, one from Christiania and one from Buenos Aires, and I have read them both, again and again. First word since Dominica, 132 days ago! All's well, all's well, but I don't know whether my head points up or down. It doesn't matter. Now I'm truly homeward bound. Now I can set out with joy incarnate toward the Bay of Isles, secure in the knowledge that you have found me, and with a confident hope that I may receive another letter, in reply to my messages from Porto Grande and Fernando Noronha, or even to my first report from South Georgia.

The letter I now clutch tightly in my hands was written between August 17 and September 11, and is postmarked Providence, September 12. That is not yet two months ago! It is also within a few days of the date on which I sent you my log from the Cape Verdes.

The circumstances of my blessed fortune were dramatic enough. I was up in the mountains skiing with the doctor and the secretary. We were alternately toiling up and flying down a valley filled with the snow of uncounted years. Needless to say, I kept off the terrifying declivities chosen by my companions, but even at that I went quite fast enough to suit me, and I more or less shifted between sliding on my borrowed skis and my nose, which is now skinned from forehead to tip. Fortunately, the snow was probably two hundred feet deep and still soft on top, so that my tumbles were comparatively painless. At some earlier date the whalemen had built a mound on the steep slope, and over this Willberg made

several jumps that carried him sixty feet or more through the
air. He insists, nonetheless, that he is not a very expert skier,
coming only "from the south of Norway"!

Suddenly a distant whistle came to us through the still
mountain air. Willberg and the doctor

> Look'd at each other in a wild surmise—

but they were not silent on their peak. *"Harpon!"* they yelled
with one voice, as they immediately began to make tracks for
home, soon leaving me far behind.

Everything was excitement among the South Georgian
populace. All work apparently stopped, and while scores of
men pored over letters from their loved ones ten thousand
miles away, others were ripping open newspapers and chattering about an attempt on the life of Theodore Roosevelt,
the election of Woodrow Wilson, a war that Greece and other
Balkan States are waging against Turkey, and about precarious conditions in the Old World generally. With British,
Russians, Germans, and other Europeans amid the larger
group of Scandinavians here, the stage was all set for stirring
discussions.

The Old Man had come ashore and, as soon as I saw him,
I whooped to him to join me in a cheer for President Wilson.
He called me the second-worst name he knows—Democrat—
and assured me that I was a highly undesirable citizen. He
had had Old Glory all ready to hoist in honor of "President"
Roosevelt, but he was enough of a good sport to fly it for Wilson, even though he loudly protested that he had never hoped
to live until a day on which he would celebrate for a Demo-
cratic Chief Magistrate over New England and the lesser
parts of our great republic.

The *Harpon* brought sixteen bags of mail, numbering
several thousands of letters, so South Georgia is now only
about a month behind the rest of Mother Earth. I had tried

earnestly to suppress the hope that I might hear from you. Even before Mr. Wilson had stopped to read his own wife's letters from Scotland, he sent word that there was at least one for me at headquarters, and that others might turn up during the sorting. The message reached me after I had gone aboard the *Daisy*. I clambered down into the dory, cheered on my oarsman, jumped ashore among the stinking whale skeletons, and ran all the way to the magistrate's home. He had two letters, and an armchair by the stove, all ready for me. I know now that everything is well, and I believe that my chance of receiving your letter written after Election Day is excellent. All's right with the world!

DECEMBER 11.   Johnny, the egregious cabin boy, came aboard in high glee last evening, bringing in his pockets five very young goslings of the upland goose, which he had captured at the West Fiord lakes. For once, I had to dash his hopes and explain the taboo. So this morning I carried them home again, searching until I saw several pairs of adult geese on the far side of the water. One of the goslings peeped, and immediately a throaty clucking came in answer. A barred goose then began to swim straight toward us, followed at a discreet distance by the milk-white gander. I put the young brood in the lake, but each gosling attempted to scramble back to me until it heard the call of the approaching mother. Then all five turned their tails and swam bravely forth. The parents gathered up the restored family, and the flotilla disappeared around a point of land with the youngsters well guarded, side by side between the goose and her pompous mate.

We are now heaving up our anchors in the rain, and the old *Daisy* is shaking like a decrepit trolley car while her hooks stick firmly in the muck on the bottom of King Edward Cove. It will probably take us most of the day to get under way. Parties are over now. I am going ashore to mail the last let-

ters from the Old Man and me, and to accept Mr. Wilson's
invitation for a "wee sma' nip of the auld kirk."

I am reasonably well satisfied with my stay here because
I have a fairly representative herbarium of South Georgian
vegetation, a collection of invertebrates and fishes, various
rock samples, some seal skulls and whale embryos, and more
than a hundred bird skins.

DECEMBER 12. Well, here we are! Where? Still at anchor in Cumberland Bay.

With much song and toil yesterday, we had our cables
shortened and one anchor atrip, only to have to let everything
go again when the williwaw suddenly raked down from the
mountains with such terrific force that the *Daisy* heeled over
under bare spars, and the air was filled with sleet and water
smoke on which a rainbow formed. Spray was carried up to
the ridge of the hills on the lee side of King Edward Cove.
Never before have I felt winds so strong as during some of the
puffs. The mountain valleys appeared to be filled with flying
snow, although we received very little of it at sea level. All the
whale-chasers were driven into the bay for shelter, and one
of them came perilously close to being cast on the rocks. In
the outer bay, the water was scooped up from the surface in
sheets that scudded off for miles to leeward.

The storm continued all night and has slackened only
slightly today. Nobody has been able to leave the brig because
a whaleboat would probably be bowled over by the gale. Trying to possess my soul in patience, I have been also trying to
read polyglot newspapers in the cabin. Fortunately, Captain
Larsen made a particularly thoughtful effort to supply me
with a long run of an English sheet published in Buenos Aires.

From this press assortment I learn that it is not safe for
me thus to turn my back on the world, because many things
then go agley! A bumper crop of train wrecks in the United
States, I note. Hetty Green reveals that the way to live long is

to chew onions. Is it worth it? Jack Johnson has been "read out of the Negro race," which is a neat solution. Andrew Carnegie says that New York taxes are confiscatory, alas! Since last New Year, 106 children have been killed in roller skating accidents in New York City alone, 60 per cent of all juvenile accidental fatalities. The Hamburg-American Line threatens to quit the port of New York. The Japanese are putting the screws on the unhappy Koreans. Motor trucks are going to supplant the army mule, and the Red Sox have beaten the Giants for the world's championship. You see now that I know all the bad news.

On the brighter side, I learn that Jacques Loeb has grown a "fatherless frog," Grand Central Station is finished, and ships will pass through the Panama Canal next year. A Zeppelin has flown over the Baltic Sea to Sweden. An aeroplane has carried mail across Long Island Sound, and Glenn Curtis predicts ultimate speeds of close to 200 miles an hour. Herschel Parker has attained the summit of Mount McKinley. The ladies are sure to win suffrage soon. The opera season in New York opened "brilliantly," with Caruso and Bori in Manon Lescaut. And Harvard beat Yale 20-0 for the first victory in eleven years. Not that I care, but it was high time. Moreover, Mayor Gaynor warmly congratulated the New York police on their capture of Gyp the Blood.

And William Sulzer, this new Governor of New York— should that go in the mournful or the cheerful column?

But the spontaneous Balkan conflagration seems to be nothing to take lightly. It is exasperating not to know the end of it, which may by now have come. One paper tells that the Turks started the fighting without a declaration of war. Subsequent scattered and confusing accounts refer to Greeks, Serbs, and Montenegrins piling upon them, driving them nearly out of Europe, and of the feats of an inspired Bulgar army that only cholera—not cannons—could stop.

Then I found an ominous headline about the mailed
hand of the Triple Alliance rising between the Balkan states
and their fruits of victory. In the paper of latest date, Ambassador von Bernstorff observes that the conflict can still be
"localized," while some other German spokesman forecasts a
general European war.

Two years ago, President David Starr Jordan, of Stan-
ford University, had me nearly convinced that there could
never be another war. Perhaps he meant only wars between
the great and enlightened powers, rather than explosions
among Ottomans and neighbors no longer willing to be
vassals. I still try to believe that Dr. Jordan was right, and
that international business has now done to war what
Cervantes long ago did to the cult of Chivalry.

6 Ambassador
to the Penguins

DECEMBER 13.   We glided out of Cumberland Bay at ten o'clock this morning, towed by one of the whale-chasers. Old Glory, the Union Jack, and the Blue Cross of Norway dipped thrice in gracious farewell. Whistles blew, hats and handkerchiefs waved, and the crew of the *Daisy* gave three long cheers as we rounded Sappho Point and left King Edward Cove astern. From the clouded snow water near shore we passed to the blue outer bay, where we hoisted sail and were cast off by our tug.

In parts of the fiord, grand tabular icebergs had been massed by the recent storm. Mushrooms of spray and vapor, springing from their crevices, slowly fell back onto the battling ice and sea. At first the mountains were clear and sunny, but now fog has once more veiled the land. After so long a rest on an even keel, I hardly know how to walk upon the gently swaying deck.

About noon it fell calm and we had to lower three of our whaleboats with full crews in order to tow the *Daisy* slowly ahead and avoid the risk of drifting toward a lee shore. It was a struggle to get around the long point into the open sea, when for minutes at a time we seemed scarcely to move at all, but at last we gained the weather gage of the headland. We are now free and the sails are bellying, although the wind is still barely perceptible.

One of our forecastle Portuguese fell overboard on our way out—nobody knows just how. Fortunately the forward speed of the *Daisy* was so slight that we were able to toss him lines from the quarterdeck and haul him aboard again. There were chunks of ice in the water all about, so that his chances of survival would have been slim if the brig's headway had gained several lengths on him. Another sailor had a fit on deck, falling down, losing consciousness, and jerking his limbs violently. It is probably not epilepsy, because he has had no previous attack of the kind during half a year's service on the *Daisy*. The conditions on board and the poor health of many of the men, due to their own fault and to plenty of other causes, lead me to fear that we shall not carry all of these boys back with us to the West Indies.

Evening. A thick, wet, calm, nasty, aggravating fog is closing about us. It is snowing thinly, the feathery flakes falling straight down, and our sails are flapping from the gentle roll and pitch of the brig. I am turning in early to amend the bad nocturnal habits acquired in the metropolitan anchorage of Grytviken.

December 14. During the quiet but impenetrable night, we had to lower whaleboats again into black water filled with growlers, in order to tow the brig. Finally a breeze came up, and we stood eagerly offshore. This morning is fresh and sunny, with a head wind from approximately southwest. The coast lies forty miles to windward, and we are starting to beat back toward it.

I have just stood a two-hour trick at the wheel. There

was a jolly, shifting wind, with casual flurries of snow. I steered by the wind well up toward the coast, and brought the brig about on the offshore tack just before I was relieved. *Daisy* is a good weatherly ship.

DECEMBER 15. Brisk southerly and southwesterly winds have held since yesterday, and again I have had the wheel for two hours, bringing the *Daisy* close in toward the entrance of Prince Olaf Harbor. This now lies astern, and we are beating down into the extensive Bay of Isles.

A more desolate coast than that which lies off the port beam would be hard to describe. Instead of being green and sheltered, like so much of the country around Cumberland Bay, it is bleak and frozen, and marked by snowfields that stretch from the edge of the sea to the crest of mountains four thousand feet above. It looks to me as though I shall require my Indian snowshoes for inland travel in this part of South Georgia. I can't yet make out any gorges or valleys on the coast, but I hope that we shall find a few green spots. It seems to be much colder here than in the fiord from which we have come, but the feeling may perhaps be more psychological than thermal. The ocean and the bay are dotted all about us with icebergs, some of which are old and worn into fantastic shapes because they have overturned several times. One particularly pleasant thought is that in this part of South Georgia I have virgin territory. There is not yet even a map of the Bay of Isles, so the first sketch, and the naming of its promontories, glaciers, and islands, will fall to me.

About two o'clock in the afternoon we dropped anchor in thirteen fathoms not far from shore and under the shelter of the high walls and encircling kelp fields of two small islands. The kelp, which sends forth long, brown, rubbery strands from the bottom to lie afloat for many fathoms at the surface, acts as an efficient natural breakwater by disrupting waves with whitecaps and flattening the great swells. Our sail

toward the anchorage was exciting, because the passage
through the outer islets gave little sea room. The Old Man
had been here before and knew his course, but to me it
seemed as though we barely cleared certain points of rock,
besides ploughing through the edges of kelp fields and nearly
scraping with our yardarms tall columns that were covered
with orange lichens.

The snowy appearance of the mainland is at least partly
tempered by the emerald green of the larger islands. Their
tops seem to be a lush pasture of tussock grass, broken only
where rocky outcrops rise above the soil. Wandering albatrosses stand all over the greenery of these islands, looking in
the distance like scattered flocks of sheep. The nearest beach
of the bay shore, which is now in plain view from deck, seems
to be covered with penguins and giant fulmars. Little heaps of
sea elephants are lying here and there. The weather is cold
and gray, and the shoreward landscape is depressingly dull.
Only the séracs of three glaciers, and the high snowfields,
which might be called an invisible scene because of the way
in which they blend with the sky, gather and reflect a certain brilliance.

Evening. I have been off in a whaleboat to the largest island in the Bay of Isles and have seen wonderful sights in
spite of the fact that it snowed heavily all afternoon. At the
landing place, walking on the sand and the stranded kelp, I
found my first South Georgian pipits, a species which I believe to be the southernmost land bird in the world. Incidentally, it is the only songbird found at South Georgia. I also
strolled among innumerable nests of the wandering albatross,
and for the first time met the great birds face to face on their
own territory. We found that the grass-covered island
abounds in sheltered hollows, many of which contain exquisite fresh ponds. The men lanced several sea elephants and
brought back the blubber. After our long labor in the open air,

two or three hours of it in snowfall, a hot supper tasted particularly good at eight bells.

DECEMBER 16. Today has been very filled with exciting experience, but my summary of it will be brief. I have been out in several directions from our anchorage, both in the whaleboats and alone in my dory. By the best of good fortune, there proves to be, close to our anchorage, a tiny rock-rimmed cove which makes a perfect landing place because it is quiet even when the surf is leaping high on the coasts outside. I can row the dory into this, skimming over the kelp that helps protect its narrow entrance, and step ashore with no trouble whatsoever. The kelp is at least thirty fathoms long, and a tiny channel between the ledges of the cove mouth permits me to ride through on the swell.

This afternoon the Old Man lent me three sailors to lay a foundation for my tent in a mossy gulch on the headland just west of the landing cove. The site offers considerable protection from the raging winds, and the outlook faces the front of a wonderful glacier that enters the bay about half a mile across the water. I am naming this Grace Glacier (paradoxically) on the map that I have started.

We carried up shingle from the beach at the foot of the hill, and built a wall along the downward edge of the slope. Then by making a fill with more stones, and with turf pulled up from the grassy hummocks round about, we completed a level platform and set up the tent, well braced. Thereafter we brought a table, a chair, and an oil stove ashore from the *Daisy*, which provide me with the essentials of a workshop on terra firma. Within a stone's throw of my front door is a pod of sea elephants, mostly wallowing in the water of a glacial stream. I very much regret that these creatures are not likely to be there long, because the gang will probably soon shed their blood and leave them as hideous stripped carcasses to undergo slow rotting in the cold.

No farther away in the other direction, or uphill behind my tent, is a small colony of wandering albatrosses and giant fulmars, which are nesting in the grass of this mainland promontory instead of on the islets. This is a reflection of the fact that there are no native predatory mammals in the far south, nothing to take the place of the wolves and foxes that range in arctic wildernesses. Among the birds incubating eggs so near at hand is a white giant fulmar, the first I have seen at close range. Penguins waddle past on the beach below and stop to peer at me when I walk between my tent and the landing cove. On the neighboring rocks we also saw today our first sheathbills, known to the whalemen as paddies, or sore-eyed pigeons. They are really very curious shore birds, distantly related to such things as oyster-catchers, but as they trot along the rocky ledges they look as much like white pigeons as anything else.

On the small island closest to the brig is a colony of the blue-eyed shags, or cormorants, which have gleaming white throats and breasts, iridescent blue backs, and large orange warts at the base of the bill. They fly continually past *Daisy* at her anchorage. A pair of them alighted this noon on our foreyard, from which both birds watched the activity on board with evident curiosity but no trace of fear.

DECEMBER 17.   This morning I finished equipping the tent, taking a lot of necessary gear ashore. I then joined three boats' crews on the prowl along the beaches in search of sea elephants. Eighteen were slain, skinned, and stripped. It is a most harrowing experience, particularly because such a large proportion of each huge animal becomes sheer waste. The skin, which might make a single piece of leather large enough to line the tonneau of a motor car, is flayed off the blubber in small quadrangles and wasted. Then, after the beast has been deprived of blubber, the huge red carcass, with its meat and bone, is likewise wasted. The ghastly wastage of former years still lies on the sand and among the tussock hummocks. The birds, such as skuas and giant fulmars, may obtain a brief banquet from an occasional freshly killed carcass, but after the remains have frozen or have dried for a day or two, they no longer serve any active purpose in the economy of nature, and it may be years or decades before such sorrowful remains can disappear.

Later in the day we went again to Albatross Island, as I have named it, where I collected five teal, which the Old Man calls widgeons, and five pipits. Shooting the latter was particularly brutal because I had to run away from them to obtain enough distance so as not to blow them to atoms, even with the small auxiliary shell in my shotgun. However, the pipits are very abundant here, and there is not yet a single example of the species in the collections of the American Museum of Natural History, or, so far as I know, of any other museum in the United States. Nobody yet knows the relationship of this pipit to the species of South America, from where its ancestors were presumably blown by the wild west wind. So a few of them, willy-nilly, must become martyrs to science.

I had my trusty Graflex, and took considerably more pleasure in photographing albatrosses and giant fulmars on their nests than I did in drawing a bead on unsuspecting pipits. I would have had a field day for pictures but for the fact that a blizzard came shrieking up without warning, and it was a stiff struggle back to the brig across a couple of miles of choppy water. I pulled stroke oar both ways. I can feel my thews strengthening day by day, and when I return you will perhaps mistake me for Sandow.

DECEMBER 18. A day of countless snow flurries and boisterous southerly winds. My negatives, developed last night, came out well, and they fire me to make further pictures of the life history of sea birds and other creatures. I worked in my little tent, which rattled and flapped in the breeze but stood firm. It was easy to learn more about the habits of sea elephants without stirring from my table, because many were the fights between bulls in my front yard down below, and all waged over a single diminutive brown cow, apparently the only female that has yet hauled out on this beach.

DECEMBER 19.   Strong easterly gales all day, with much snow in the morning. The freak shifts of wind emphasize that "westerlies" signify little more than an average direction. By and large, the winds at South Georgia, and elsewhere in the west wind zone, do come from a westerly quarter, but they are also likely to blow all around the compass within a period of two or three hours.

As I was rowing back toward the *Daisy* about seven o'clock this evening, through combers with white crests, a sea leopard came to the surface close by my dory and just off the cormorant rock. This is a ferocious seal that feeds chiefly on penguins. I hope before long to make a closer acquaintance with it.

I find it disconcerting to have the sun continue shining long after eight o'clock in the evening. Sunshine makes it difficult to think of going to bed, even when one's work is done.

DECEMBER 20.   No sun today; only a leaden sky.

All morning I worked in my tent, making study skins of several teal, two sheathbills, and other birds. Then Captain Cleveland walked in and told me it was after three o'clock. I had not looked at my watch, and had no idea that noon had arrived.

For the most part, I plan now not to row out to the brig for midday dinner. I take ashore albatross-egg sandwiches, cook a duck breast on my little stove, and make tea. Your tea ball is one of my most useful possessions. My larder chest in the tent also holds loaf sugar, condensed milk, pilot bread, and maple syrup, so you see I shall be faring well for at least a while. I like best to work alone, for then I can philosophize and sing while the job hustles along. Across the cove is the Grace Glacier, where the blue ice rises sheer more than two score feet. (It resembles you in its shining countenance rather than in its temperature!) Every hour, or even more often, bergs break off its front and crash into the sea with the sound of a presidential salute. Then the waves spread out and for a few minutes a lively surf dashes on the shore below.

This recurrent event moves me to yell my head off in song. No particular words, but just a noise to fling back at the glacier and let it know that I'm on this side of the cove. Here is a glacial melody that has grown out of my larynx, lungs, and midriff. You have my hearty permission to play it on your violin, or even to transcribe it and build up a symphony, if you wish!

Sometimes my inclinations run toward the grisly, which fits certain moods of the South Georgian weather. For example, it gives me special glee to improvise musical variations that fit the so so merry words of Isaac Watts' Day of Judgment, which happens to have found immortality in the *Oxford Book of English Verse* rather than in the hymnals. I don't know the tune for the jolly old paean-in-reverse (if it ever had one), but I can surely delight the devil and me with my renderings.

—Such the dire terror when the great Archangel
        Shakes the creation;

Tears the strong pillars of the vault of Heaven,
Breaks up old marble, the repose of princes,
Sees the graves open, and the bones arising,
        Flames all around them.

Hark, the shrill outcries of the guilty wretches!
Lively bright horror and amazing anguish
Stare thro' their eyelids, while the living worm lies
                                Gnawing within them.

Hopeless immortals! how they scream and shiver,
While devils push them to the pit wide-yawning
Hideous and gloomy, to receive them headlong
                                Down to the centre!

Johnny penguins and king penguins both trot along the
icy brook that flows only a few paces below my vantage point,
and bull sea elephants still gurgle and fight all day long, because our bloodthirsty boys from the *Daisy* have not yet come
questing for this particular group. Skuas fly down and peer at
me through the open tent flap. They clean up all my refuse
and eat my castaway carcasses, regardless of the arsenic in
which some of them have rolled on the skinning table. Giant
fulmars, antarctic terns, and kelp gulls with white-edged
wings all cross and recross above me while I sit here on the
job.

In the midst of these antarctic surroundings, my mind is
very much on quite different scenes. When one is utterly alone
except for one's thoughts, the latter seem to run a curious
course. Every little corner of my memory is ransacked, but
most of it has to do with our all-too-short life together. The
flashes are unimaginably vivid. When I think of something
funny, I laugh aloud; then I most mysteriously hear your
laugh too, and I burst awake and realize where I am.

The sun has not shown his welcome face for a day or two,
and my camera has been idle. The easterly gale of yesterday
has continued until this afternoon. There has been a great
swell in the bay. It is fun to pull the dory and ride high, but
also hard work because of the buffeting air and rigid water. As

I bear down toward the *Daisy*, watchful eyes see me coming, and not one but three or four men stand by the bulwarks with coils of rope that may be tossed, in case I fail to make fast at the first attempt.

Through all the description of cold and snowy weather, I have never told you what I wear at South Georgia. Outside my tent the temperature is just below the freezing point, and inside it is not more than eight or ten degrees higher, so this is a good place to say that I sit here quite comfortably, clad as follows: two suits of medium weight, Jaeger wool underwear, woolen stockings, gabardine windproof breeches, and soft leather boots that come all the way to the hips. The latter are now lowered to the knees, and I often replace them when I am in dry surroundings by a pair of the leather slippers known on the *Daisy*'s slop-chest list as "pumps." In particularly cold and windy weather, I slip on oilskin trousers over my long boots. My "top hamper," over the underwear, is protected by a gray short-sleeved sweater, a double-breasted blue flannel shirt, a windproof Russian vest, my Brown varsity sweater, and the dogskin coat purchased at Cumberland Bay. Sometimes an oilskin is added outside all that. In fair weather I like to go bareheaded, but a felt hat or a sou'wester is available for worse meteorological conditions. I usually have two pairs of heavy woolen mittens tied to my belt. They have one great advantage over leather in this climate, namely, that one may wring the water out of them when they are soaked and they will still afford a certain amount of warmth.

DECEMBER 21. This is the longest day of the year at South Georgia, and I hope the windiest, because if the blizzard raged any harder it would blow the hills down. I have not seen the sun, but I know that he is starting home again toward you, and it will be a happy day when we finally weigh anchor to follow and overtake and pass him.

Dr. Lucas and the other scientific men now sitting in their offices at the American Museum of Natural History haven't a ghost of an idea of what we are up against here. My tent, for example, is in the most sheltered spot to be found in our neighborhood, but I am continually fearful that it will be ripped to bits by the frightful winds. Would you or the museum men believe that after we haul our thirty-foot whaleboats high up on these South Georgian beaches we don't dare go a mile away from them without first half filling them with sand or cobblestones? If we neglected that precaution, a sudden williwaw might roll them over and batter them to pieces on the rocks or whisk them back into the bay.

This morning I worked in considerable discomfort, with the whole tent fluttering and rocking, despite the fact that the door was tightly lashed. Just before noon Mr. da Lomba called me out in a hurry, saying that the immediate recall signal for all hands was at *Daisy*'s masthead. We ran to the boat cove where the men had already pulled out the *Grace Emeline*, which I had anchored offshore. They were now nailing her down with stones.

We sprang into the whaleboat and pushed off, with two men at each oar. The gale was blinding, and there seemed to be as much salt water in the air as in the sea, but we reached the brig safe and wet.

Evening. It seems that about noon the barometer dropped to 730.4 mm., and the Old Man sensed the approach of the southwesterly gale even before it reached us. At three o'clock it began to snow, the wind still remaining high, and for the past several hours, the snow has not been falling, but has, rather, been traveling parallel with the surface of the sea. Most of the birds have sought shelter, but the Cape pigeons still contrive to stay on the water alongside and to feed, with a continuous clamor, on the sea elephant blubber that is soaking there on raft-tails. I don't know when I shall have a chance to do an uninterrupted day's work, and there are times when I wish that I might have the shelter of a room in one of the whaling factories.

DECEMBER 22. The gale still blows, and we are stormbound on board. The entire mainland, down to the edge of the sea, and even the green islands in the bay, have turned white and smooth with their load of new snow. Practically no work is possible, and days like this on board seem even more lonely than on the high seas. I have just read Shakespeare's *Cymbeline*, and now I have started Captain Cleveland on *A Midsummer Night's Dream*, which seems appropriate for a midday blizzard in the Antarctic! He gives the appearance of being thoroughly absorbed, and no doubt we'll hear more about it later.

DECEMBER 23. Late yesterday afternoon the weather cleared, and the wind dropped off enough so that we could go ashore. Toward evening the sun broke through and I was able to make a few photographs. Happily these include pictures of king penguins incubating their eggs. I may never be able to obtain any more because our sailors seem determined to gather every fresh egg for the larder, and to break every other with the hope that the penguins thus deprived will lay a more edible second egg. I have protested to the Old Man about this destruction of the very resources that I came here to study, but he doesn't seem disposed to do much about it.

We found that the wind had broken one of the guy ropes of my tent and had made a short tear in the canvas, through which an amazing amount of snow had entered. I brought all my prepared specimens out to the ship after the men had emptied my dory of sand and rock and had washed her out for me.

Today we have had the blessings of Old Sol throughout, which has permitted me to make some photographs that ought to be superb. I also showed Captain Cleveland how to use a box camera which he has finally broken out of his luggage, and I have offered to develop his films. So for the first time the Old Man resembles a news photographer very much on the job. He has been busy snapping his own officers and crews while shooting or bashing in the skulls of sea elephants, and subsequently skinning and flensing them.

An evening of full, or nearly full, moon should have followed such a glorious day, but in these unpredictable latitudes the weather suddenly turned warm, and now the rain is pounding.

DECEMBER 24.   It is night and Christmas Eve. I have just hung up my stocking on the bookshelves at the foot of my berth, and have put in it your Christmas letter, written seven long months ago. Four other sealed letters or cards that you so phenomenally collected are along with it, so I am sure to have a surprise in the morning.

There will not be any particular Christmas celebration on the *Daisy*. So far as I can determine, the Cape Verde Island Portuguese don't know what Santa Claus means and have nobody in their folklore who corresponds to him.

During the day I made some more photographs, including my best of sea elephants to date. In a rather gloomy gulch beside a glacier, I found also an undisturbed colony of about 350 king penguins, including more of the incubating birds and various yearlings in the process of shedding their long brown down and showing their first suit of feathers. Mr. da Lomba was out scouting with me, and he has promised not to reveal the location of this colony. After watching the birds at great length and making many photographs, I slew ten examples of assorted ages and sexes. We carried these only a short distance from the colony because the adults weighed, I judge, about forty pounds apiece, and then we skinned them out on the ground.

How long did Mr. da Lomba tell you it took him to skin a

king penguin, at the time he was bragging on the subject in New Bedford? Four minutes, if I remember rightly. I was therefore interested in checking up on him this morning, though without making any comments. I find that he required about twenty-five minutes to skin each of his specimens, or in other words, he averaged one bird while I was finishing two and one half. It was job enough to carry even the empty skins across the two miles of rough plain and beach to my tent, where we left them.

DECEMBER 25.   Merry Christmas!

I have had a busy and happy day, and here we are at the end of it already, and I am the only man below decks who hasn't turned in.

The first thing I heard this morning was a cheerful "Merry Christmas" from the Old Man. I read the letters at once, but waited until after breakfast to fetch my Christmas box up from the run. Your letter is marvelous, and I know that it expresses your present sentiments as completely as though you had written it yesterday. I can't comprehend how you have developed the imagination to project your thoughts ahead for many months and thus enclose your vivid living presence in a tiny envelope. The other communications were also entertaining and gratifying. Francis Harper sent me a series of his photographs of Long Island ducks and shore birds, which have an extremely nostalgic appeal at this time and place. Your mother's letter recalled countless happy memories, and her enclosed check is most surprising and generous, although I have decided not to take it to the bank today!

Among my other Christmas mail was this drawing from Dwight Franklin which gives a practically photographic idea of my goings-on with the penguins. If you have previously had any difficulty in conjuring up an accurate picture of them and me, your troubles are now over!

Christmas
with the
Penguins

Your 1913 calendar, with a sheet for every day in the year, is a particularly cheerful present. I shall take infinite pleasure in tearing off the dead records of days past, crumpling them up and tossing them overboard. Ultimately they will melt away like the "forty-nine blue bottles hanging on the wall" until no date remains to separate you and me. I now suspect that this calendar was the mysterious object that caused you such endless running around in New York last May.

When the box was opened, I found on top the package of peppermints and the teacup marked for the Old Man, and he seems altogether delighted with the presents and with the fact that you remembered him at Christmas. He then proceeded to dig out a long-forgotten package that you had given him last July, with the expectation that he would open it then. I laughed to see another package of mints unrolled, but that wasn't the end of it, for he subsequently opened Mrs. Cleveland's Christmas package and found six boxes, all mints in different styles, so the joke is on him.

My own box proves to be jammed with about everything that I have not tasted for a long while. The maple sugar, hard candies, preserved ginger, sweet biscuits, concentrated soup, milk chocolate, and the huge carton of glacéd fruits all make my mouth water. After dinner I passed the fruits to the skipper, officers, steward, cooper, and Johnny boy, and the palates of most of these individuals had never before been tickled by such luxuries. I hope that you will buy yourself half as nice a present with my check that you found in your stocking this morning.

We had boiled potatoes for dinner—a rare treat because our stock is almost gone—and also reasonably good apricot pie, which proved a palatable change from the dried-apple pie. The skipper opened his first jar of the muctuc prepared at Cumberland Bay. My unprejudiced report is that it has not much tang, and is a definitely over-advertised dish. Before the Old Man climbed into his gimbàl bed, which is now gently creaking while it swings to the roll of the *Daisy*, he and I topped off our Christmas celebration with a couple of bottles of good Danish stout.

I stood at work on the middle-deck, not eating peanuts by the peck, but fixing up my penguin skins, which soon I'll stow away in bins with lots of salt and fluffy cotton to keep the skins from going rotten. The Old Man helped me with a will; the first mate, too, and Sailor Bill. (It *wasn't* a sailor of that name, but the word fits in here just the same.) King pen-

guins are as plump as skunks; we scraped off fat in enormous
chunks; and, though we toiled from morn till late, we were
able to finish only eight. (We finished only seven, indeed, but
"eight" made a rime in a moment of need. Yet, since I am a
truthful boy, I must confess that I told a loy.) Tomorrow I'll
tackle the other two, and, after that I shall be through. (As a
matter of fact, there are still three more, since we did but
seven, as I said before.)

The birds flew round the brig today in a truly wonderful
feathered array. Skuas, petrels, gulls, and widgeons; stinkers,
shags, and smart Cape pigeons; whalebirds, albatrosses, paddies; half-grown terns and their red-billed daddies; and penguins in the water below—'twas a sight to beat a Wild West
show!

Well, I've had a Merry Christmas here, and a merrier
one's in store next year. So think of your lad and smile for
him, and now, in the words of Tiny Tim, "God bless us every
one."

DECEMBER 26.   Today the bay was full of growlers, and
of small bergs calved from the glaciers. One chunk, half as big
above water as our ship, drifted slowly upon us. Since its
weight and inertia could easily rip off our copper sheathing, or
grind into our planking, we met it with poles, oars, and spars,
in the hands of as many men as could crowd at the bow. Con-
certed pushing against the ice slowly widened the gap between hull and berg, until it passed astern.

Growlers are stony blobs of old and greatly worn ice.
They are dangerous to my dory, and particularly to the thin-
skinned whaleboats, rather than to *Daisy*. They are often
bowl-shaped, with staghorn-like fronds projecting around the
rim. Other pieces are roughly spherical, but in either case the
surface is evenly pitted with polygonal facets—like an insect's
compound eye. They are devilishly hard to see from the boats.
Miles from the ship, and almost as far from land, in murky

weather, I have become first aware of the blood-chilling presence of a growler by seeing a submerged thin blade of ice that
has just missed the delicate cedar planks between our boat's
crew and the hereafter!

DECEMBER 27.   Christmas already seems a long way
past, and it will soon be another year.

Today I stood knee-deep in the glacial brook, with rain
and snow afalling, and roughed out the skeleton of a bull sea
elephant that our men had killed and stripped at the spot. It
was hard work and, before I finished, very cold work. I have
become so well acclimated, however, that keeping my hands
in icy water causes me no discomfort and little inconvenience.
My fingers swell, so I now have to wear my wedding ring on a
necklace of cod line, instead of where you properly placed it.

This evening I have been initiating the Old Man into the
mysteries of developing negatives. He is as enthusiastic as a
small boy over the results obtained with his inexpensive
camera. On previous voyages he has carried his exposed negatives home through the tropics, and at the end of a voyage of a
year or two the corner drug store has delivered him nothing
but fog and blanks for all his pains.

DECEMBER 28.   Sea leopards are common here at the
Bay of Isles, and I have been awaiting an opportunity to kill
one of the beautiful and snaky creatures in a place where I
could be sure of recovering it. This morning I found one lying
at the surface in the kelp, almost under the counter of the
brig. It floated just awash, with a small island of its back in
the air, and from time to time it lifted its head and opened its
nostrils roundly to inhale. Now and then it also opened its
mouth to an extraordinary angle, showing clearly the terrible
trident-shaped cheek teeth with which it seizes penguins
under water. Watching my opportunity, I finally shot it in the
brain with a .22 long-rifle ball, but to my great regret and discouragement the creature, which had been floating so buoy-

antly; sank like lead. I watched it go down, slowly turning
over and apparently stone dead. The next sea leopard that I
try to collect will have to be firmly ashore or on the ice, because my conscience keeps me awake when I take life to no
purpose.

I am in my tent as I write, and big blocks of Grace
Glacier are tumbling off over yonder. I have been here most of
the day through frightful weather and a pounding mixture of
rain and snow. Now I am preparing myself a snack of hard-
tack and maple syrup, and a cup of your excellent beef tea.

DECEMBER 29.   Today was mostly clear and bright,
with westerly winds and tattered cumulus clouds until mid-
afternoon, when the sky suddenly became overcast, and
rhythmic snow squalls followed. Periods in which the air was
almost solid with flakes alternated with clear gray spells. The
rapidity with which weather changes seems to be the out-
standing characteristic of South Georgia. At least twice I
have seen a strong breeze shift halfway round the compass
within ten minutes. Many times during the past week we have
had an easterly gale in the morning and a southwesterly gale
in afternoon. Much of the feeling of grimness here is due, of
course, to the fact that there is so much less shelter than in
the Cumberland Bay neighborhood.

This morning I made the difficult landing on the lee side
of Shag Islet (in earlier notes called the cormorant rock), near
our anchorage. By letting the *Grace Emeline* float away on a
long painter, I was able to scramble up the wall to the flat
summit.

The islet was a rugged little pile of strata tipped on edge,
cut by many gorges in which long strands of seaweeds
swashed. On top it was covered with black soil and tussock
grass, alive with millions of the tiny, leaping insects called
springtails, and here I found my first pipit's nest. It was made
of fine roots, partly covered with a dome. No eggs had been

laid, but a pipit flew out of it just before I would have stepped on it.

The blue-eyed shags or cormorants were, however, the principal inhabitants of the rock, nesting on ledges all over the northerly or sunny faces of the cliffs. I filled fourteen pages of a notebook with observations on the behavior of these little-known birds.

Their courtship was in full blast while the nests were still building. I saw one pair standing side by side on their unfinished home, and curtseying. The enraptured birds would press their cheeks together, bow down their heads, then twisting their necks, put their other cheeks together in the same way and curtsey again. After this graceful minuet had carried on for several minutes, the male would launch off on a short, ecstatic flight, from which he would soon return to resume the love-making.

I sat beside one shag that was brooding a naked, black, newly-hatched young and one green egg. (I had to lift her—or was it him?—off the nest to find out what was underneath.) She settled back and watched me with blue-rimmed eyes. Her only note was a barely audible croak—such as Keats calls "a little noiseless noise." She kept her bills parted, the mandible and throat trembling as when one's teeth chatter, but I doubt that she was afraid. At any rate, she had no cause to be. I can shoot them at shotgun range, but they are safe when I'm a guest in their homes!

DECEMBER 30.   Last evening we were all up late. I developed two dozen negatives after supper, and three of our whaleboats did not return with a large blubber raft in tow until ten o'clock. So this morning we were served breakfast at seven o'clock instead of five, an experience in the nature of a most slothful luxury.

I walked to the king penguin rookery by the Lucas Glacier (another of my new geographic names). The presence of the birds is still a secret that belongs to Mr. da Lomba and me, but I can hardly hope to keep knowledge of it from our boys much longer, because they are now scouting for sea elephants at that end of the long beach and among the hummocks behind its crest.

The day was leaden until late afternoon, when the sun suddenly burst through filmy clouds and the whole vault of the sky cleared up as if by magic. Then followed a rare evening for this inclement zone. The northwest wind died down to a soft breeze, the slanting rays of the sun illumined the many green isles of the bay, and the crest of the western mountains was drawn with a fiery line. The nearer slopes, made up of vast fields of unbroken snow, turned to lovely purple shadows, which softened and deepened on their descent toward the great Brunonia Glacier that stands cold and sharp and rugged at their base. The islets all reflected an increasingly bright yellow-green after the sun sank. The mountains to the south turned an ochre-red wherever rock pierced the snow. All else was white, yet not quite white because every color that enters into sunlight played upon the endless mantle of the hills. Here we can well appreciate such an hour, because a gray ambiance and blustering, tingling winds are our usual portion. Whenever South Georgia puts aside her sterner aspect and relaxes into smiles, it is astonishing with what clearness faraway objects can be seen. Distance, moreover, becomes amazingly difficult to judge. At this moment the range of hills behind the surf-lined beach looks from deck as though it were only a stone's throw from the edge of the bay, yet I know after much tramping that it stands a mile back. In the last light of the day, now that the sun has gone down beyond the water, the mountain peaks of the main range seem so close at hand that I imagine I could run and climb them in no more time than it takes to think the act. Actually, many a

toilsome mile and rocky gorge and never-thawed crevasse lie
between them and me.

DECEMBER 31.   It is well that I unloaded my rhapsody
on beautiful weather yesterday, because today it has been
hard to see more than a boat's length. The cold has been particularly penetrating, and there has been no letup in a shower
of snow crystals that sting the skin like needle pricks. Nevertheless, the wind has not been too strong for boat navigation,
and the crews have wandered widely along both island and
mainland shores. A great day, the captain calls it, because his
men have slaughtered eighty-six sea elephants and have
brought all the blubber to the vessel before dark. It is horrible
business, but, after all, it is what has beckoned the crew 7,000
miles from home, so I suppose that I ought to be tolerant
about it.

JANUARY 1, 1913.   Happy New Year! The anniversary
was introduced by the heaviest snowfall I have yet seen at
South Georgia. The new blanket lies nearly hip deep, and the
rising tide is now making a straight cutbank of snow along the
beach.

Our boat's crews were able to work all day because the
wind was not high, even though visibility was cut to very
short range. The men killed seventy-seven sea elephants and
brought every scrap of blubber to the ship. I was with them
during part of their hunt, and I wasted a good many rifle balls
in order to prevent the brutes from being tortured by the
ghastly lances. A bullet through the brain does the trick instantly, and the bleeding that the sealers regard as necessary
for the production of clear and light-colored oil flows just as
effectively from a freshly killed animal as from one still living.
Cow sea elephants and young males can be numbed by a club-
bing on the head, and then so treated with lance thrusts
through the chest that they never wake up. The big bulls are,

however, almost impossible to stop in their tracks unless a
bullet pierces the parietal bone at the side of the brain case,
between the huge crest on top of the skull and the massive
bony arch below the eye. The Old Man has four Springfield
muskets, shooting a 45-70 lead bullet propelled by black
powder. These are used only by himself and the officers. They
produce a thundering roar and a tremendous cloud of white
smoke, and yet they are not as effective as the much smaller
modern rifle and ammunition in my own outfit.

The joke about the sea elephant club, or "manduc'," of
which I wrote while we were still at sea, has at last become
obvious. You will remember that our boys produced on the
ship's lathe an assortment of parlor ornaments with which
they proposed to belabor the heads of countless sea elephants. When we really began the hunt down here, Mr. da
Lomba produced seasoned "elephant clubs" from the *Daisy's*
hold. They proved to be herculean weapons, from five to
seven feet long, each one weighing two or three times as much
as a heavy baseball bat. All the toy clubs were then
promptly stored in the men's sea chests. With them in
their hands they would not have dared to approach a sea
elephant close enough to hit it, and the blow in any case
could have had no more than an annoying effect. But when
Long John da Lomba swings his proper manduc' on the
noggin of anything smaller than an old crested bull, the
victim is, as he says, "knocked stiffer'n a loon's leg" and
never stirs again.

Another echo from the past concerns Cadella who, as an
unsophisticated puppy in strange surroundings, was afraid of
the *Daisy's* rats, and for this reason won the scorn of the Old
Man. Well, Cadella is still with us and, now that she has
waxed mature in a hard school, she no longer has a trace of
timorousness. She has been going about in the boats and taking part, so to speak, in the slaughter of sea elephants, at least

to the extent of daintily lapping from the pools of hot blood. Today she rushed yelping at a twenty-foot bull seal, which she seized by the snout. The men shouted frantically, thinking that Cadella was at the point of being bitten in half, or at least flattened like a pancake. Instead, she was tossed through the air for about fifteen feet, from which point she started back for more punishment, but we succeeded in calling her off.

"My soul and body," said Captain Cleveland. "That bitch ain't afraid of anything."

"Portugee dog," commented Mr. Almeida, with a meaningful look.

Thus was the Old Man hoist by his own petard.

Cadella is not the only creature whose moral stature has increased. Conrad, who once trembled on the ratlines and who was nearly scared into the next world the first time he came into close quarters with a whale, is now one of the most fearless and competent men of our crew in the sea elephant hunting. When he joined us in the West Indies, he was not only the youngest of all our boys, but was also one who seemed to have enjoyed an unusually sheltered home life and much more schooling than any of his fellows. He was by no means a tough guttersnipe, who had had the conditioning of life's hard knocks. But he always wanted to do his duty and he soon recovered both from his terror of a whaleboat battle and from his fear of going aloft. During the latter part of our southward voyage, there was no better member of the watch to slide out on the highest yardarms for taking in sail, even in the middle of the night, with the puffs nearly shaking him out of his clothes. Conrad has grown husky too, so that he pulls a strong oar and wields a deadly lance. He does a man's work and uses his head, which is one of the best in the forecastle. He can always be relied upon to finish a job, and Mr. da Lomba says that he will make a first-class boatsteerer for "next voyage." I haven't yet sounded him out on his future plans, but I suspect that he is more likely to become a teacher in Dominica.

I was able today to select eight heads of adult sea elephants, both male and female, of which I am going to prepare the skulls. Salome, the daughter of Herodias, would not dance very far with one of these trophies on a silver charger. It took two strong men to carry the head of a big bull from beach to boat, which they did by thrusting a lance handle through a loop of the tough hide, and swinging the burden between them.

One sea leopard was observed sleeping just below the snowbank on the beach, about twenty feet above the water's edge, but I was not with the crew that saw it. I hope to capture one soon and to save both skin and skeleton, as well as to make a dissection of the whole animal.

JANUARY 2.   Today I visited Albatross Island in one of the whaleboats, despite hard weather. While the men were sealing, I searched the crevices and fissures of a cliff for breeding places of petrels but without success.

The combined kill of sea elephants was thirty-six animals. Many of them had wandered a long way from salt water, and these were driven back to the shore by men who shook pebbles in iron buckets. The tradition is that this sound is particularly frightening to sea elephants, and at any rate I can testify that it works. The aim of the treachery was merely that the beasts might meet their doom close to the water's edge, so as to lessen the toil of lugging blubber. All day long terrific gusts of wind blew from the southwest, bringing rain and sleet and an occasional snow flurry.

JANUARY 3.   There is no doubt about its being a tough life. My brawn is now equaled only by my beard, which has not known a razor for nearly a month. Almost every day I get from a mile to six or seven miles of hard rowing, either in the dory or in one of the whaleboats. Neither is it rowing such as we undertake on a trip across our harbor to the beach of Long Island Sound! Here we pull like the companions of Odysseus or Leif Ericson. You lie back and put your heart into each stroke, for the winds of South Georgia are like a strong hand that changes so as to push against you, both going and returning. It is a wind that picks up the bay water in sheets and dashes it over us, while ashore it starts roundish cobblestones rolling. Calm spells come only every week or so, and if they last ten minutes, we are lucky. Now and again the sun takes a peek through a hole in the clouds but, not liking the look of things, he may then neglect us for the next two or three days. We have seen no neighbors yet, except for a distant steamer that passed far offshore on New Year's Day.

On days when I have been working ashore alone, I usually row out to the *Daisy* about seven o'clock in the evening shouting, "Ho! Dory alongside!" as I approach. The men then drop the boat tackles, and when I hitch them on and call "Fore and aft," the *Grace Emeline* is hoisted out of the boisterous sea until the cranes can be swung under her. I always make myself responsible for every detail in handling my own boat, and I always do a full seaman's share when in a whaleboat.

JANUARY 4.   Forty-two sea elephants were killed today. Some of them, particularly the cows, had recently hauled up from sea and were extraordinarily fat, which means that they will yield the maximum amount of oil. The Old Man's license, received from Mr. Wilson at Cumberland Bay, forbids him to kill any females or young, but he cheerfully disregards all agreements and makes the slaughter universal, even down to the winsome and playful pups born last October.

Today I made my first photographs of South Georgian teals, among the hummocks of grass near the landing place. Correia and I stumbled upon the little ducks, which seemed unconcerned and continued prodding about in the mud of a glacial streamlet. When I stepped within six feet, they quacked softly, raised their heads, and waddled farther off among the tussocks, from where they peered out through a screen of drooping grass. All but their bright eyes and yellow bills blended completely with the surroundings.

It is obvious that the creatures in the Garden lacked all fear of Adam merely because he was the first man they had ever met. The same rule holds here.

Later I rowed the *Grace Emeline* to Albatross Island, and spent a wonderful afternoon among the courting wandering albatrosses. Indeed, I nearly filled a new notebook.

At this season many of last year's young albatrosses still linger on the nesting ground. These fledglings are no longer fed by the adults, so they must go without eating—for many weeks, perhaps—until they have moulted their gray down and have learned to fly and to catch squids for themselves.

But, if they grow thinner, they also grow lighter. They stand on the hillsides facing the breeze, spread their long, weak wings, and jump into the air. Poising for a second, they then glide downhill, tumbling head over heels when alighting. In the bright lexicon of albatross-youth there is no such word as fail. They patiently repeat the bumping process until they have reached the bottom of the slope; whereupon they toil upward on foot, and shoot the chute all over again.

The show put on by the adults is a marvel. The sexes are of different appearance, at least among fully mature birds, and every unattached female now appears to be besieged by several suitors, which dance about her, gobble, squeal, caterwaul, stand on their toes, and puff out their chests. They also click and fence with their beaks, and ardently spread wide their great wings which, as I have now learned, sometimes have an expanse of more than eleven feet from tip to tip.

The end of all this, of course, is a mated pair. The humus

and soil are raked together to form a nest mound that may measure eighteen inches in height, and on or beside this both birds remain until the single big egg appears. Then one begins to sit, and the other flies off over the ocean for a few days of fattening up before relieving guard on the nest.

Our gang, unfortunately, is now raiding the albatross colonies as a new source of omelets. The other day Mr. Vincent outwitted three boats' crews by obtaining a basketful of eggs, while the other seventeen men gathered only about a dozen. They all landed on the island together and started rampaging, each sailor shouting in triumph when he found and picked up an egg. But the pawky Tagalog rushed rapidly from nest to nest along his course, and always yelled "Nothing!" Then he backtracked for half a mile and garnered an egg from at least every other nest that he had passed!

The Old Man blows a large proportion of all albatross and king penguin eggs brought to the *Daisy*, because he can sell the shells for a dollar apiece to the curio dealers in New Bedford and on Cape Cod.

The egg of a wandering albatross is good food, and yet from an epicurean point of view it proves a delusion and a snare. I can compare it with nothing better than beaver tail soup, and this entirely because of its effect upon the appetite rather than from any similarity in taste. You boil your egg, which weighs a pound, until the contents are of just the right consistency. You snip off the smaller end, sprinkle with salt, and dig in. It is delicious! But by the time you have progressed halfway to the bottom, you begin to wish that the bird had laid a somewhat smaller egg, and if you have the stomach to scoop the shell clean, you are sure to hope that you may never see another. However, that first rich taste soon wipes out the memory of what had followed, and within a few days you once more fall a victim to the insidious temptation that never fails to cloy.

JANUARY 5.   The holocaust today accounted for sixty-six
sea elephants.

In dark pools among the fields of kelp, I saw pulsating
jellyfish, many of which were at least a yard in diameter, or as
large as an open umbrella. They had an aster of brown petals
under the transparent mantle and a fringe around the periphery. With a net I captured several curious crustaceans among
their tentacles, and several times I saw small fishes in the
same place.

Since such jellyfish, like the Portuguese man-o'-war, have
potent stinging cells, why do they not kill the small guests
that live among their gelatinous trailers? My theory is that
the stimulus which produces the sting is not tactile but chemical. By this I mean that some acid or other reagent in the
skin of their victims is the trigger that discharges the shock.
The creatures that normally abide with them presumably
lack this chemical stimulus, for which reason they may touch
the tentacles with impunity.

For a change, the weather was mild and calm. Over the
tussock grass and wet moss, countless tiny flies oscillated in
the still air.

Nothing has surprised me more than the insects, or
rather the terrestrial arthropods, that I have found on this
snowy island. I already have one or more mites, one spider,
bird fleas, springtails, midges from the grass and their larvae
from the pools, scavenger flies and beach flies, and two
species of beetles. Large beach flies are common under
stones and seaweed alongshore. They are always sluggish and
I have never seen one fly, even though they have fully developed wings. An overturned stone sometimes reveals fifty or
more huddled together. When thus exposed to the light, they
scatter and walk stickily to some new and cold hiding place.
What a life! Yet, no doubt, they are as nebulously happy as
only non-human animals can be. Kinaesthetic contentment;

no craving for warmth; no inhibitions; no urge without its gratification; no glimmering of an end or of death.

The most intriguing insects are the springtails, or Collembola, which swarm by inconceivable numbers in the vegetal mould among the tussock stalks. I have collected them by placing a saucer of alcohol on the soil. Then the little skippers, leaping pell-mell hundreds of times the length of their bodies, shower down into the saucer as if they were spontaneous creations of the atmosphere. If there are a thousand springtails on each square yard of grassland (a conservative estimate), how many of them live on all South Georgia?

The cove between my tent and the snout of Grace Glacier is now filled with an ice floe. This morning I found a sea leopard fast asleep on a large cake within twenty-five yards of shore. He dozed restlessly, as the sea elephants also do, moving his flippers about and stretching and writhing while his icy bed rocked on the gentle swell. When I whistled, he raised his head and gave a yawn that would have done justice to a crocodile. But he showed no uneasiness at the sight of me. I could easily have killed the animal with a rifle but was afraid of losing his carcass because it would have been impossible to row the dory in among the crammed rafts and growlers of ice. So I left my friend dreaming in peace.

I have been prospecting on the moraines of Grace Glacier, where slabs of slate and other rock, red from iron oxide, are heaped up in great mounds on a foundation of ice. Here and there the fragments have been cemented into huge masses by what looks like silt. This binder seems to have almost the strength of Portland cement because I find it difficult to break up the conglomerate with my geological hammer. A stream that is now flowing off the glacier, enclosed within a bed and walls of ice, is swallowed up in the very center of the moraine, plunging down into an apparently bottomless ice pit about thirty feet in diameter. It is an awe-inspiring spot, with a noisy flow of water pouring into the hole, doubt-less to find its outlet to the sea under the straight wall of ice that stands in the bay. The moraine extends upward along the crown of the glacier as a dark line running all the way to the distant snowfields. It must be of great age, because luxuriant moss and lichens are now growing on rocks that have no con-tact with the soil.

JANUARY 6.   A clear, warm day, with light northwester-ly winds and an almost cloudless sky over bay and sea. Heavy clouds fringed the crest of the mountains, but we had the blessing of continuous sun, only a straggling wisp of cirrus occasionally dimming, but not hiding, its face. In sheltered spots, the weather at noon might almost have been described as hot. The young giant fulmars in their nests thought so too, for they opened their bills and panted. The water sparkled in the sunlight, just as it does in summer at home, and the ocean looked as blue as in the tropics, not from an intrinsic color but as a result of reflection from the azure sky.

I went to Albatross Island in the dory. Later two of our boats' crews landed and followed the tracks of unfortunate sea elephants up to their sleeping places in the tussock grass. For the first time I walked through the hordes of nesting alba-trosses to the northern side of the island, which terminates in a high cliff. A rocky peninsula extends from the northeastern corner toward smaller islets, the line of a former land connec-tion now being marked by the tall cylindrical columns past which the *Daisy* sailed on the way toward her anchorage.

I dug out eleven blue whalebirds from their burrows in the black soil, and found my first occupied pipit's nest. There were four young in it, and the bottom contained remains of beetles and marine amphipods. I know now why the pipits often stand in water up to their feathers on the floating kelp. Presently one of the parents fed the chicks within a few steps of me, picked a beakful of feces from the nest, and flew away.

This nest was only two yards from that of a giant fulmar. Why didn't the latter eat the pipits? The same question applies to the skuas, which gobble up everything else that they can swallow, yet the pipits on the beaches practically run over their toes. In the midst of such chivalrous attitudes, the little pipits seem to have no enemies whatsoever at South Georgia.

The pipits have a nostalgic appeal, being the only relatives here of our land birds at home. They are afraid neither of a man nor a dog, and can easily be caught in the hand. The report of a gun over their heads doesn't even cause them to look around. Their music is rather like that of our song sparrow, only the refrain is softer and longer. Best of all, dour weather does not quash them; from my tent I hear their gay melody on the rainiest and gustiest of mornings, ascending from where the pipits run along the edge of the glacial torrent.

Before returning from Albatross Island to the brig, one boat stopped to fish in a pool of the kelp beds, using sea elephant blubber as bait. The weird-looking fish, all species of an antarctic genus called *Notothenia*, bit ferociously as soon as the hooks were three or four fathoms below the surface, and the bottom of the whaleboat was soon filled with them.

While writing these entries, I have been having a cup of tea, made with your silver ball. Now I can keep awake no longer, so good night from your dirty, bewhiskered, and adoring husband.

JANUARY 7.   Calm, and a useless day from the Old Man's point of view because dense fog, mist, and swirling sky cut down visibility to about the length of the ship until evening, when the fog lifted and the vault cleared just as the sun sank behind the western ridge. By the time the stars peeped out, there was scarcely a wisp of cloud to hide them. I stayed late at my tent because there was neither breeze nor snow flurry to mar the beauty of the night. After dark I climbed the promontory above the landing cove, startling a pack of giant fulmars which had settled there to roost. The clumsy birds, squawking in alarm, dashed over the brink and down the long bank to the sea, like the swine of the Gadarenes. For the first time at the Bay of Isles I saw all the southern stars and the nebulous Clouds of Magellan.

Up until eleven o'clock in the evening, when I last went on deck in order to drink in the experience of sparkling darkness at South Georgia, the islands in the bay and the peaks of the mountains showed almost as plainly as in daylight. From every isle and headland came a sweet, bell-like piping—the singing of numberless whalebirds, shoemakers, and other petrels in their burrowed nests. At South Georgia it took the place of the katydids, the whippoorwills, and the frog choruses of summer nights at home on Long Island.

The weather curtain of the day mercifully protected the sea elephants and only a single bull was slain. Mr. da Lomba declares that he saw a sea leopard killing a pup sea elephant, turning the water gory for yards around.

JANUARY 8. I have spent the day on board, making up fourteen skins of sea birds, and I still have five albatrosses that need attention.

Thirteen sea elephants were taken by the crews. They brought me a male sea leopard's head, of which I have taken a plaster mould. It will be useful when the museum taxidermists mount the whole animal which I yet hope to obtain.

JANUARY 9. Still busy on board. Very strong southwesterly winds limited the movement of the whaleboats, but at least we had sunshine.

Rather late in the day I got ashore and began my ambassadorship to the gentoo or Johnny penguins, the smaller of the two common species at the Bay of Isles. They make me think of the Eskimos who would be my companions if I happened to be up near the other end of the earth.

The gentoos have blue backs, breasts like starched white

shirts, coral-red bills, orange feet, and across the crown of the head they wear white fillets resembling the caps of trained nurses.

By taste they are hill dwellers. No matter how much available space there may be near the water, no matter how wearisome the scramble up the steeps, most of these penguins select the summits of windy, shelterless ridges for their homes. Many deeply-grooved winding avenues extend through the snowbanks to the highest parts of the colonies. Processions of adults can be seen coming and going at all times between their nests and the sea. They meet and pass each other without a sign of recognition, each bird trudging gravely along on its own business.

I sat quietly among them for about an hour, and found that the general attitude toward such a strange visitor as myself was one of indifference or of curiosity unmixed with fear. Then I pulled on leather mittens for safety's sake, seized a passing penguin, lifted it off the ground, and tried with all my might to prevent it from struggling. The outraged bird screeched, beat a tattoo with its flippers that stung even through thick polar garments, bit, squirmed, kicked, and fought like a demon. The tussle continued for about a minute, and I was just about to give up and drop the furious armful when it abruptly quieted down. There it rested in the crook of my elbow, unhurt, bright-eyed, and as contented as a well-fed baby. I stroked it from head to tail and it seemed fascinated or hypnotized. I placed it gently on the ground, whereupon it looked up serenely, as though nothing unpleasant had occurred between us.

From this and other observations I conclude that the gentoos are creatures of the moment, not readily holding one mood after the novelty of the stimulus has worn off. One penguin that was at first excited by my sudden appearance in the colony presently lapsed into a yawn, shut its eyes, and fell asleep. I understood, as soon as I saw that ardent cock and hen penguins took naps in the very middle of their courtship antics, that there was nothing intentionally rude in their behavior toward me!

JANUARY 10. Today I visited two colonies of the gentoos, and learned where good penguins go when they die! We have often remarked upon the extraordinarily few dead penguins encountered among the large populations. Now I have discovered their romantic sepulchre.

Near the summit of a coastal hill I came upon a lonely pond in a hollow of ice-cracked stones. Several sick and drooping penguins were standing at the edge of this pool of snow water, which was ten or twelve feet deep. Then, with a tingling of my spine, I perceived that the bottom was strewn, layer upon layer, with the bodies of gentoo penguins that had outlived the perils of the sea to accomplish the rare feat among wild animals of dying a natural death. By hundreds, possibly by thousands, they lay all over the bed of the cold tarn, flippers outstretched and breasts reflecting blurred gleams of white. Safe at last from sea leopards in the ocean, and from skuas ashore, they took their endless rest; for decades, perhaps for centuries, the slumberers would undergo no change in their frigid tomb.

JANUARY 11. Eighty-four sea elephants were slain today, including some extremely large bulls. They were all taken in Sea Leopard Fiord and Beckman Fiord, five or six miles to the east of our anchorage. So the boats, which returned to the ship late in the evening, have had a long cruise. Forty-two of the animals killed were cows, which is wholly illegal and unjustified, as I have remarked before. Mr. Vincent tells me that many of these cow seals had climbed to the top of a grassy plateau, about forty feet above sea level, and that some of them escaped by sliding and falling over the brink while the men with clubs and lances were rounding them up.

The fat creatures swam away as though not in the least incommoded by their long tumble.

JANUARY 12. I have spent most of the day in my tent but, contrary to usual custom, I rowed out to the brig for dinner. While wrapping specimens in old newspapers, I noticed the following item in the Buenos Aires *Standard*, an English language sheet.

BIRTH.

MOFFAT.—On the 20th May, at 19 Manor Place, Edinburgh, Scotland, to Mr. and Mrs. J. S. Moffat—a daughter (by cable).

It must be a very convenient way to have a daughter, and if there were only a cable station at South Georgia, we might try it!

Every day, my darling Grace, I regret that I have been unable to send you another letter. From time to time we sight whaling steamers from our anchorage, but they are always miles and miles away, and probably not one of them knows that an ancient windjammer from New Bedford is lying in the lee of these islands. Sooner or later I hope that one may discover us and pay a call.

After a bright morning, the day has turned blustery and bitter cold. That should be regarded, however, as only a reversion to normal. Nature has been unduly clement lately, and has given us the sun for the greater part of the past four days.

JANUARY 13. A terrific southwest gale has raged since noon, continuing into the evening. A hard frost has followed the dying down of the wind. Snow fell all day, driving on the deck and water with a sharp hissing sound. During the height of the blizzard many sea birds that we seldom see so far within the Bay of Isles were astern of the ship in great numbers.

Although we were completely stormbound, the mincing
and boiling of sea elephant blubber continued on deck. Occasionally men had to knock off and go below, to thaw some of
the numbness out of their mittened hands.

I took the opportunity to write a long letter to Dr. Lucas,
Director of the Museum, telling him of the progress of my
work to date and also something of the trials and difficulties,
as well as of the joys and successes. It would hardly be wise to
let him wax too optimistic about what I am supposed to be
accomplishing in faraway South Georgia. Some day I hope to
find means of sending off my letter to Dr. Lucas along with
one to you.

JANUARY 14.   Recurrent ice storms all day, though with
less wind than yesterday. The deck and the world ashore are
ankle deep in diamond crystals. The temperature dropped so
low before noon that the Old Man ordered all work knocked
off for the day. You may take your choice about attributing
this to kindness of heart or to the perfectly obvious fact that
the frozen sealers could no longer hold a knife in their hands.

The weather did not slow me down, however, and by this
time I believe that I am acclimated to South Georgia better
than anyone else on board. At any rate, while ashore I
achieved one of my highest hopes by killing and saving a huge
female sea leopard (the females of this species are larger than
the males, which is just the opposite of the relation in the
sexes of the sea elephant).

This morning I walked from the landing cove over the
crest of the main beach of the bay, and there on the shingle
was my prize, sound asleep. I tiptoed away, ran to my tent for
the .22-caliber Winchester, and stalked back. My victim gave
never a wriggle after I had put a long-rifle ball into the brain
through the thinnest part of the skull. The process of skinning
in the intense cold was made possible by the body heat of the

seal itself. Every few seconds I would thrust my bare hands against the hot blubber under a flap of skin. Within about an hour I had the skin off, although, of course, a great amount of work on the flippers, and other trimming, still remains to be done before it can be safely salted down.

I next made a quick dissection of the carcass, discovering some extraordinary anatomical facts which I believe have never been reported. The most remarkable relates to the trachea, or windpipe, of this seal, which is a flat band because the cartilaginous "rings" are straight bars. The windpipe opens only when the sea leopard breathes, whereas in all other mammals it is always a tube. This formation leaves plenty of room for the gullet and enables the sea leopard to swallow penguins nearly whole. The mangled remains of four king penguins were in the stomach of today's victim, a 140-pound meal!

Next I eviscerated and dismembered the carcass, and cut the greater part of the meat off the skeleton while the remains were still warm enough to keep my hands from freezing stiff. Finally, I brought the entire skin and skeleton off to the brig in my dory and, when the weather has moderated somewhat, I shall complete the skinning out of the flippers so as to obtain every bone down to the last phalanx of the fingers and toes.

I feel pretty smug, because if any museum in the United States yet possesses a sea leopard, it is certain to be ancient and hideous, probably dating from the United States Exploring Expedition of 1838-1842. From a museum man's point of view, a sea leopard is just about as rare as a pine in Pine Street!

I have never described for you the sea leopard in action. Swift, crafty, graceful beyond any other antarctic seal, it is a devourer of penguins both along the coasts of their breeding grounds and in the pack ice. Males may reach a length of ten feet, females of fourteen. They lurk in wait beneath the ice foot of the penguins' thoroughfares to the sea. They likewise cruise about offshore from the rookeries, sometimes making astounding leaps out of water to land and rest upon pans of ice, on which they move about by an eel-like wiggling instead of by crawling. Sea leopards capture penguins by bursts of speed, usually seizing them in the depths. Before eating their prey, however, the brutes bring it to the surface and tear it out of its skin by violent shaking, which makes the foam fly. Most of the skin and feathers then float off before the wind, and the hot, stripped carcass is bolted with very little dismemberment.

7 Blubber on Ice

JANUARY 15. Another howling sou'wester, and it has been impossible for anybody to leave the ship. I have been doing whatever I could on board, but the important jobs at the moment are ashore. It is now two o'clock in the afternoon, and I can see no prospect of being able to land today.

The mincing and boiling of blubber has been going steadily ahead, despite the weather. Sea elephant blubber has much less waste than whale blubber, by which I mean that a larger proportion of it can be converted into clear and limpid oil. Sufficient scrap rises in the trypots to serve as fuel for the boiling, but the Old Man and I have been figuring that we recover at least 180 gallons of oil from every 200 gallons of the blubber. In other words, the loss by volume is only 10 per cent, and the loss by weight is probably even less.

Now for the first time, I can understand the tradition current among the old-time Yankee sea elephant hunters at Heard Island, in the southern Indian Ocean. This was to the effect that "a cask of blubber equals a cask of oil." Heard Is-

land has no safe anchorage, and the custom was to sail down
from one of the harbors of Kerguelen Island, slaughter sea
elephants, flense and mince the blubber, and then fill the
casks through their bungholes. The cold was sufficient to
keep the fat from turning rancid before it could be conveyed
back to Kerguelen for boiling. Here at South Georgia we are
spared the double labor, the *Daisy*'s lads handling the business as follows:

The first rule, as you know, is "Get 'em to the beach," as
close to the water as the animals can be driven without risk of
their escaping. There they are clubbed or shot, and lanced
through the great arteries near the heart.

After the blood has fountained out, the hide is slit lengthwise down the middle of the back, and then transversely in
several places from the dorsal incision to the ground. The
flaps of hide are next flayed off on each side. Curved butcher
blades are used, and two of these, along with a knife steel,
hang in a wooden scabbard from the belt of every sealer. The
knives are whetted so frequently that the ring of steel on steel
runs like a metronome through the skinning process. Four
men usually work together on a large carcass.

Free of skin, the investment of white blubber, which may
have a maximum thickness of about eight inches, is dissected
away by sweeping strokes from the underlying muscle, and
cut into squarish blanket-pieces. The animal is then rolled
over, before rigor mortis makes this impossible, and the ven-
tral side is divested in the same manner.

The blanket-pieces are floated and strung on short ropes
called raft tails. These are towed to the anchored ship, where
each laden raft tail is looped around a hawser that extends
from bow to stern along the waterline. The blubber then
soaks for forty-eight hours or thereabouts, until the remaining
red blood corpuscles have washed out. During this blanching
process a proportion of the oil is lost. Moreover, ravenous

Cape pigeons, with an interminable hubbub, feed upon the blubber night and day as long as it remains exposed.

Hoisted aboard, the blanket-pieces are cut up and minced, the process differing from that of sperm whaling only in that the fat is sliced as thin as possible. At this stage a further loss of oil occurs, particularly if the temperature of the air chances to be well above the freezing point. The trying out is done exactly as with sperm oil.

JANUARY 16.   Gales from the west and northwest, and a heavy sea all over the Bay of Isles. The temperature is mild, and after the wind died late this afternoon a warm rain fell and a dense fog steamed up from the surface of the water.

The men killed fifteen sea elephants, of which all but two were cows. Some of the latter were amazingly gentle, refusing to be alarmed or disturbed even when they were slapped on the back. It irritated the crews to have to murder several far from the sea, and then have to tote hundreds of pounds of blubber swung on lance poles.

JANUARY 17.   Strong sou'westerly gale, and once again we are completely stormbound. I have made up a packet of the letters to Dr. Lucas and my mother and a long section of the log for you. These are all sealed and I have left orders for them to be turned over to any whaling steamer that might call on the *Daisy* in my absence. From time to time I will add a date on the outside of your envelope, so that you may have the latest possible indication that I am still in the battle. We have had no communication with the outside world since we left Cumberland Bay thirty-five days ago. It is lonely and isolated which, however, is the way I expected to feel on the entire voyage from the West Indies and back. What great good fortune we really have had!

This is the third day on which it has been impossible to lower the *Grace Emeline*. The strength of the wind here exceeds that of all the blizzards I can remember in Long Island or New England. Let me recount one example of the pull of the wind on a buoy no bigger than a soup tin.

Some days ago I put a sea leopard skull in a wire fishtrap in order that the industrious isopods or sea lice might eat off the residue of flesh and thus share the labor of producing clean white bone. I put also a round stone in the fishtrap so that the combined load weighed somewhat over fifteen pounds. This I sank in thirteen fathoms of water, attaching a one-quart tin as a float. The can was enclosed in a net and was tied to the trap by cod line. My plan was to leave the seal skull at the bottom for three or four days, and then to haul it out in condition for a museum cabinet. Well, the wind blew so hard on the tin can that it dragged the skull and fishtrap two miles and a half, and Mr. da Lomba discovered it, quite by accident, at the lee end of the Bay of Isles. At any rate, the isopods had done their job well, and the skull has esthetic as well as scientific appeal.

In weather like this I find that the Old Man is very attached to your Christmas teacup—and also to my Formosa tea, of which I have, fortunately, an abundant supply. I believe that he has engulfed twelve or fifteen cupfuls today. He is as close-mouthed as ever about future plans. But by checking up on the rate of our increment of sea elephant oil, realizing that the seals themselves will all go back into the ocean before the end of the antarctic summer, and diplomatically wheedling whatever vague ideas I can get from him, I now believe that we shall set sail from South Georgia about the first of April. In the meanwhile I always remember that I am on the homestretch, even now. And just so you won't forget, let me remind you that I have a long, scraggly, curly beard of four colors (not counting the blends), and that I manage to keep myself about half clean.

The skipper and I are the only ones who have access to an honest-to-goodness lavatory, and I don't know how other members of the crew manage their ablutions, particularly below the neck and above the wrists. To their credit, I must say that most of them appear more than reasonably clean. If they were not, our cabin would soon become too rammish to endure, because the stove now roars full blast, except at night.

JANUARY 18.   For variety's sake we have had an easterly storm today, and the heaviest fall of snow I have yet seen at South Georgia. In the afternoon the wind began its old trick of boxing the compass. This made no difference to the snowing, and it was odd to see the bombardment of hard flakes swing around from east to southwest all within the course of a single hour.

A whale-catcher came into a far corner of the bay for shelter, and lay tantalizingly at anchor several miles away during a period in which it was out of the question for us to lower a boat.

JANUARY 19.   Continued snow and sleet, with a particularly vicious burst of southwest wind in latter afternoon. I got off to the *Daisy* just in time to avoid having to spend the night in my tent. That is where I keep my sleeping bag in order to be provided against such an eventuality.

Mr. da Lomba took my letters away in an oilskin bag with the hope of delivering them to the whale-catcher, but she had departed long before our boats neared her anchorage. The crews killed fifty-six sea elephants along the coast toward Prince Olaf Harbor. Of these, one was a rather thin, beach-lain bull, and the remaining fifty-five were fat cows that had recently come from sea. "Good pickings," the Old Man calls it, but all these female animals were killed in direct contravention of his agreement and, what is worse, at serious risk to the future existence of the seals at South Georgia.

It has been exceedingly cold, but I am delighted to find that I can now make plaster casts with the icy sea water, or pull an oar through the strong winds with bare, wet hands and still feel glowingly comfortable, while the West Indians and Cape Verders shiver. I infer with regret that the difference has something to do with clothing as well as with conditioning, because the undergarments from the *Daisy*'s slop chest are somewhat shoddy. They certainly do not compare with my expensive and efficient Jaegers. I find a sort of gratification in working under all sorts of difficulties, with the snow pelting down and scant shelter from the blinding wind. There is a sense of triumph in learning that you can do things in spite of malicious weather.

JANUARY 20. Today forty-three sea elephants were killed in Sea Leopard and Beckman Fiords and one more on the beach close to our anchorage. I spent several hours measuring and sketching their internal organs, examining the contents of the stomach and intestines, and writing up notes. My manuscript records are not exactly immaculate, because it was hard to wipe the blood from my hands when the thermometer stood exactly at the freezing point and a fairly brisk wind was blowing.

The Old Man himself went off with his whaleboats this morning, leaving Mr. Vincent in charge of the deck. At Beckman Fiord we found an unusually large bull sea elephant surrounded by a harem of twenty-five cows. This group seemed so contented and stable that it was left alone while the men first rounded up and slaughtered scattered seals. However, when Captain Cleveland approached within thirty or forty paces of the family cluster, the old bull charged him, humping over the sand like a gigantic inchworm. He repeated these tactics whenever any member of our crew came within a stone's throw. After a while a second bull came swimming alongshore and hauled out near by, but the aggressive and jealous beachmaster at once attacked and drove him off.

To bull sea elephants, fighting is a profession, and the only known means of settling the wife problem. The average

number in a seraglio may be about fifteen, but a truly successful gentleman gathers more. In the code of the bulls, the correct number of wives is just one more than you've got.

Each bull aspires to be beachmaster, even though no
beachmaster is ever left in peace. Other bulls, possessed with
the urge and personality to win ladies who don't care who is
their husband, are forever swimming alongshore and hauling
out in the other fellow's preserve.

The first stage of combat is bluff. Defender and challenger begin by roaring, gargling, strangling, retching, and
seeming to be nauseated (or so it sounds). Next they rear up
like a pair of rocking horses, even though they be still out of
each other's reach. Crawling closer, they bump, raking rival
necks and chests with their heavy canine teeth. When opportunity offers, they endeavor to clamp jaws and tear. Marquis
of Queensberry rules are not observed!

One of the fighters may trounce the other quickly, or
they may carry on until both collapse from exhaustion, to go
at it again when they have sufficiently revived. It is rather
slow-going for a heavyweight battle, and yet the bulls have a
rabidly furious aspect because it appears to be normal for the
arteries of the palate to rupture during the violent "gargling,"
so that the combatants are presently spewing out blood with
every breath.

More rarely, there is plenty of ripped hide, or possibly a
mangled snout, or even an eyeless socket. The captain says
that about one big bull in every hundred encountered looks as
though he had been bounced through a stone crusher.

At any rate, the object of such a battle is to win, not to
kill. When one bull retreats to sea, the other resumes control
or takes over, as the case may be, and peace reigns until the
next interloper lumbers ashore.

While our men were at their bloody work in Beckman
Fiord, I found two nests of sooty albatrosses on a cliff. One

was directly over the other, and the lower about a hundred feet above the beach. On each ledge I could see a brooding bird, asleep with its bill tucked under the wing coverts.

I managed to scale the wall to the lower eyrie, meeting my first sooty albatross at home. It was covering a downy chick, and it grunted softly and snapped its beak with a hollow "chop." When I backed away about six feet, to one end of the rocky niche, the parent snuggled down and began to draw blades of grass through its bill, watching me with a solemn, wide-eyed expression caused by its white orbital ring. Presently the youngster also took an interest in the strange intruder. It stuck its funny head out from beneath its parent, snapping its bill at me just as the old bird had done.

JANUARY 21. A mighty easterly storm raged all day. Captain Cleveland states that it is the most violent and sustained gale that he has ever experienced at South Georgia. Our only shelter to the east is offered by some of the outer islets of the bay, so we experienced a swell more disconcerting than any westerly wind can produce at this anchorage. We have been pitching and rolling about almost as severely as though we were on the open sea, but both our anchors have held. No boats, of course, could be lowered. It took me the greater part of the day to trim, scrape, and salt my complete sea leopard skin, which is now packed away in perfect condition. I have also cleaned up the entire skeleton of the same animal.

Regardless of weather, the steward showed an extra burst of pride and ambition, producing a creditable cake, rich with the beaten whites and yolks of penguin eggs. It evidently warmed the cockles of the Old Man's heart because, when he and I had adjourned to the aftercabin, he ordered two more slices of the cake and dug out two bottles of stout, which he and I finished off with our second servings.

JANUARY 22.   Today we have the proverbial calm that follows the storm. A light northeast wind is blowing this morning, and there is a fairly dense fog, but the temperature is mild.

I pulled in the Old Man's crew on a long row to Allardyce Harbor on the northwestern side of the Bay of Isles, where we killed twenty-two sea elephants. Our two other crews gathered forty-six in Sea Leopard Fiord. In the poke of one cow I found the remains of about a dozen fish, eight inches long. Hitherto I have taken only squid beaks from their stomachs.

On our trip back to the *Daisy*, the fog became increasingly thick and we were in a bit of a pickle, because the boat's compass had been left on board! The Old Man couldn't damn anybody, because he himself was boatheader of the day and the responsibility was his own. Snow began to fall, and we had before us a row of seven or eight miles with no land in sight. The gentoo penguins presently began to leap out along our course, all heading in the same direction. We judged that they were returning from sea toward the colony on the west side of Grace Glacier, and by keeping our bow pointed at an angle across their line of march we figured that we might head consistently southeast.

Then suddenly I remembered that somewhere in my jeans I had tucked a little toy compass which Marion Mumford had put into a letter recently taken from your exhaustless mail bag. I searched my many pockets, fished it out in triumph, and by such means six men, one boat, and a load of blubber, reached the brig in safety!

On the voyage, I was surprised to find that the temperature of the bay water, despite its ominous load of growlers, was only 36° F. The air was at least five degrees colder, and such a difference favors the production of fog, regardless of whether water or atmosphere has the higher temperature.

JANUARY 23.   The snow continued in spells this morning, blown before strong southeasterly winds. In the afternoon the weather fell absolutely calm.

I found several nests of the South Georgian terns on the
lateral moraines of Grace Glacier. They can hardly be called
nests because the birds lay a single egg directly on the
pebbles. During the snow squalls I found that the sitting terns
could scarcely be driven away. I knelt beside one bird and
stroked it, without causing it to fly, and also made some
photographs.

In the afternoon I went eastward with the whaleboats to
Beckman Fiord, where the mountains on one side rise sheer
to a height of 2,000 feet, ending in pinnacles and sharp ridges.
The lower parts of the cliffs have massive rock buttresses, and
between these are labyrinthine gulches down which the snow
water tumbles. The rock is rich in color, particularly in various shades of red, which is set off by spatterings of green moss
and orange-tinted lichens. We anchored our boats offshore in
this cove, because there was no suitable beach on which they
could be dragged out.

For safety, one of the boatsteerers stayed with the boats.
He also passed his time appropriately by fishing. At noon the
cook built a fire under an overhanging cliff, using West Indian
cordwood carried from the *Daisy*, and fried in fresh sea elephant blubber the fish which had just been cleaned alive.
They were delicious. Boiled sea elephant's tongue, hard bread,
and coffee in our pannikins completed the menu. Nobody had
plates, or forks or spoons. Our sheath knives and fingers conveyed the food to the mouth, after which it was taken care
of automatically!

Our picnic ground was one of the most picturesque and
impressive spots I have encountered in South Georgia. Rows
of white-breasted shags were nesting on ledges and niches

along the lower parts of the rocky wall, while higher up were several strongholds of the sooty albatross.

The day ended clear, bright and summery, the sky filled with minute, fleecy clouds, the blue sea sparkling, and all the mountains sharp and cold.

Some of the locality names that I have been using in this log require a word of explanation. They are my own geographical terms, taken from the chart I am making of the Bay of Isles. Today's trip to Beckman Fiord (commemorating the captain of the *Don Ernesto*, who was killed during our stay at Cumberland Bay) enabled me to take much needed bearings from the eastern end of the bay. My draft is now nearly completed, and when it is published you will find not only Grace Glacier but also one named for Brown University and another for Dr. Lucas.

JANUARY 24. Today has presented another rare and glorious spectacle. The sun has shone from rising to setting and the distant mountains have seemed piled up to heaven, ridge beyond ridge, and peak beyond peak, against the blue. I had a long walk over the coastal plain, taking angles and cross bearings, making pictures, and basking in the sunshine.

I have now become extremely intimate with my friends, the gentoos. As an ambassador, I seem to be persona grata.

On land or ice they appear unprepared for danger, doubtless because they have never had experience with an enemy able to harm them out of water. By this I mean that ashore they know no animal that attacks a full-grown, healthy penguin. The flesh-eating skua, which is a gull with the plumage and habits of a hawk, is an ogre in their colonies because it steals and devours penguin eggs and chicks. The gentoos fully appreciate the role of this foe. They guard their nests solicitously, rush at every skua that lands near by, and swear vainly at those that fly overhead. But, although concerned for their offspring, they have no fear for the safety of their own persons unless they become too ill to strike back.

But the ocean is different, because of the lurking sea leopard, which dotes upon penguins. Its presence gives the gentoos a fixed association regarding peril in the sea and safety ashore. Cadella often rushes at a group of penguins standing at the water's edge. If the silly birds deign to show any concern at the approach of the yapping terrier, they invariably respond not by taking to the bay but by deliberately running up the beach, heading for the nearest bank or hillside. Even after the dog has seized one by its bristly tail, and has swung it around and around merely for the fun of teasing, the dazed bird still persists in scampering away from the water. The surest way to keep gentoos ashore is to try to drive them into the sea.

Such behavior is sufficient to cast doubt upon the intelligence with which penguins are often credited. The real basis of their human resemblance lies rather in their upright carriage and inability to fly, their strong bump of curiosity, their peering nearsightedness (due to eyes adapted for clear vision under water), the readiness with which captive birds become tame and companionable, and the fact that everlastingly, even if unconsciously, they play the clown. Devoid of the convolutions in the brain and of the gray matter by which man sets so much store, they rely, like bees or ants, upon their heritage of instinctive behavior, and are certainly capable of very little thinking. Almost invariably they exercise a more than Chinese tenacity in clinging to the ways of their ancestors, even when repeated experience should have taught them better.

This afternoon I stood knee-deep in the Bay of Isles and looked down upon four gentoos playing about my feet. The water was clear and brilliant in the sunshine. The quartet dashed hither and thither, now and again almost brushing my boots. Frequently they rolled their backs above the surface, and more rarely they leapt out. I presume that they were feeding, although I could not see their prey. Whether for sport or for a more purposeful reason, they occasionally balanced in the ridge of a swell, being carried so far up the beach that they were momentarily stranded. Presently three of them walked out of the sea together, shook the water from their spiny tails, and became so immensely interested in watching me that they afterwards pursued me for a hundred yards or more along the beach.

Ordinarily the gentoos feed upon krill, or opossum shrimps, captured far from shore and often fathoms deep. They swim with the flipper-like wings, which work with amazing rapidity and power. Toward evening, we see countless penguins "porpoising" back from distant feeding areas to their regular landings. The habit is so dependable that whenever we are overtaken in our whaleboats by impenetrable afternoon fog we can rely upon the homing Johnnies to point us toward a smooth shore. Beneath the surface they swim incredibly fast—about ten yards a second, as I have determined by stopwatch timings—but periodically they leap out, giving a gasp for air, to be gone again within a twinkling.

Courting penguins give up eating and remain ashore hungry, but too much in love to realize it, for periods of at least two weeks. The lady gentoos select nesting sites, after which they await the attentions of suitors bearing gifts in the form of pebbles or ancestral bones, which make the foundation of the nests. Males and females appear exactly alike, and sex is evidently recognized by a process of trial and error. Cocks sometimes make mistakes, with dire results, by offering pebbles to other cocks. The presentation to a hen is a pantomime of bowing, accompanied by soft hissing sounds and later by either angry or joyous trumpetings, according to the outcome. The hen is the builder of the home, the cock the bearer of bricks, and acceptance of the first pebble is the symbol of success in wooing. Today a cock bird laid a pebble at my feet, a compliment properly followed by ceremonial bowing and, I hope, by mutual sentiments of high esteem. (That, I believe, is an expression to be expected from an ambassador.)

The steward has been in irons for twenty-four hours. It began last night when the Old Man went to a locker in which he thought he had a five-gallon demijohn of West India rum. The demijohn was there, but not a drop within it. I heard the now familiar ominous, rumbling, grunting sound in the Old Man's throat, but he soon recovered sufficient composure to call Mr. da Lomba. The two then talked softly for a while, and the mate went out and fetched the steward into the after-cabin. The Old Man pointed to the open locker without saying a word, and the steward's knees began to knock together. "Out with it," ordered the skipper, but the snivelling, shaking suspect denied all knowledge of what was referred to.

He was put in shackles and sent down in the steerage, the lazaret being too cold for safe incarceration here in South Georgia. Hard bread and water were ordered as his fare, and the skipper announced that he would break any man found slipping other food to the culprit.

This evening the steward sent word that he wanted to talk, so he was brought again to the aftercabin, where he confessed that he had drawn off the rum in pint and quart lots, after obtaining empty bottles from the Norwegian whalemen at Grytviken. He had received no money, but had acquired various articles in barter, including four dogskin jackets, a number of Eskilstuna knives and other Scandinavian gear, all of which have now been found in his chest and sea bags in the steerage. When he had finished talking, the Old Man ordered his bracelets unlocked and taken off, a job which fell to me. He then had him pack up his personal property, under the eye of Mr. da Lomba, and remove from the steerage to a bunk in the forecastle. Johnny, the cabin boy, was next called aft and informed that he would function as steward until further notice.

JANUARY 25. A westerly gale in the morning, which kept us all on board. This afternoon I worked ashore, although the weather was rainy, cold, and penetrating. In one of my traps, set in kelp, I captured a species of fish new to my collection.

Later, on board, I came to the inescapable conclusion that a shampoo and personal scrubbing were indicated, so I made the best job I could of it under difficult climatic circumstances, and ended by snipping and shaving off my brown, black, and yellow whiskers.

JANUARY 26. Calm, and a mixture of snow and rain.

This morning Mr. da Lomba completed an inventory of supplies and reported to the skipper that we have hard bread and flour to last at most three months longer. The news is not without its brighter side, because it means that we can't possibly stay here much later than the end of March. It would take us several weeks after that to reach the first port, which might be Cape Town.

The evening has been clear and quiet, and there is not enough motion of the ship to make me realize that we are afloat. I have been checking our slaughter through the daily entries in the *Daisy*'s log, and find that during December we killed 297 sea elephants, and, since January 1 an additional 797, or a total of 1,094 to date. If these had all been big bulls, we might now be loaded to the hatches with oil, but the larger proportion has been made up of cows, and no negligible number have been babies which could be killed only by men capable of crushing the skull of a friendly puppy.

JANUARY 27. A wet day, with frequent brief showers all morning and a heavy and prolonged rainstorm, driven before westerly winds, in the afternoon. Forty-four sea elephants were killed on Markham Point, of which only one was a bull.

Despite the weather, I walked to the king penguin rookery near Lucas Glacier and collected six adult birds which appeared to have neither eggs nor young. I skinned these out at the spot, but I have long since learned better than to spend hours and hours trimming away the thick blubbery coat of fat that lies between hide and muscle.

Instead, I now enlist the labor of skuas to undertake that part of the work. I simply sew up the slit, with the skins inside out, and toss them on the pebbles. Then down come thirty-five or forty of my pets, the skuas, which pick off every bit of fat and flesh, completing the job much more quickly and very much more thoroughly than I could. Don't you think I have grown bright? The first time I brought such "processed" penguin skins to the ship, the Old Man wondered how I had succeeded in cleaning them so thoroughly. I merely have to keep an eye on the skuas so that they will not carry their work too far and begin to nip holes in the tough hides with their bills.

The skua is cock-o'-the-roost at South Georgia. It is capable of killing and eating any bird no larger than itself, and of plundering the nests of all the others. It can drive Cadella into hiding and is just as quick to assault a man who happens to approach the neighborhood of its nest. When I go up into the grasslands behind the shore, I am never left long in doubt regarding my invasion of breeding territory. The old skuas become quite frenzied, swooping at my head so that I have to duck, and varying their attack by standing on the ground close by, wings pointed upward and heads downward, and screeching at the top of their lungs. Today, when I was banding a skua chick in the nest—he protesting lustily all the while—both parent birds struck with their wing quills the barrels of the gun that I held up as a protection against their furious stoops.

Buccaneers usually command a sentimental admiration,

and the skuas are no exception. Energy is apparent in every movement—in their restlessness, rapacity, the quantity of food they can ingest in a few moments, and in the volume and continuousness of the screams that issue from their throats. They look like small eagles much more than like relatives of the gulls. They make the most impressive picture when they stand with wings held upright, in the posture of those on ancient Norse helmets. They are then the apotheosis of defiance, and they fairly split the air with their shrill cries.

They are as close to wholly intrepid as birds can possibly be, and, when I sit beside my inside-out penguin skins, they will actually crowd against my legs in their eagerness to pick at the fat. They snip it off in small bits with the hooked tips of their beaks, swallowing the pieces one after another as rapidly as a chicken gathers strewn corn. During the process they are also quick to attack each other, springing up like gamecocks and pulling out feathers half on the ground and half in air.

When they deign to notice me at all, they glance up with bright, fearless, unsuspicious brown eyes, accept from my fingers any food I offer them, and show no concern over the loudest shouts, whistles or hand claps. Then I quite succumb to their charm and, regardless of their rapine and cannibalism, I subscribe to the principle that such supremacy of might must be deserved.

JANUARY 28. The rains of yesterday have continued coldly and steadily, with occasional step-up in intensity when northwesterly squalls lash us. Here at South Georgia I have an involuntary assurance of wearing clean underclothing, because I change it as often as I get soaked to the skin. That is an almost daily occurrence, and Johnny always washes my wet clothes.

JANUARY 29. Rain throughout the day, the weather clearing slightly at evening. Seventy sea elephants were killed in the western corner of the Bay of Isles, near the great Brunonia Glacier. All but three of these were cows that had recently hauled up from sea. The shores along which we worked had a large number of carcasses of big bulls from last year, or from some earlier period. It would be hard to date them because disintegration is extremely slow in this climate. At any rate, there is every indication that the Norwegian and British whaling companies, which were probably responsible for the slaughter, observe the law and do not take cows and pups.

JANUARY 30. A relatively clear day, but with an especially penetrating southwesterly wind. The bay is filled with a mush of fine ice that has suddenly crumbled away from the glacier snouts, and the layer of wind near the water is no doubt chilled and dampened by the melting. Whenever a cloud has passed across the face of the sun, the temperature has felt extraordinarily shivery, and it seems to me that the sun itself wears a wan and unnatural look. Nevertheless, the water and the hills have been especially beautiful in the clear air, and this morning the colors of the king penguins gleamed with a splendor not to be forgotten. I have never seen any other animals that appeared quite so chic and magnificent as these royal birds. The movements of their white breasts and golden gorgets stir me as the daffodils stirred Wordsworth.

I have been reading about the king penguins in the account of James Weddell, the British explorer who visited South Georgia in 1823. The details of his story have long been overlooked, or perhaps disbelieved, by ornithologists, but they actually comprise the best account of the bird's life history that has yet been published. Nothing in my own observations would lead me to change a line of Weddell's almost forgotten history. "In pride, these birds are perhaps not surpassed even by the peacock," he writes, quaintly and truthfully.

The principal colony of king penguins here at the Bay of

Isles is in a waste of morainic stones close to a sloping edge of the Lucas Glacier, at the point where it fans out on the plain behind the beach. It is a cold and cheerless site, constantly swept by southerly gales that howl through a rift in the mountains. Last year's young birds, now full grown but with much down attached to their feathers, are still hanging about. They resemble college boys in raccoon coats.

Our men cleaned out nearly all the eggs in December, but some of the penguins seem to have laid anew. The sitters, each of which carries an egg on its feet, stretch up to full height when men approach. Last month, after a pile of stolen eggs had been built up on the ground, some of the robbed penguins approached and slyly appropriated an egg to replace the lost one. Others gathered up stones to satisfy the "sitting" propensity. Still other birds, which did not have recourse to such cold solace, shuffled around flat-footedly after losing their egg, instead of rising at once to the ordinary walking gait, which is on the toes. It evidently takes them some time to become accustomed to an empty egg repository.

While incubating, the kings like to crowd up together, even if with no better object than to facilitate quarreling! Perhaps their squabbles are merely a method of keeping warm. At any rate, this morning I was watching a dozen birds all asleep, all snoring softly, and all swaying very gently back and forth as they snuggled their eggs. Then one bird waked up and, without provocation, jabbed its sharp bill against the back of another's neck. The latter penguin, grunting vehemently, retaliated by delivering backhand blows with one wing, without turning to face its opponent. The fracas was enough to wake up all the others, which joined in with both rapiers and broadswords until every member of the group was exchanging thrusts and whacks. The mêlée died away about as quickly as it had flared up, and within a few minutes all the sitters were snoring and swaying once more.

King penguins have an indubitably lofty and martial bearing. Their regimental characteristics, such as standing at attention, marking time with their feet, and marching in single file or in doubles, are almost too realistic to sound true. Their voice also has a military sound, for the call is a series of long-drawn bugle notes, highly musical and almost worthy of being called a tune. When delivering this the king stretches up to his full stature and points his bill skyward, after which the volley rings forth from an expanded chest. At the close of the song the head is tilted forward with a smart jerk and the bugler stands at attention for several moments.

Below is a summary of my personal and purely descriptive meteorological records for the balmy summer month of January, 1913, at the Bay of Isles,
lat. 54° 02' S., long. 37° 20' W.

Prevailing Weather Conditions	*Dates*	*Number of Days*
Clear	6, 9, 10	3
Fog	7, 16, 22	3
Rain or snow	1, 3, 13, 14, 15, 16, 18, 19, 21, 22, 23, 25, 26, 27, 28, 29, 30, 31	18
Heavy and prolonged snowstorms	1, 18, 30	3
Gales { Southwesterly	3, 9, 13, 15, 17, 19, 30	7
Westerly and northwesterly	16, 25, 27, 28	4
Easterly	14, 18, 21	3
Southeasterly	23	1
Calm	7, 22, 26, 31	4
Frost	12, 13, 14, 15, 17, 18, 19, 20, 21, 22	10

JANUARY 31. Dirty weather, though extraordinarily calm. I find myself suffering from a sore throat and a lame chest, one of the few touches of indisposition that I have experienced during seven months aboard the *Daisy*.

The Old Man called the steward aft from the forecastle and restored him to his post. No forgiveness is involved—it is merely a matter of convenience, because his services are needed to provide meals for the after-guard. At the time of the final settlement in New Bedford, the Old Man can, and doubtless will, take it out of the offender's hide for mooching. It will cost him at least the price of five gallons of rum.

FEBRUARY 1. Happily, this is not Leap Year, so February will be properly short.

After an easy day, spent partly in salting down my penguin skins and partly in completing my records and reading, I feel sufficiently recovered.

The forenoon was calm and cloudy, but an easterly gale, driving snowflakes of especially large size, began shortly after midday and increased in violence throughout the afternoon, while the wind gradually swung toward the southeast. I had a hard pull from the boat cove to the brig against the wind, and once again was drenched to the skin by salt water torn from the surface of the bay. Some of it beat through the worn creases in my oilskins, but more found its way, most incredibly, down my collar and up my sleeves.

My latest worry concerns the health of Mr. da Lomba, who has spent a large part of his time here in never-dried clothes. He is no doubt tough, but he is likely to remain permanently in South Georgia unless the Old Man puts a stop to his constant and undue exposure. Ever since we arrived, Mr. da Lomba has had to work in leaky boots, because there are no others in the *Daisy*'s slop chest to fit his size 13 feet. The skipper, however, should have provided against this, because the mate has been his right-hand man on many a voyage

before. In spite of his wiriness and vigor, he has a small chest
and, during our stay in Cumberland Bay, he had an attack of
bronchitis that might have finished him off but for the minis-
trations of the German physician.

It is now long after dark and two of our whaleboats, containing twelve men, are still away in the wild night. It is such
a night that "mine enemy's dog, though he had bit me, should
have stood . . . against my fire."

FEBRUARY 2.   Last night was the most anxious one we
have spent since the beginning of our voyage. There was nothing we could do for our missing crews except to hang extra
lanterns in the rigging. Even that was an empty gesture, because we knew that the men were either ashore somewhere or
else drowned. The storm continued in full force. Coming from
the east, or the direction of the open ocean, it had kicked up a
sea of maximum size. I sat up with the Old Man, who was
greatly agitated, and worried over the probability that there
was no compass under the thwart of either whaleboat. Being
unable to do anything else, I read the last five cantos of the
Paradiso while the infernal east wind howled overhead.
Finally I turned in and immediately fell asleep, but the Old
Man didn't go to bed at all. About midnight, according to the
anchor watch, the snow ceased, and within an hour the wind
died away.

Calm, clear daylight broke about three o'clock. The westward shores soon brightened, but no boats could be discerned.
By five o'clock the whole bay was brilliant under an almost
cloudless sky, the atmosphere transparent, the water calm except for the heavy easterly ground swell. I went to the mainmasthead, and scrutinized all the miles of the long coast
through my glasses, but made no sign of a boat. Below, everyone was nervously agaze toward the northwest, from where
the lost comrades should appear.

The captain decided not to leave the ship to look for the

missing crews, but to have all hands watch for a signal fire. So I went ashore in the dory about eight o'clock, and climbed to the summit of the promontory above my tent. Then I sat down on a hummock, rested my elbows on my knees, and minutely swept the shore of the whole west bay through field glasses. On a distant rocky point beyond Grace Glacier, I saw indistinctly a little group of penguins, but by straining my eyes I transmuted them into men. I stood up against the skyline, waved my oilskin jacket for several minutes, and then ran to the east point and signaled the brig for a whaleboat. Instead of understanding what I wanted, which should have been perfectly clear, the captain sent in a boat with orders to come right back to him.

But we finally got started, the Old Man in the stern, I at after oar. We went through a dangerous hole in the rocks and were almost swamped by a roller, but eventually we safely passed a field of drift ice and spied the fire of the wrecked crews. We eagerly counted the men, when we had come near enough, and found all twelve and Cadella. So nobody was lost. We took the sad and bedraggled boys into our whaleboat with considerable difficulty through nasty surf, leaving there two damaged boats on the shingle. The poor fellows were almost dead from their cold wettings and fatigue, and there was no comfort for eighteen men in a craft built for six. Ten of them manned the five oars and the rest of us huddled wherever we could.

Nobody said a word on the way home except Mr. da Lomba, who told how the boats had started off laden, after killing eighty-nine sea elephants and leaving two boatloads of blubber buried. The sea proved too much for Mr. Almeida's crew, so the boats ran before the wind to the distant corner of the bay. A collision caused by a wave turned what might have been a successful landing into a wreck. Both boats had to cut their anchor warps, and Mr. da Lomba and Mr. Almeida, with

hands greasy from throwing out blubber, both slashed themselves badly in the palms. The crews, with the exception of a
man or two, turned limp in the crisis from cold, exhaustion,
discouragement, and fear. As a result, both boats were stove,
the guns, lances, oars, and all other gear were swept into the
sea, and twelve men and the dog had to swim and wade
through floating ice to get ashore. Somebody had hung onto
the lantern keg with its supply of sulphur matches, and subsequently they made a fire of hard bread, scraps of blubber, and
a splintered plank from the bottom of a whaleboat. After a
long, long night of unalleviated misery, they saw me wave
from the hilltop and waited as patiently as possible for our
arrival at ten o'clock.

When the men had changed clothes and eaten aboard the
Daisy, Mr. da Lomba insisted upon taking his own crew and
Mr. Almeida's, with several replacements, right back to
Allardyce Harbor to recover the buried blubber, and the Old
Man has foolishly allowed him to do so. In my opinion,
all these men should have been tucked into their berths
for the day and the following night. Several of them look
fagged out, and one, the Dominican called William Elwin
or William Stephens, is in an alarming condition. The Old
Man is now sighing for his pilfered rum, which he says that
William needs. However, I never knew him to dish out any
while he still had it!

The weather has been our salvation—mild, bright and
relatively warm until late afternoon. Toward evening the
wind began again to blow freshly from the east. It is now half
past seven o'clock, and three boats are nearing the *Daisy*, the
first and third mates' laden down with the blubber that had
been cached ashore, and Mr. Vincent's dragging the two
whaleboats that had been patched with sailcloth and towed,
nearly awash, all the way from near Brunonia Glacier. We
now have one good boat, one in fair condition, one very much

battered, and two that look quite thoroughly wrecked. With the worst of the misfortune behind us, the Old Man, the cooper, the officers, and the boatsteerers are all ready to go to work on deck to patch up their craft. A whaleboat seems capable of taking any amount of rebuilding, so long as she has not become thoroughly hogged or "back-broke."

Altogether the past twenty-four hours have been hectic and depressing. I came within an ace of making myself one of Mr. da Lomba's crew yesterday morning because he told me that he had found another sooty albatross in an accessible part of the Allardyce Harbor cliffs.

Aside from the damage to boats, outfit, and men, the blubber of about forty-five sea elephants was jettisoned. This seems to tear the Old Man's heart more than any other aspect of the catastrophe. For my own part, I am more inclined to mourn the futile loss of forty-five of these wonderful animals than I am to weep over the skipper's spilled oil at 50¢ a gallon. His point of view is probably not out of harmony with his calling, however. Roderick, our sprightly Dominican tailor, the only man in the crew who has a repertory of blubbery ballads, sings one that goes in part like this:

> The fust mate's boat was the fust boat away—
> The whale guv a sweep with his tail
> (And he swang it like a flail.)
> Then daown went the boat with our five Brave Boys,
> Never to rise no more, Brave Boys,
> Never to rise no more.

> When the Old Man heerd of the loss of the whale,
> Quite loudly then he swore
> (For it grieved his soul full sore.)
> When he heerd of the loss of his five Brave Boys,
> He said he'd ship some more Brave Boys,
> He said he'd ship some more.

FEBRUARY 3.   Continuing easterly winds and a chilling mist. A heavy surf breaks on the beach. It is doubtful whether a boat could be safely lowered, but at any rate the crew is divided into two groups, one busy at mincing and boiling blubber, the other devoting the day to boat carpentry.

Frank, the boatsteerer, who was not on yesterday's fiasco, has collapsed again and has gone gleety and feverish. The Old Man's medicine appeared to pull him up for a while, though he has not been fit for any heavy duty.

FEBRUARY 4.   A westerly gale has kicked up a short sea that batters against the big swell still rolling in from the east. It has been sunny, but hazy, all day. The whaleboats have been partly replanked, and, as the fresh paint goes on, they begin to look almost new again.

FEBRUARY 5.   Yesterday's strong westerly winds continued through the morning but fell away later, and died down to a comfortable breeze before nightfall.

After dinner I obtained the Old Man's rather reluctant permission to lower the *Grace Emeline*. It was somewhat tricky and exciting getting launched, but quite comfortable as soon as I had swung away from the *Daisy's* hull. I went bouncing over the rollers, surfboarded through the rocky entrance of the landing cove, and beached the dory without difficulty.

Then I visited the rookeries of both the king and the Johnny penguins, and walked up, for the first time, the crown of Lucas Glacier. This is quite different in surface structure from Grace Glacier, which faces my tent across the water. Grace Glacier is so rugged with séracs that no one could possibly cross it on foot. The rounded top of Lucas Glacier is prevailingly smooth, although much seamed with crevasses and drilled by wells, into which water melted out by the sun pours down through depths of ice to the glacier bed.

I watched with utmost caution for snow-covered holes

but found none. Everywhere the ice seemed to be solid and glassy except for thin patches of half-melted granular snow. The lateral moraines are vast dump heaps of broken stone and silt, long breastworks of debris piled evenly, and boulders balanced precariously on the scratched bedrock of the hills. The murmur of subterranean streams can be heard everywhere.

As I proceeded southward and upward on this vast smooth causeway, which seemed to lead toward a valley or pass in the main mountain range, the bottomless funnels in the ice became more numerous and terrifying. When I finally slipped on a bit of the wet and trickly surface, and began to slide down the barely perceptible slope in the direction of one of the unfathomable abysses, I realized that it was time to stop traversing such terrain alone. I have no hankering to melt out of the seaward end of this glacier a hundred years hence, even though that would offer the only way for me to preserve my youthful freshness and ruddy complexion for so great a length of time!

I long for the opportunity to cross South Georgia to the still wilder and more antarctic southerly coast. It would be quite safe to undertake such a trip if three men with sufficient rope were to travel together. The difficulty, of course, is to yank anybody away from the endless murder of sea elephants. Once in a while I have the company of the cooper or of Mr. da Lomba for an hour or two, but it is hopeless to try to organize a party for an expedition.

FEBRUARY 6. Calm all day. All the whaleboats but one are back in service. It is really phenomenal to see how self-sufficient a whaleship can be, even under the most trying conditions, and to realize the competence and ability represented in this tattered horde of unlettered, raffish, and abused men.

I have made an excellent photograph of the site of my tent, which I call Camp Chionis (the generic name of the

sheathbill). The picture also shows the landing cove with the
Grace Emeline on the beach, and the mighty ridges near
Beckman Fiord at the eastern end of the Bay of Isles.

Collecting scientific specimens with a gun is no amusement, like shooting quail. It is the bird, not the sport, that you
are after and you pot him squatting or asleep if the chance
offers. Nevertheless, I have found a means of combining duty
with the gratification of my sporting instinct. Late every
afternoon the skuas and giant fulmars glide high in the air
across the flat tussocky land below my tent. I need a series of
each of these species, so I have decided to collect them only
with a .22-calibre rifle, and only on the wing! My luck this
afternoon was better than I had anticipated, because I
brought down two fulmars and five skuas, each of which
dropped cold dead, and without a single splash of blood upon
its feathers.

FEBRUARY 7.   Calm all day, with more or less fog.
Seventy-one sea elephants were killed in Allardyce Harbor.
I have been busy preparing fresh tissues of the seals for subsequent histological study, running pieces of liver, pancreas,
kidney, and other glands and viscera through mercuric chlo-
ride, glacial acetic acid, and alcohols of increasing strength.
The technique is necessary for the preparation of stained
microscopic sections.

Today the skipper, with the help of the cooper and several others, repaired the remaining damaged boat on the
beach of the landing cove. He still allows his Jeremiad
lamentations about all his recent ill fortune to break out once
or twice a day. I have been trying to worm out some information about his plans after leaving South Georgia, but he always ducks out from under by saying that he hasn't yet been
able to decide on the next step. There is no use getting hot
under the collar about it, because he is built that way and can
no more help his taciturnity than his gray hair. I don't know

just how I arrive at approximate conclusions after beating my head as tactfully as possible against his stone wall. Nevertheless, I am inclined more and more to the opinion that we shall be in the West Indies not later than May.

This evening I have had a strong attack of homesickness. I think of a big, comfortable chair and a fireplace, and of our familiar possessions, and long for an evening together with no thought of a five o'clock breakfast. Here there is nothing that can properly be called an evening, because it is usually after eight o'clock when supper is finished by the first table of wind-burned, weary men, and the only way to escape the dim, cramped cabin is to crawl into one's berth and fall asleep.

FEBRUARY 8. Rainy all day, made worse by westerly winds in late afternoon. These began in the form of violent gusts and then settled down to a steady screamer, which soon had the whole bay boiling. Once again two of our boats were caught on the far side of the Allardyce Harbor, but this time we were less worried because it was improbable that they could have started back before the storm struck. At any rate, the poor devils will have to be out in the wind all night.

FEBRUARY 9. Strong variable winds, with continued rain, but the bay was navigable and our boats returned in the forenoon, bringing the blubber of forty-nine sea elephants. The officers told me that many of the animals were killed on a hill over a cliff on the northern shore of Allardyce Harbor. After the carcasses were flensed, the blanket-pieces were tossed to the beach below. Mr. da Lomba says that two cows flopped over this same cliff in attempting to escape from the sealers. He estimated the drop as "mast high," or about 125 feet. One of the cows broke her neck and never budged again after hitting the beach, but he declares that the other bounced like a rubber hot-water bottle and scrambled right ahead into the sea.

By this time you know that in the lingo of sealers the off-

spring of bull and cow sea elephants are "pups." The latter
had all been born before the *Daisy* reached South Georgia. In
December we found great numbers of them here at the Bay of
Isles, mostly lying on their sides or backs, and often piled one
upon another like so many sausages. It was rather hard to
wake them up enough to persuade them to open their mouths
and look fierce. Even this gesture was merely congenital bluff,
for I found that most of them had no objection to being
patted and tickled. Among themselves, though, they show
contentious dispositions, and very early in life they begin
their sparring practice for the bouts without which no old
beachmaster can get along.

With older animals one cannot afford to take liberties.
They have extensible necks and are very quick. Even the cows
have been known to kill men. On the other hand, if you let
them alone there is little to worry about.

On a level surface the adult sea elephants can bob along
faster than a man can walk. They arch the spine and jerk forward the side flippers so rapidly that the resulting gait might
almost be called a gallop. It is comical to see a fat bull bounce
ahead at full speed, with his head jerking up and down and his
ponderous sides quaking until he splashes into the bay.

In the water sea elephants remain submerged most of
the time, progressing by wide sculling sweeps of the hind flippers. With unbelievable ease their huge spindle-shaped bodies
pierce thickets of giant kelp that would slow up or stop a ship.

Sleeping seems to be the principal business of sea elephants during the antarctic summer months. The bulls wake
up to fight, but the others slumber nine tenths of the time.
Some of them doze in their baths, lying at the surface of coves
and ponds with their backs just awash. More of them snooze
ashore, usually lying belly up. For long periods they refrain
from breathing by keeping the nostrils tightly closed, just as
though they were under water. Still more often they make use

of one nostril only, spreading and closing it with each breath while the other remains shut tight.

A sea elephant's slumber suggests either nightmares or a guilty conscience. The inspirations are irregular gasps, the expirations tremulous wheezes. The whole body shakes violently from time to time and the fore flippers are forever pawing about, now scratching the sides, now the head, now crossed over the breast so that one hand may be scratched by the nails of the other. The hind flippers are now and then spread fanlike, brandished in the air, or rubbed and clasped together. Whether awake or asleep, the brutes are fond of flinging sand or mud over themselves. All this activity often goes on while they are in such total oblivion that it is difficult to arouse them even by kicking their fat ribs.

If I approach a wide-awake bull too closely, it will rear up on the fore flippers, thrash its hinder parts about, contract its trunk-like snout into tight bulging folds, open its pink mouth to show the great canines, and finally utter its rather anticlimactical vocal expression of displeasure or warning. The process appears painful, because the first step is a period of nearly noiseless choking. Then the rush of breath seems to squeeze out of the windpipe, the soft palate vibrates violently and forth comes the strangled bellow.

Mammals lack our human "brains," including our inhibitions and self-control. But they share a large proportion of our emotional nature, as revealed by their tantrums. When a bull sea elephant chooses to regard itself as really annoyed, it gives way to uncontrolled passion, flounces and squirms about like a child kicking the floor, bites the ground, and finally runs amuck and snaps at every living or inanimate object within reach.

I was ashore for an hour or more near the anchorage, where the men killed two exceedingly large bull sea elephants.

Between 10:45 and 11 o'clock this morning I had an opportunity to observe the most remarkable shift of wind that I have ever seen. Without any noticeable change in velocity, it swung from south of east through north to a little north of west, or half way round the compass within those fifteen minutes.

I have discarded my first suit of oilskins, which were no longer impervious to driving rain, and I have learned a useful trick from the Old Man about treatment of the trousers. This is to sew an extra piece of sailcloth over the seat, and to give it a coat of linseed oil to waterproof both the canvas and the stitching. I shall now have more hope of keeping a dry bottom, even when the boat thwarts are running water.

Cadella has become an inseparable member of Mr. da Lomba's crew. The men say that she killed seven mice at Allardyce Harbor but, unfortunately, they did not bring me the specimens. I take it for granted that they were the young of the ordinary introduced brown rat, which has been acclimated here for a century. The boats brought me a real treasure, however, in the form of the only downy duckling of the South Georgian teal that I have been able to add to my collection. It is probably the first specimen of its kind ever discovered.

FEBRUARY 10.   Another day of very limited activity because of the weather. I went ashore in a whaleboat this afternoon, but it was so exceedingly stormy that I could do little that was useful. Stinging granules of snow were being driven down from the mountains before southwesterly winds, and from time to time there was a little rain as well. We came off to the brig without labor, merely bracing our oars apeak and square to the wind so that we flew along like a silent launch.

FEBRUARY 11.   Strong westerly and southwesterly winds, and snow falling during most of the day. The temperature has remained four or five degrees below the freezing point.

FEBRUARY 12.   Extremely foggy all day, and raining almost continuously. The morning was calm but an easterly wind arose in afternoon, increasing in strength into the night.

FEBRUARY 13.   Cold and dark under a low canopy of dense clouds. Westerly and southwesterly winds and frequent snow squalls all day.

I went to Albatross Island in a whaleboat and had a profitable experience merely squatting and watching the nesting habits and some of the belated courtship antics of the wandering albatrosses. The snow beat a tattoo on me most of the time, but I was well protected. The beastly weather is growing monotonous, nevertheless. I had brought with me some jars of fixing reagents, and I collected a graded series of albatross embryos for subsequent sectioning and staining. It is unlikely that anyone has yet studied their early stages.

The men killed a small female sea leopard on the beach, of which I have trimmed out the skull, which will be further cleaned up by the isopods in one of my fishtraps. The blubber of sea leopards is relatively thin, although it is said to yield a particularly fine grade of oil. Our men, however, toss it in with the sea elephant blubber, making no distinction.

FEBRUARY 14.   I dreamed this morning of telling you that St. Valentine's Day always seems close to spring. Then suddenly I heard the Old Man's voice announcing five o'clock and breakfast time. My valentines from your mail bag were very cheerful, and I suspect that I know the source not only of yours but of two others. I also had a special local valentine from you this afternoon in the form of a rainbow that arched the whole eastern end of the Bay of Isles.

This evening the rain and snow, which have given us a visitation of seven continuous days, have ceased enough to allow us a casual glimpse of the bright half moon hanging over silvery mountains beyond Allardyce Harbor.

Today we killed our biggest sea elephant of the season. I suspect that some of the bulls of largest size are just beginning to come ashore from their winter wanderings. I am eager to make photographs of these gigantic males before the men slay them, but recently the weather has made photography impracticable.

FEBRUARY 15.   Quiet and foggy during the morning, the weather lifting just before noon. Light and pleasant north by west winds, and a clear moonlit evening.

A great deal of ice, probably from the disintegration of Brunonia Glacier, has drifted into our section of the bay. It travels back and forth in floes with the wind and the tide. The pieces mostly range in size from tiny particles to cakes as large as a boat, but now and then they include a small berg with a tonnage as great as that of our ship. The worn surface of old ice is covered with regular concave facets about an inch in diameter, so that the rounded or oval pieces look like huge berries carved from rock crystal. Some of the growlers are big enough to be a hazard to the anchored brig. This morning we sent down a boat to attach an ice anchor and to tow off one that was bearing toward our bow. It proved very difficult to warp it from its course, but ten or twelve of us aided by pushing against it from deck with a spare whaleboat mast and other poles, and it finally grazed past us without ripping off any copper sheathing.

FEBRUARY 16.   Calm. A vast amount of ice in the bay. The moving floes make a continual soft crackling noise that sounds like the patter of large drops of rain. The Old Man is grateful that a gale is not blowing because he believes that this massed ice might easily grind into the *Daisy*'s planks.

FEBRUARY 17.   Clear and fair, as it ought to be on this greatest of anniversaries. Mare's tails and shattered cumulus clouds fleck the sky. The westerly breeze is gentle, though a heaving swell is dashing to spray on the rocks. The sun is warm and unusually bright. The Old Man has appeared on deck in a straw hat, which looks extremely quaint against the background of glaciers and perpetual snow. The tussock grass seems a brighter green, the water a richer blue. It is a calm, deep-breathing day. The pipits are singing like skylarks, but I am happier than either the pipits or the sunshine. I have been trying to extract a faint odor of orange blossoms or lilies of the valley from the fragment of your bouquet taken from the letter bag. There is not much of either now, but what a beautiful bouquet it was a year ago today! You are unbelievably thoughtful, my love, and Nature is in sympathy, for this is surely the most inexpressibly beautiful day that South Georgia has ever seen.

I have read your letter for today, only to rediscover the miracle that 6,000 miles interpose no barrier to the semaphore that flashes in both directions from heart to heart.

I worked all morning in the tent, revelling in and drunk with my own thoughts. I'm coming home soon. Time is rushing now; I hardly know where the days have gone when evening comes. My work is all mine, too, for I find it harder and harder to get from the captain any of the assistance specified in the agreement.

At noon I had an unforgettable and somewhat queer experience for a wedding anniversary. From the platform in front of my tent I saw an unusually big bull sea elephant come out of the cove and work his way up among the tussock hummocks. "Ha ha!" thought I, "here's my chance to demand that the Old Man give me help in roughing out the whole skeleton of a big one I've just killed for him!"

I had left my rifle aboard the brig. However, as soon as the lazy beast had found a satisfactory berth and had fallen asleep, I descended with a camera and a seal lance. Making ready for a head-on snapshot, I whistled to awaken him. The effect was greater than I had bargained for. The brute opened its eyes casually enough, but instantly rolled over with a snort and bounced toward me so rapidly that I had barely time to avoid the charge. I dodged aside, but he continued humpety-bump after me, with homicide in his eye.

Setting the camera on a hummock, I came back with the lance, and attacked as soon as the sea elephant had pulled into the clear on the upper beach, where I had room for action. Then began the nimblest five minutes of fighting that have ever fallen to me. Although ponderous, my adversary was quick as well. Snorting and bellowing, he reared up on his after-belly, stretching three feet above my head, and then hurled forward in an effort to crush me to a pulp. I staged a Fabian offensive—always retreating—but also impaled him with good Arthurian thrusts until he collapsed in a pond of his own blood and expired, ten feet from the water's edge.

As for me, I fared slightly better, because I collapsed only to catch my breath. Then I rowed out to the brig to change my wet, cold, and clammy underwear.

The skipper came ashore with the mate and two boat-steerers to take the blubber. He was loud in his praise when he saw the magnificent size of the kill, but the old robber said that nobody had time to work on the skeleton with me at present, because it would take a crew of six all day. I told him that the museum wasn't paying him just for my bed and found, but he said that we'd get plenty of skeletons later.

February 18.   Stormbound again all day by a south-westerly gale. For a time an attempt was made to continue mincing and boiling blubber on deck, but it finally had to be given up because of the wind, the cold and the heavy snow. Great flocks of birds were around the stern of the brig, as is usual in this kind of weather. It is only under such circumstances that I see two or more species of gray-headed albatrosses, an abundance of snow petrels and antarctic fulmars, and several other exciting kinds of sea birds of the far south.

In the afternoon I took a long nap, which is a rare luxury here.

FEBRUARY 19.   Very high westerly winds and stinging snow flurries. The boats went forth, but had great difficulty in making landings and found only two sea elephants ashore.

FEBRUARY 20.   Stormy west winds and much rain. From late afternoon until early evening there was an extraordinarily soaking mist, which seemed to wet clothing more rapidly than rain. By eight in the evening this had disappeared, the mountains became visible at long range, and the sky was full of glowing translucent windows, which showed where the clouds were thinnest beneath the full moon.

I packed away in a cask a good series of sea elephant skulls that I have been preparing for several weeks past. They comprise both males and females, and show the stages of growth from the youngest pups we have found up to the largest bulls.

FEBRUARY 21.   Weathercock gales, swinging back and forth between northwest and southwest, but never letting up except for a short lull at noon. During most of the morning it rained with the force of a thunder squall at home. I managed to get ashore because Victor, the senior boatsteerer, who is also the best oarsman and probably the strongest individual on the *Daisy*, manned the second pair of oars. The wind blew harder than any I have ever rowed through before.

This evening I have prepared in the cabin four mollymauks that I had already skinned out in my tent. This means a ten o'clock bedtime hour, which is scandalously late for Bay of Isles.

FEBRUARY 23.   A wintry morning, the land and ship being rimy with frozen snow, which is falling in the form of hard globules about the size of BB-shot. High westerly and southwesterly winds blew all day, but not so hard as to prevent me from going ashore.

I have been trying to learn the range of the sea elephants' food. Only once have I found fish in a stomach. Most other freshly killed examples have contained only the horny beaks of squids, remaining long after digestion of the soft parts. Every stomach opened, however, has revealed mawworms. We call these unattractive creatures parasites, which no doubt they are. At the same time such inhabitants are absolutely normal in nearly all mammals and, under ordinary circumstances, they do their hosts no harm. Every blackfish head that I dissected in the West Indies last summer had clusters of roundworms in the ear passages. Most whales also harbor these, as well as barnacles, small crustaceans called whale lice and other infesting organisms, inside and out. Only man shudders at the thought of "personal vermin," and it is likely that most men, even of the first families, have done so for only the past few generations.

FEBRUARY 24.   Fair, with light southerly winds.

Everybody was routed out for breakfast at 4:30 A.M., whereupon the Old Man announced that the *Daisy* would move her berth if favorable wind and weather held. I therefore went ashore immediately and worked hard at breaking camp and getting all my equipment and specimens off to the brig.

The sunlight seemed to penetrate into the quiet depths of the water more than usual today. Looking down from my dory into the pools of the kelp, I could see millions of tiny wraithlike crustaceans and other organisms to an extent that I have never previously beheld them.

At four o'clock in the afternoon, we weighed anchor and we are now at sea, running before a fair offshore wind toward Possession Bay. The shift will bring us closer to the whaling stations, which is a matter of avid interest to me because this

morning we saw on the horizon a large steamer bound toward
Cumberland Bay. I feel certain that she has letters for me,
and I want to get as close to them as possible.

When we passed the easternmost islets of the Bay of
Isles, I took final bearings and finished the sketch which I
hope will lead to a respectable chart.

FEBRUARY 25.   Easterly winds; fog and snow during the
morning.

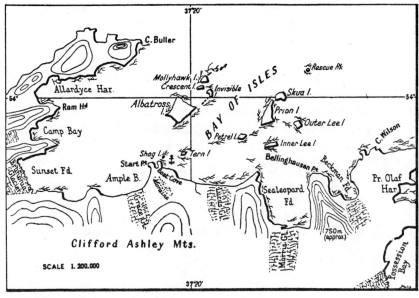

THE BAY OF ISLES

In 1914, the author's map was published in *Petermann's Mit-
teilungen,* thereafter serving as the international hydrographic
chart until the issue of the British Discovery survey in 1931.

I had the wheel for a watch, while we beat eastward past
the mouth of Prince Olaf Harbor. Inside, we saw a whaling
station of which we had no previous knowledge. We entered
Possession Bay where, 138 years ago, Captain James Cook

took possession of South Georgia, and in early afternoon we dropped anchor not far from a sandy spit that divides the bay into outer and inner harbors. Beyond that, to the south, a large and very steep glacier reaches the shore.

The whaleboats immediately set off in search of sea elephants, though with no great success. I landed in the *Grace Emeline* on the western side of Possession Bay, and found a spot at the base of a cliff where a natural wall of rock nearly encircles a small patch of green meadow. The site offers more shelter from the wind than any place I have yet found in South Georgia, and tomorrow I shall pitch my tent there.

As I look along both shores of this wild fiord, which has a paucity of good landings, I infer that my beach and meadow probably mark the very spot at which man first set foot on South Georgia. I have with me a typed translation of the Swedish record kept by Anders Sparrman, who accompanied James Cook in the *Resolution*. He wrote:

> "On the 17th [January, 1775] I went ashore with the Captain, Mr. Forster and a cadet. . . . With a salvo of musket fire and the hoisting of the flag, the territory was taken possession of for his Britannic Majesty, in whose honor this island (31 leagues long, 10 wide, and of less value than the least cottage in England) was named Georgia, and the bay was called Possession Bay."

In my opinion, these discoverers were none too complimentary to our great and good friend, George III, who gave us Yankees our Fourth of July!

FEBRUARY 26. Well, I have not pitched my tent, after all. Furious southerly gales raged all day, except for one short and mystifying slatch in the forenoon. The sun shone brightly, but the wind, sweeping down from ice-covered mountains close at hand, was penetratingly cold. Our whaleboats had difficulty in making landings because of the dangerous surf. The men killed seventeen sea elephants, most of which were small or thin.

Possession Bay seems extraordinarily cheerless and desolate. It wholly lacks the feeling of spaciousness that we had at the Bay of Isles. From our anchorage we can look toward the sea only through a narrow gap between headlands. In every other direction the icy mountains shut off our view. There is little green to strike the eye, and animal life seems to be scanty.

FEBRUARY 27. My tent is ensconced, well stayed and remarkably well sheltered. The enclosure is quite elfin, for it was created in the primordial world to fit a tent of 1913. You pass through a narrow gate in a natural monolithic wall, enter a green snuggery shut off from the wind, and there stands my shore base in just enough "lawn" to make a front yard. The bordering "garden," along the foot of the cliff and under a sprinkler of dripping icicles, includes two plants that I have not previously found at South Georgia. One is a buttercup, of the same genus as ours at home, the other a *Callitriche* closely resembling our water starwort. I have also a lush bed of the little rosaceous herb with a red flowering head, which Captain Cook called wild burnet and which his distinguished successor, Captain Cleveland, knows as diddle-dee. It is supposed to be good medicine for whatever you've got! Just make a tea of it, and all will be well.

To my great surprise, I find also that earthworms inhabit the soil of my small private bog. I discovered them while digging a hole to plant a tent pole.

The beach here is much like that at the Bay of Isles, except that it is sandier and more shelving. The same stony, wind-swept plains stretch from high-water mark to the hills. Tussock grass is scanty on this western side of the bay. A few hummocks of it grow on the rocks, and many of the stalks have been bitten off close to the ground by the rats, which have a much-burrowed stronghold here. Every hilltop near the water is strewn with limpet shells, the spoil of abundant and noisy kelp gulls.

South Georgia boasts only nineteen kinds of vascular plants (flowering plants plus ferns), and I now have herbarium specimens of most of them. There are, of course, many species of mosses, lichens, and hepatics, and I have added an orange toadstool never previously reported. But there is no bush or shrub or other woody vegetation, or, as the great discoverer put it, "not wood enough to make a toothpick." The most conspicuous of all the plants is the famous subantarctic tussock grass, which forms a pure stand of wonderful but unused pasture, and builds up dense hummocks six feet tall.

In a wet meadow, and close beside a brook which has slope enough to make a pleasant gurgling sound, I have found eight steel drums of gasoline. It now turns out that these were left here four years ago by Captain Cleveland, after he and his officers had made a vain effort to utilize a motor that had been fitted at considerable expense into a whaleboat. It was a happy thought, but as an innovation to sea elephant hunting it proved a dismal failure.

These drums of gasoline must have been discovered by the Norwegian and British sealers who periodically scour the coast of South Georgia. Such is the code among sailors, however, that they have regarded the fuel throughout these four long years as property temporarily cached by its owner, and therefore not to be disturbed. I am now glad to have the opportunity of using some of this gasoline for washing the skins of such extremely fat and oily specimens as penguins and petrels. The bulk of it, however, will be left here by the Old Man to lie through further antarctic winters.

This morning the southwest wind was so cold and biting that not a man on board could hold his face against it for more than a few minutes at a time. It moderated toward noon and then increased again, but also shifted in direction and became warmer. By night nearly level raindrops were being blown before it.

A week or two ago I dreamt that I discovered a bank full of holes in grassy soil, out of which I dug specimens of diving petrels, which are one of the rare desiderata of my voyage. The American Museum of Natural History has, for example, only one imperfect specimen of this group of birds. Today I walked up a deep valley on the eastern side of Possession Bay, and after tramping for about two miles over a surface of shattered stone, varied here and there with scanty tussock grass and saturated moss, I came to a gentle hillock, greener than the rest of the terrain, and noticed many small burrows on its slopes. My dream picture at once flashed back to me, and, strange as it may seem, within the next two minutes I had dug out the first diving petrel ever to come into my hands. It was a fledgling youngster with patches of gray down still clinging to the plumage of its head and breast. It had been sitting near the entrance of one of the burrows, as though anticipating the early date of its first flight to sea. Tomorrow, or at first opportunity, I am going back to the site with a pick and a basket, in order to see whether I can exploit my joyous discovery and collect a series of diving petrels, including examples of the adults.

FEBRUARY 28.   The Old Man is already becoming disgruntled with the hunting prospects in Possession Bay. Forty-three sea elephants were slain today, but most of them were either small or disgustingly thin. The latter are chiefly bulls that have lain ashore for weeks, or even months, during the rutting season, without returning to the sea to feed. They therefore look skinny and flabby, the hide hanging in lappets from the snout, the flews, and the wall-sided head, while the blubber yield, as the skipper grumbles, makes it hardly worth the labor of killing and flensing. Most of them are unsightly beasts in other ways also, because they are shedding their hair and have a particularly sleazy and moth-eaten look. Some of these bulls are still surrounded in their wallows by five or six cows, but their generally woebegone appearance indicates that the jolly season has passed, and that they would be wise to go back to their winter migration in the nourishing ocean before the goblins get 'em.

MARCH 1.   May this be the final month at South Georgia!

Screeching southerly winds; raw, dark and blustery; snow in frequent spells all day. I have turned to fishing, but the game here seems to be less abundant than in the Bay of Isles. At any rate, it does not bite as well, although I have found two or three small forms of "dragons" not previously captured. I have also obtained more diving petrels in my dream valley, but only three of them are adult birds. I likewise saved the head of a bull sea elephant that measured more than twenty feet in length, and I have preserved it entire in a barrel of formalin.

Tomorrow, if the weather is favorable, I may at last be able to post my letters, because we are scheduled to make a trip by whaleboat to the station in Prince Olaf Harbor. I dare not hope that a letter from you has already been delivered there.

MARCH 2.   At six o'clock of a bright morning we started out before light southwesterly winds in two whaleboats. I sat on the stern cuddy, beside the Old Man who held the tiller, and he waxed extraordinarily confiding while we skimmed along. He told me—in strictest confidence, because that is the only way he can disclose anything—that he expects to leave South Georgia within two or three weeks and to resume sperm whaling on the way toward the West Indies. He thinks that we can count on reaching either Barbados or Dominica early in May.

We were warmly welcomed by the skippers at Prince
Olaf Harbor, where the plant is called The Southern Whaling
and Sealing Company of North Shields, a British concern.
The Old Man and I were entertained at dinner in the fine dining saloon of the steamship *Restitution* by four captains from
as many vessels. Our officers and other men were equally well
treated by the steamer's crew.

It is not cheerful to compare our miserable business
on the *Daisy*, murdering pup sea elephants and living on
penguins and skilly, with the mode of life of these South
Georgian Britishers and Scandinavians, who do things on
a grand scale, have proud, upstanding men for crews, and
live in a civilized or almost luxurious manner even though
they are in a forgotten corner of the world. At times like
this it makes my gorge rise to think of our penny-pinching
skipper, who is willing to exist like a coolie. The contrast
between his daily fare on the *Daisy* and in his rather distinguished white home on Pleasant Street, where the flag
flies from a mast in the yard, is appalling. I suppose his
point of view at sea must be attributed to the hard life which
he began as a twelve-year-old cabin boy. Another element
is that our old Yankee whaling has long since passed its day
of glory, and the few present participants represent anach-
ronisms of the old calling.

At least the Old Man had the grace to take the opportunity of replenishing his stock from supplies at the Prince Olaf
whaling station. The agents sold him whatever he wanted, not
from preference but out of hospitality. We have laden the two
whaleboats with flour, rice, potatoes, butter, and several
other commodities. It is weeks since I had tasted potatoes until today's dinner.

From the big steamer where we dined as guests of Captain Anderson, a cheerful red-headed Englishman named
Captain Rochester took me over to his four-masted barken-

tine, which has painted ports and the hull of an old-time many-gunned frigate. Her main cabin is a gorgeous example of the passing shipwright's art. Captain Rochester produced three large bottles of Danish Carlsberg beer, for the consumption of which we were joined by the plant's physician, a very lordly looking Irishman. All these men seemed to be interested in boxing, even the elderly doctor, who, in fact, is the master among them in the manly art of self-defence. They asked me whether I was proficient with the gloves. I replied that I possessed no great skill, but, holding out my right hand, I remarked that there was a paw which had clasped the paw of Terrible Terry McGovern. The Irish doctor and Captain Rochester both seemed positively awestruck at being in the presence of a hand that had had physical contact with so great a man, and they insisted upon vicariously shaking hands with Terry.

There are no letters for the brig *Daisy* at this station, but the officers believe that they can get them for us from Cumberland Bay within the next ten days. The most important news from the outside world is that of the tragic death of Captain Scott and his four comrades on their return from the South Pole. E. A. Wilson, who was probably closest of all the men to Scott, was, in my opinion, the best naturalist who ever worked in the Antarctic. Under the circumstances of the sad end of Scott's great and successful effort, I am glad that the party had Amundsen's records to establish their glory beyond any possible doubt.

The steamship *Restitution* is the floating factory for the manufacture of oil and whale guano, and Captain Rochester's barkentine is one of several sailing vessels which carry the product back to Great Britain. During our visit six finback whales and one humpback were brought into port by one of the company's two chasers. We were told that the guano, which consists of ground and dried meat, viscera, blood, bones, and the stomach contents of the whales, can be manufactured here at a cost of about two shillings a ton, whereas its market value at home is more than six pounds a ton.

Near this station are some graves of American sealers dating from early in the nineteenth century. They are at the top of a little tussock-grown knoll, only a few yards from the shore, and their epitaph is pricked on a sheet of brass. I neglected to copy it, but my memory is that they were members of the crew of the schooner *Elizabeth Jane* of New York, who died here in 1835.

The promontory between Possession Bay and Prince Olaf Harbor is greatly waterworn and is pierced along its base by numerous deep caves that we could see from the whaleboats. In one of these, we were told, an ancient skeleton of a man was found only a few weeks ago.

Because today is Sunday, a good many of the workers at the Prince Olaf Station had gone off across the mountains on a skiing jaunt to the south coast of the island. We were surprised to learn that a trip of only four miles will bring one to the head of a great fiord on the polar side. I am itching for the opportunity to make such a trip, but see little chance of so doing.

We returned in late afternoon with our booty for the larder, and reached the *Daisy*'s anchorage about dark.

MARCH 3. Fair and mild, with light southwesterly winds.

Because of the increasing scarcity of sea elephants in Possession Bay, Captain Cleveland asked Mr. da Lomba and me to make a land journey to Antarctic Bay, which lies over the mountains to the east. This plan suited me to perfection, and we were put ashore immediately after breakfast.

The way began through a valley leading toward a pass, or col, paved with a mosaic of broken stone, on which there is almost no vegetation. We crossed the ridge without difficulty, except for a few short, very steep climbs.

Antarctic Bay has until recently been far more thoroughly glaciated than at present, because the rock formations along its shore are smooth and rounded, without the pinnacles and knife edges so characteristic of our side of the divide. A very large glacier bounds the whole head of the bay, which is filled with floating ice from it. A small glacier lies midway on the eastern shore. Extending for half a mile near the head of the bay on the western shore, is a beautiful, broad and level sandy beach. Two similar beaches could be seen on the far side, with extensive stretches of tussock grass behind them. Our search of the near side, and our examination of the far side through field glasses, revealed, however, a total of only eight small sea elephants. Our report will certainly end all Captain Cleveland's hope of adding substantially to his catch during the present summer season.

I surprised one large sea leopard, which I left in peace because there would be no way of carrying any part of it back to the brig. The beast snorted when I disturbed its sleep, then looked up with a stupid expression and opened its jaws to an angle that appeared impossible. It finally wriggled snakewise down the beach into the water, keeping its fore flippers pressed back against its body as it oozed along.

But the most exciting discovery of our journey was a new species of penguin! For the introduction I am indebted to Cadella. While we were threading our way down a rugged slope to the beach of Antarctic Bay, the dog took a side route, and was presently greeted by two penguins that made such a strident clatter and uproar as never could have issued from the throats of gentoos. To my delight, they proved to be ringed, or chin-strap, penguins, cousins of the gentoos but far more cocky, pugnacious, and swashbuckling. They were quite prepared to whack the hide off Cadella, if she had dared to toy with them as she does with other kinds of penguins.

Upon returning to the *Daisy*, we found that only a single

sea elephant had been found and killed today by the crews of all four boats.

MARCH 4. There was a hard frost during the night. Pancakes of new ice are afloat in Possession Bay on this fair and bright morning of light southerly winds.

During a good part of the day I worked on specimens in my tent. I had to wear a hat to keep my hair out of my eyes, because my mop is now like Kubelik's. In fact, if I were seen carrying your violin case, I should certainly be taken for a virtuoso.

In latter afternoon I made a long climb to the summit of my first South Georgian peak, just west of the head of Possession Bay. I had no barometer, but angles taken from the ship indicate an altitude of about 1,700 feet. The summit was exceedingly sharp, with just about room for my feet (less than half an acre, as you will infer). Toward the south I could see row after row of completely snow-covered ridges and pyramids, stretching and climbing away for miles—a still, white land, beautiful in the sunset light, but fear-inspiring, too, because of its cold and tracklessness. The descent from the peak proved worse than the climb. Several times I sank up to my hips in the snow, but I finally reached the beach after dark, launched the *Grace Emeline* and rowed home to *Daisy*.

MARCH 5. Strong northerly and northeasterly winds all through an overcast day. Our boats worked the nearer coasts of Prince Olaf Harbor and also those of a large cove between Possession and Antarctic Bays. They took twelve sea elephants, of which only two were adult bulls.

MARCH 6. Strong easterly winds, with rain which began before dawn and continued all day.

In afternoon a disagreeable looking iceberg floated in from sea and bore down ominously toward the *Daisy*. We lowered a whaleboat, made fast to the berg, and endeavored to tow it off. For fifteen or twenty minutes, it seemed not to budge one inch from its course, but it finally passed just to leeward and later ran aground, where within a few hours it broke into half a million pieces.

MARCH 7. Continued easterly storm, and a high swell rolling in to the very head of Possession Bay. In afternoon there was a brief lull; then the wind shifted to west and it is now blowing a gale, with rain.

MARCH 8. Still stormy, and the highest surf we have yet seen on the lateral beaches as well as on the long bar that runs across the head of Possession Bay.

In afternoon the wind died down somewhat, and we endeavored to go ashore in one of the whaleboats. The surf proved too much for even Mr. da Lomba's steersmanship; we took a good portion of one breaker over the stern and had to retreat, carrying plenty of water in our bottom.

For three days I have been mostly stormbound in the dark cabin, and have taken naps both morning and afternoon. I have also found time to read from the *Divina Commedia*, the whole antarctic portion of Moseley's account of the *Challenger*'s cruise, *All's Well That Ends Well*, and *Othello*. In addition, I have started writing up the notes that will ultimately constitute a life history of the sea elephant. During this loafing time, Johnny has given me an artistic haircut. He wanted to trim it round behind, and shave the periphery, but I drew the line at that!

We must be close to the end here, because the Old Man has given orders to make ready for watering ship, which means to fill our empty casks from the brook for the long voyage home. I now earnestly hope that we shall not start before letters reach us, because I have received only one since the second of last July.

MARCH 9. All hands busy at fetching out water, in spite of the continued bad weather. The wind is right to let the casks blow ashore, and some of them skim and roll in at racing speed toward the beach, where our men retrieve them from the surf. They are then filled through the bungholes in the brook, plugged, rolled back to the beach, and hauled off on a whale line to which many casks are attached by running bowlines. They are tremendously heavy to handle ashore, but, since the density of fresh water is less than that of salt, the filled casks float just awash in the bay. The chine hooks are caught on alongside, after which the casks are hoisted to the deck by block-and-fall, and lowered into the hold.

MARCH 10. Still watering, under great difficulties of weather. The *Grace Emeline* is an excellent surf boat and I am no tyro at handling a dory, but when I went ashore we swamped in the surf, and I lost four oars and the thwarts, while busy saving my craft from being smashed on the rocks. Fortunately, one of the whaleboats later recovered every piece, caught in the kelp half a mile away from the site of my mishap.

MARCH 11. The weather has subsided after five very rough and trying days. Today we were able to travel by boat and to land without undue difficulty, but only two small sea elephants were taken.

In the evening a whistle sounded through the darkness astern of us, and everyone on board came awake with a bang and an indescribable feeling of excitement. I slipped on trousers, boots, and an ulster over my pajamas, and skipped on deck where the searchlight of an approaching steamer had turned the whole scene bright. Then the whale-catcher *Southern Sea* eased alongside, with Captain Rochester and two other officers from Prince Olaf Harbor aboard, and a small packet of letters was passed across to us. Our visitors stepped on deck and shook hands with several of us, but said that they must hasten right back to their station. They would not even come below. We did our best not to allow the feverishness about our mail to prevent us from being courteous to the friends who had gone to so much trouble on our behalf.

Alas! there was no letter for me, nor for any other soul on board except the captain. Two of his were in answer to letters sent from Cumberland Bay—one from Mrs. Cleveland, dated January 12, the other from his New Bedford agents, mailed on January 17. Mrs. Cleveland mentioned that she had not seen you, nor heard from you, since autumn, so that is all the word that I have to satisfy my longing.

I shall try to keep cheerful and hopeful. Mail for South Georgia starts from any port only at long intervals, and it would have been very easy for your letters just to miss the ship if, for instance, you had been in Florida and had thus received my letters even a few days later than the skipper's reached New Bedford. But the promised November letter, referred to in the one of September 11—I cannot understand why that hasn't arrived. That is the one lack that makes it very difficult to rise above my bitter disappointment.

MARCH 12.   Cold and blustery during most of the night. I heard the howling of the southwesterly wind and the sizzling of snow on deck because it took me a long and lonely, and almost despairing, while to fall asleep. This is the month that portends winter at South Georgia, and there is no doubt that the days are rapidly growing colder.

In the letter bag I had found an envelope addressed "For Bob, when he worries about his wife." The message is undated, but I judge that it was written on a bench in the Plaza at Roseau, Dominica. At any rate, when you tell me how marriage has conquered your restlessness, and how, throughout this long year, you will await my return with confidence and patience, I am bucked up to make the same sentiments my own.

MARCH 13.   Alternation of fair but windy weather and

fierce snow squalls. I believe that we have had fifty of them since yesterday morning. In latter afternoon the wind veered from southwest around through west to north, and then died away. Immediately thereafter, snow began to fall very quietly and heavily and has continued into the evening.

I have perhaps set foot for the last time on the soil of South Georgia. This afternoon, when I had loaded my final camp effects into the dory, I most sentimentally fell prone and kissed the cold stones of the icy but beautiful land where I have learned so much, and upon which I always expect to look back with a sort of nostalgic affection, provided you and I are together again at home.

After dark this evening, two diving petrels were captured in the snow on deck and brought to me. The birds were evidently dazzled and attracted by lanterns in the hands of members of the crew who were working at our anchor chains. This reminds me that Captain Anderson of the steamship *Restitution* told me that hundreds of divers had covered the decks of his vessel one night in January, just after he had entered Prince Olaf Harbor and dropped anchor while his ports were still alight.

One sea elephant was killed today. If this represents the end of our slaughter, I shall be truly thankful, and I hope with all my heart that no sealer from the United States will ever trouble these shores again.

MARCH 14. Blustery winds arose during the night and are continuing this morning. They probably have a higher velocity than any I have known before in South Georgia (and therefore anywhere in the world). The strongest puffs have come from the southwest, but the storm veers and whirls in a bewildering manner, so that the vessel swings in all directions. We have had the wind in the northwest, then north, and then east.

The snow has turned to rain and a heavy downpour is

now under way. My dory on the davits is half filled with rain water because I neglected to pull out the plug in her bottom.

We had one anchor up and had expected to make sail to-day. That anchor is down again, however, and the toil at the windlass has all to be done over. At least I now know that at the first opportunity we shall put to sea for the long home-ward voyage. No doubt we shall spend weary weeks cruising for sperm whales, but I will try to hang on to my patience which now, for the first time, is straining to jump its bounds.

My business is over except for what I hope to be able to accomplish at sea. There is still much undone at South Geor-gia, of course, but I can honestly say that I have done my best. The last end drags out slowly, but, if destiny is in our favor, we may meet even sooner than we had dared hope.

The Beachmaster

8 Back Through the Roaring Forties

MARCH 15. The chain cable is clanking and groaning up again. The weather is vicious, however, and I am not at all sure that we can sneak out of this narrow fiord even today. These are the most trying of all times; lingering stormbound, with nothing to do except to translate into action the yearning to get away. The day is biting cold, the wind is cutting, and we have had a score or more of snow squalls since daybreak. Possession Bay is no place for either a dory or a sailing ship at this season. We have almost reached the end of what is called summer. The sun has a big start over us on his northward course, but I still hope to beat him to the Tropic of Cancer and you.

It is now two o'clock in the afternoon, and, thank God, we are bound toward the open sea.

2:45 P.M. We have crossed the long harbor bar, and are passing a grounded iceberg and the pointed mountains at the entrance of Possession Bay. The glaciers that have hemmed us in so long are now white rivers, far far astern.

3:00 P.M. A whaleboat is being lowered, and I am

about to accompany Mr. da Lomba and his crew to the station in Prince Olaf Harbor, in order to post letters. My log to date will go, if it can be registered.

MARCH 16.   We were hilariously welcomed at the station last evening, where the skippers and Dr. Leach, the physician, wanted to keep us interminably for drinks, a game of chess, and many other things which were, of course, out of the question while the *Daisy* was standing offshore in an ocean that is rarely calm. The next steamer from Cumberland Bay to Buenos Aires is to sail soon, and everybody was of the opinion that our letters would reach the United States within six weeks. We hurried away, with Irish "God bless yous" following us across the water, and had a most eerie and soul-stirring trip to the brig, which we joined after dark six or seven miles off the coast.

The evening was perfectly calm, and the white peaks of the mountains seemed to float without bases on the darkness. As soon as we had left Prince Olaf Harbor, I observed that the ocean twilight around me was absolutely alive with small petrels. They were mostly whalebirds, diving petrels, and Mother Carey's chickens, the latter including countless thousands of Wilson's petrels and equally large numbers of their relative, the black-bellied storm petrel. The scientific name of the latter is *Fregetta tropica,* which is a thoroughgoing misnomer, because it breeds only in the far south and enters the tropics only in the role of a migrant. There are probably millions of its nests in the grassy soil of some part of South Georgia, but, alas!, I was never able to find one, and I never even saw the species here until last evening. The sight, the whirr and splash and twittering of these incalculable birds, like bats in a vast black cavern roofed with the firmament and floored with the ocean, so stirred my imagination that I was jumpy throughout the night.

Calm weather is precious here! About midnight a strong

southwest wind began to blow and to kick up a sea. This morning South Georgia was still visible far astern, and our old friends, the oceanic albatrosses and many other sea birds, were in our wake. Our course is north by east.

I took a nap of several hours, following a feeling in my stomach that was suspiciously like incipient seasickness. You must remember that it is a long while since I have spent my days on the bounding main.

Later, the southerly wind died away. Although we are bouncing around badly, I had regained my equilibrium, and I have spent the evening mounting a diving petrel for Captain Cleveland's New Bedford home. It is six years since I have turned my hand to taxidermy, but the Old Man is inordinately tickled with my product, which is in a flying attitude (to hang from his parlor ceiling, above the case of seashells!). The bird is now complete, save for its glass eyes.

In sailing for home from Possession Bay, without reporting at Cumberland Bay for the clearance of his ship and the payment of dues on seal oil, Captain Cleveland is playing a foxy game for his own advantage. He has been entirely frank about it with me because he apparently enjoys pulling the wool over the eyes of the British magistrate. When he arrives at the first port in the West Indies, he will merely use his clearance of last September from São Vicente, Cape Verde Islands. This will seem entirely reasonable for a whaleship, and, even if the officers learn that he has visited South Georgia, nobody is likely to realize that a port of entry exists at that half-mythical island. It is barely possible, though not at all likely, that the long arm of international shipping regulations may some day catch up with Captain Cleveland and his co-owners of the *Daisy*. But he evidently thinks the chance worth taking, because, although he expects to go to sea until he is "to the north'ard of seventy," he has no intention of ever returning to South Georgia.

MARCH 17.   The top of the mornin' to you, mavourneen!
I am celebrating St. Patrick's Day by being in the homeward
parade, although I'm afraid it will not be the "straight wake
for home" in which sailors rejoice.

The night was one of tumbling calm, always the worst
kind of weather at sea, but this morning we have a good
southerly breeze and we are ploughing along gloriously at
eight knots. It is a cheery prospect to think of the sun sinking
again on our port beam, day after day, and to realize that we
are chasing him toward God's country.

> Blow, blow, thou winter wind;
> Thou art not so unkind

as the refrigerating breath of the glaciers. It has been exceedingly rough, but the seasickish tendency has vanished, and I
have been happy, at least on top. Down lower, I have troubled
depths.

Already the air has a different and milder feeling. I love
to suck it in and to anticipate its changing temper. I got rid of
my old ulster today, and shall nevermore have to wear it.

Our friends, the blackfish and right whale porpoises,
were around us again this morning. A skua flew northward
overhead, and four sooty albatrosses have been accompanying us. Only one of these is the gray, light-backed form that
nests at South Georgia. The other three are dark on back and
belly, of browner plumage generally, and have an orange, instead of a blue, stripe on the bill. These markings are characteristic of a subantarctic race of sooty albatross, which nests
at Tristan da Cunha, far outside the zone of floating ice. Our
present latitude lies within the mingling belt.

A slight snow squall after dark.

MARCH 18.   Lat. 49° + S., by dead reckoning.

Reasonable weather, and we are skimming northward. I
look longingly at my tropical helmet, which has hung in a bag

of cheesecloth all through the South Georgian summer. I hope soon to give away my greasy old felt hat, to take off my woolen undies and thick stockings, and to realize that once more I am approaching equatorial climes. You can't imagine how I begin to love the tropics.

The Old Man, believe it or not, has had one of the little volumes of my *Divina Commedia* in his hands during every spare moment of the past several days. You will remember that these have the Italian text and Wicksteed's English translation on facing pages. The skipper has had his nose in a volume for at least eight hours today. He has finished both "Hell" and "Purgatory" and is now halfway through "Paradise." I have been waiting for some profound comment, and it has finally been forthcoming. He has remarked, "Dante had a head on him."

MARCH 19.   Lat. 48° 30' S.; no sight for the meridian.

> The sun now rose upon the right;
> Out of the sea came he,
> Still hid in mist, and on the left
> Went down into the sea.

Today we had a northwesterly gale to retard our course somewhat, and it has been exceedingly rough. This evening the wind is down and we are in the throes of another uncomfortable rolling calm. It strains all your muscles either to sit, stand, or lie down, and beans and things roll out of the dishes into your lap. Nevertheless, the Portugee can balance the most rolling of all beans, once he gets it on his knife!

We are almost in midocean. Ouch! The lashings of the stool I'm sitting on just gave way, and I nearly broke my larboard arm, as we slammed across the cabin floor. Rough weather is quite livable so long as the wind blows hard enough to steady the ship, but it's maddening when a gale ends abruptly in a calm. The temperature is fairly comfortable, though—about the same as it would be off Newfoundland in

September. If we cross the line in April, as I sincerely hope, it will be jumping happily from autumn to spring, from "October" to April. All my trials may then fall off like autumn leaves and all my hopes renew like April buds. Ho for the equator!

MARCH 20.   Lat. 47° 20' S., long. 34° 26' W. West wind, light rain, and an evening rainbow.

Many of the gray petrels that the whalemen call "pediunkers" darted in Indian file above the cabin roof, and large numbers of other sea fowl, from albatrosses down to Mother Carey's chickens, were about. The skuas seem to be bent on a regular migration toward the equator.

MARCH 21.   Lat. 45° 50' S., long. 33° 52' W. Very rough; seas have been slopping across the deck, and on one lurch we shipped water over the bulwarks, but the strong, cool west wind has been driving us northward, which is all I care. I've been working on the life histories of South Georgia birds and seals.

Tonight the big golden moon came up as soon as the sun went home. The Lady, who has been capsized so long, is beginning to right herself. She looks straight down now, but when we cross the magic line she will raise her radiant countenance.

Now that my South Georgian notes are closed until such time as I can study and compare my specimens in a museum laboratory, I am giving most of my attention to the abundant ocean birds.

Your calendar reminds me that it is Good Friday, so I am about to end the day by reading the story from all four Gospels.

MARCH 22.   Lat. 43° 20' S.; long. approximately 33° W. A bright mild day, with gentle southwesterly winds which are favorable for our northward course.

Mastheads were set for the first time, but the only life

reported by them was a large shark astern. Two yearling wandering albatrosses, all brownish black except for their white faces and wing linings, paid us a visit. I wonder whether they are old friends from Albatross Islet? At sunset a skua circled our main topmast, seeming very curious about the two men on watch, and then flew off to the east. After nightfall I could still see many mutton birds fluttering about in the bright moonlight.

From my typewritten records of the history of South Georgia, to which I devoted plenty of bibliographic study during the early months of 1912, I have been trying to build up a roster of visitors between the dates of the *Resolution* and the *Daisy*. The brave tales of Captain Cook were "best sellers" in the latter years of the eighteenth century. It is natural that his references to the abundant "sea bears" or fur seals at South Georgia should have led sealers in his wake, but it seems curious that the earliest exploiters were Yankees rather than British mariners.

This is explained, perhaps, in the book by James Weddell, who wrote in 1825 that British furriers did not know how to dress fur seal pelts. "At the same time," he adds, "the Americans were carrying from Georgia cargoes of these skins to China, where they frequently obtained a price of from 5 to 6 dollars apiece. It is generally known that the English did not enjoy the same privilege; by which means the Americans took entirely out of our hands this valuable article of trade. The number of skins brought from off Georgia . . . cannot be estimated at fewer than 1,200,000."

I don't know why the British couldn't go to China in that period, but at any rate the lads from Long Island Sound ports had a field day. At the end of a quarter century, they and the British who ultimately followed them had killed about a million and a half fur seals, practically wiping out the species at South Georgia. After that the sea elephants had to pay the costs, and everybody, up to and including Captain Cleveland, has since been doing his best to exterminate them also.

My sketchy historical summary is as follows:

1790. Two sealing vessels, names unknown, commanded by Captains Roswell Woodward and Daniel Green, of New Haven, Connecticut, arrived at South Georgia.

1799. The *Regulator*, of New York, master unknown to me. She was wrecked at South Georgia, but her cargo of 14,000 fur seal skins was salvaged and sold in 1800 to the British sealer *Morse* (meaning walrus), the first vessel of her nationality to reach South Georgia.

1800-1801. Captain Edmund Fanning, a Yankee of high standing as an explorer and author, in the armed corvette *Aspasia*. He found a bonanza, taking 57,000 fur seal skins. (Not bad, at six dollars apiece!) His report shows also that the fleet had crowded in, for it states that sixteen other American and British vessels procured 65,000 additional fur seal pelts during the four months beginning with November, 1800.

1801. Captain Nathaniel Storer, of New Haven, evidently lost or left his first ship, because he built a small schooner on the coast of Patagonia, sailed her to South Georgia, and spent two summer seasons salting down 45,000 fur seal skins.

1802. A Captain Pendleton, in the Yankee sealer *Union*, braved the rugged southerly coast of the island. He compiled the first detailed map of South Georgia. More than a century later this chart was discovered and published by an Italian geographer.

1819. Visit of F. G. T. Bellingshausen in the naval vessels *Vostok* and *Mirny*, on a Russian circumnavigation of the world. All that I have been able to learn about Admiral Bellingshausen's observations at South Georgia is contained in a brief German abstract of the rare Russian account.

1819. Two English ships under Captains Brown and

Short. These were spoken and reported by Bellingshausen.

1822. Captain Benjamin Morrell, in the schooner *Wasp*. Morrell was a great navigator, a successful sealer and merchant, a voluminous and entertaining writer, and a romantic liar in the grand manner. He is the Yankee Munchausen. He states that his whaleboats rowed all around South Georgia in four days, or thereabouts. I rise to proclaim that they did not!

1822-1824. Captain James Weddell, a truly noble British seafarer, in command of the *Jane* and the *Beaufoy*.

1829. Captain James Brown, of Portsmouth, Rhode Island, in the schooner *Pacific*. Fur seals must have been on the way out, and the sticking of sea elephants had begun, because Captain Brown left South Georgia in March, 1830, with a cargo of sea elephant oil, but only 250 seal pelts.

1834. Schooner *Elizabeth Jane*, of New York, six hundred fur seal skins. (We saw graves of the mate and one or more of her sailors at Prince Olaf Harbor.)

1870. (A long jump since my last preceding record.) Schooner *Flying Fish*, of New London, Connecticut, master unknown. She took five hundred fur seals and 210 barrels of sea elephant oil. On this voyage or a later one, the *Flying Fish* carried H. W. Klutschak, who published in German a colorful account of South Georgia.

1878. The Yankee sealer *Trinity*, master unknown, took 250 barrels of sea elephant oil.

1882-1883. German contingent of the International Polar Investigation was stationed for a year at Royal Bay, one object being to observe the transit of Venus across the sun's disk. The German party had two ships, the *Moltke* and the *Marie*. The bulk of our scientific knowledge about South Georgia, to date, has resulted from the studies and publications of this expedition.

1885. Our old friend, Captain George Comer, of East Haddam, Connecticut, in the topsail schooner *Era*, made his first sealing visit to South Georgia, which was only one of his many hunting grounds in the west-wind zone.

1887. A Connecticut sealer named Captain Fuller stayed at the island for two seasons, obtaining sea elephant oil and a few fur seal pelts.

1893. The momentous call of Captain C. A. Larsen, in the Norwegian steam whalers *Jason* and *Hertha*. This ultimately led to the modern antarctic whaling.

1901. Visit of Dr. Otto Nordenskjöld and the Swedish Antarctic Expedition. Captain Larsen was master of the vessel.

1903. Establishment by Larsen of the Compañia Argentina de Pesca in Cumberland Bay.

1904. Visit of Erik Sörling, for the Natural History Museum at Stockholm, Sweden. Sörling made collections which were reported upon by Professor Einar Lönnberg. The publication, in rather faulty English (which is much to be preferred to the best of Swedish!), is among those on my cabin bookshelves.

1906. A. Szielasko, physician of the whaler *Fridjof Nansen*. This craft struck an uncharted rock after she had made the island, and sank, with considerable loss of life. Dr. Szielasko survived, to publish in German an excellent account of his natural history observations.

1907. What's this? Captain Benjamin D. Cleveland, of New Bedford, Massachusetts, arrived for his first visit in the Long Island-built hermaphrodite brig *Daisy*.

1907. Establishment in August of the observatory of the Oficina Meteorologica Argentina, at Cumberland Bay. Eric Nordenhaag, now in charge, had previously been stationed at the South Orkneys, where the weather is not nearly so bland, sunny, and agreeable!

1909. Visit, as guests of Captain Larsen, of the Swedish

botanist, Carl Skottsberg, and of one or more other scientific men.

1912.   Appointment of the British magistrate, Mr. Wilson. This marks the beginning of "law and order" at South Georgia. "Alas!" as Captain Cleveland would say.

1912.   Passing visit of Captain Wilhelm Filchner, commander of the Second German Antarctic Expedition. He left the horses.

1912.   Visit of the geologist, Donald Ferguson, as a guest of one of the Scotch whaling companies.

1912.   In this same crowded year, along comes Murphy! There must be a rare and romantic story in all that had gone before, if only one had time to dig it out of the customhouse records and logbooks in a score of ports.

MARCH 23.   Lat. 42° 20' S.; long. 31° 45' W. Northwesterly winds held us to a course of north by east, or worse.

This is Easter Sunday, though I doubt whether anyone else aboard knows it. I hope that you are having just such a pleasant sunny day, with the breath of spring in the air, as we enjoy here on the wide ocean. I find three letters for today in your mail bag, and they make me think of everything that comes with Easter at home. I can even smell the crocuses that have already opened to the sun in the grass below your sleeping porch. There is a fine letter from Dr. Lord, who married us fourteen months ago, and I am confident that scores of friends are thinking of us today.

Blue whalebirds have been about in greater numbers than I have seen them since we left the whaling banks. I believe that they are a different species from that of South Georgia, one with a much broader bill, which nests at Gough Island and Tristan da Cunha. The sooty albatrosses, of which many were about, are also of the Temperate Zone species.

We are now almost in a southern latitude that corresponds with the northern latitude of Boston. The thermometer insists that the air is chilly, but to me it seems balmy and divine after the unending blizzards of South Georgia. Unfortunately the wind has been pushing us eastward for twenty-four hours, so that we have made very little northing. At least I now count the time in weeks instead of months. Before long the unit will become days, and finally only minutes.

MARCH 24. Lat. 43° S., by dead reckoning. A northerly storm blew up during the night and has continued all day, raising a very rough sea and forcing us to run to the east and even south of east.

Birds were about in countless numbers, keeping me busy and happy. We caught twelve wandering albatrosses on bent nails. I saved for specimens one mature male, two females and one black yearling. The other eight were released, as soon as I had locked numbered bands, with the address of the American Museum of Natural History, on their legs.

After I had killed the four albatrosses and had hung them up by the legs to cool, an entire squid, with a body more than a foot long, dropped out of the gullet of one of the adult females. "Making my specimens catch my specimens," chortled I, as the squid was wrapped in cheesecloth and tucked into a milk can of formalin.

I skinned the birds, using fresh and clean cornmeal in order that the carcasses might be turned over immediately to the steward for a "goney" stew.

Since we left Prince Olaf Harbor on the evening of March 15, I have observed and identified twenty-four species of birds belonging to the order of the petrels and albatrosses.

MARCH 25. No sights could be taken today. It is now nearly midnight, and we are running under shortened foresails before a ripsnorting southerly gale that commenced about nine o'clock last evening and has been raging ever since.

The waves have been mountainous, though happily we have been able to run free most of the time, and hence to speed in the right direction. It is always an astounding experience to stand at the stern before a high following sea, to look up at the crest of impending doom racing toward you, which seems at least as high as the crosstrees, and then to feel the stern lift up and up and up until the great comber slides past harmlessly on either side. Today, however, we actually shipped a little water through the taffrail scuppers several times, but the constantly recurring miracle was that we were never pooped. All night and all morning we carried only a single sail, the lower foretopsail. During the afternoon we set the foresail as well, and now, with the wind definitely moderating, the men have gone up in the blackness to loose the upper foretopsail and the foretopgallantsail. Every sail of the mainmast remains furled.

Birds have been about in great numbers all day, but observation has been difficult.

MARCH 26. Position by dead reckoning: Lat. 38° 50' S.; long. 31° 30' W. Heavily overcast; light southeast winds that helped us on our way. At nightfall, however, the wind veered into the northeast.

Early in the evening I obtained the Old Man's permission to lower the dory, and I remained down alone on the subsiding swells of the great Atlantic until after dark. Incredible numbers of birds were flying in the twilight, which seems to be characteristic of most petrels. I shot until I could no longer see the sight on my gun and obtained three examples of the Tristan sooty albatross (the first time I have ever collected this bird), and five species of petrels, one or more of which are new to my collection. In the relatively calm weather, the blackish yearling wandering albatrosses were having a wonderful social jamboree, meeting in gams on the water, raising their long wings and bills, screaming and squealing at each

other, just as I saw their parents do on the whaling banks off
South Georgia last December. Shooting from a dory in a
really lively swell is a sporting proposition; you don't drop a
bird with every cartridge.

MARCH 27.   Lat. 37° 40' S.; long. 30° 58' W. Brisk west
and northwest winds, with rain squalls and a heavy sea. At
five o'clock in the afternoon a brilliant rainbow formed in
the east.

MARCH 28.   Lat. 35° 20' S., long. 30° 50' W. Westerly
winds and frequent squalls all day.

We have had so much rough weather recently that restful
sleep has been hard to gain. Last night was one of the worst,
because the ship jerked and pounded harder than in the
higher seas of a few days ago. As I seesawed on my thwart-
ship bed, I was wrenched and bruised, and my skin was
tugged and stretched by the force of gravity until my head
ached and the miseries were all through me. I could hear the
seas swooshing aboard and the spray slapping the deck above.
At least I had a dry corner, whereas many another man on
board not only had the water above him but also felt it dripping into his bunk.

Early this morning it was more restful to get up than to
try to sleep any longer. Things are breaking loose more than
at any earlier time on the voyage. We have had a table and a
stove adrift, besides which a kettle has jumped its rack and
scalded the steward.

Once out of my berth and on deck, I found the outlook
somewhat happier. The wind is at least fair; the clouds begin
to have a piled-up tropical look; even these black rain squalls
bear a joyous promise. We are now in the latitude of Buenos
Aires and the Cape of Good Hope, a latitude corresponding
with that of Washington, Gibraltar, Athens, and northern California. Within a week we ought to be across the Tropic of
Capricorn. The weather is mild enough now so that one can

pace the deck without a coat, though I have not yet shed my woolies.

We have seen no whales to delay us, and I hope that they will continue to keep their snouts down out of sight, though the Old Man would not approve of such disloyal sentiments in the heart of his assistant navigator. This evening we are flying northward with a spanking breeze.

MARCH 29.   Lat. 33° 20' S.; long. 29° 52' W. Brisk southwest winds and frequent squalls, lasting into the night.

This afternoon a large, sleek tomcat appeared on deck. "Come now," I thought, "cats are not produced by spontaneous generation, and we certainly found none at South Georgia." Then I recollected the feeble kitten of last October, which had disappeared into the steerage at the first touch of cold weather. Its present lusty condition showed that somebody had remembered it, or else that the *Daisy*'s rats had contributed.

MARCH 30.   Lat. 31° 24' S.; long. 30° 56' W. The morning calm; light southwest winds during the afternoon. The first indubitable summer day of our homeward voyage.

To my great surprise, I have found in my cabin some unexpected veterans of the Antarctic, namely the whirling spiders which were my laboratory animals for experiments in the Sargasso Sea so many months ago. We can therefore add to our former conclusions that these spiders are hardy creatures! The cockroach population, on the other hand, has not been able to take the cold and rugged life of the far south. I have seen no living example since November. No doubt they will fully repopulate the *Daisy* just at the time I move out in the West Indies.

MARCH 31.   Lat. 29° 31' S.; long. 30° 42' W. At seven o'clock this morning the bright quarter moon was exactly at our zenith.

Quiet seas, genial air, and brilliant sunsets now foretell

continued summer weather. I am beginning to shed clothing
and even to think of a shampoo. I have cleaned house, put my
white helmet back into commission, and brought up my old
canvas chair to the deck. The latitude today corresponds
with that of northern Florida, the blue Canary Isles, Cairo,
the Himalaya Mountains, and Lower California. It is hard
to keep patient. Sometimes I can't shake from my mind
the dread of wondering why your November letter never
reached me.

Another month is behind us.

APRIL 1. Lat. 28° 46' S.; no sight for longitude obtained.

About sunrise the Old Man called me from my berth to
the quarterdeck to see a penguin riding on a loggerhead
turtle. April fool!

APRIL 2. Lat. 27° 17' S.; long. 31° 53' W.

Since yesterday the wind has been blowing strongly from
the northeast, reaching half-gale force. It has now veered
around most unfortunately to the north, and we are having
intermittent rains while the barometer is falling rapidly. The
Old Man prophesies high westerly winds tomorrow.

APRIL 3. Lat. 26° 20' S.; long. 31° 30' W.

During the night just ended we had heavy rains and occasional lightning and thunder, and then the puffs began to blow
from the northwest. These were followed by a steady and increasing west wind which has raised a sharp sea, thus con-
firming the Old Man's status as a reliable chief of the local
weather bureau.

In the middle of the night Mr. da Lomba, then on watch,
took the wheel and kindly sent the helmsman down the companionway with orders to call my name and awaken me. The
voice said merely that the mate thought I would like to come
on deck, by which I surmised that it would be worth while,
because Mr. da Lomba has never yet sent for me in vain.

The reason was something that I would not have missed at any price—St. Elmo's fire, the first I have ever seen. It sent the thrills running up and down my back and along the skin of my thighs. The hair of my bare head also stood on end, but I cannot say whether this was due to mental exaltation or because I, like the ship, was spurting a brush discharge of electricity into the atmosphere.

At any rate, I wore no visible halo, whereas the *Daisy* was agleam with them. Pale blue spherical glows tipped both masts, the upper yardarms and the end of the jibboom. At first they shone in the calm and intense blackness with a steady light of somewhat indefinite outline. But, when a puff blew out of the northwest, the fireballs lengthened and flickered into tapers, emitting a fizzing, crackling sound, as though the timbers from which they streamed were afire. I was spellbound until rain began to fall again and the celestial lights went out, whereupon I returned to my berth.

A few days ago I was reading about this same phenomenon in the last chapter of the Acts of the Apostles. St. Paul, aboard the ship from Alexandria, knew it as the ancient pagan symbol of Castor and Pollux, and yet he was apparently not above regarding it as a fair omen. May it likewise prove so to us, despite the many and profound differences between the apostle and your devoted servant, such, for example, as our respective views about wedlock!

APRIL 4.   Lat. 25° 00' S.; long. 30° 40' W.

Today begins my third trip into the tropics. The ocean is ultramarine again; many pairs of bare feet once more tread the deck, and I am resplendent in a clean white shirt, which is the only garment on my torso. The temperature is perfect, but the wind is not quite fair because it comes again from the northwest. It seems to me that the seas, day by day, have been considerably choppier and nastier than those we encountered on our southward voyage.

Today we met and saluted the first Portuguese man-
o'-war sighted since we left the warm oceans six months ago. I
also identified my first example of a rare petrel which nests on
Trindade, or South Trinidad. Our course makes it seem that
we are headed toward that alluring island.

APRIL 5. Lat. 23° 56' S.; long. 30° 08' W. Very heavy
rains pounded nearly all through last night. Today has been
chiefly calm. A light breeze, welcome because it was fair, blew
up from the south at seven o'clock this evening.

Spring housecleaning is a tradition in New England, but
I have now seen it for the first time on shipboard. The *Daisy*
is, of course, always kept reasonably trig and shipshape, and I
have already described the general swabbing we undergo
after boiling oil.

Yesterday and today, however, have been something
special, the general cleanup of a whole voyage. Below decks,
berths and lockers and cupboards were emptied and
scrubbed. All walls and ceilings were washed down with soap
and water. On deck and aloft, the process was just as thor-
ough. Men in boatswain's chairs swabbed the whole length of
the masts. The doublings were scrubbed, all painted surfaces
received a going-over, and even the planks of the deck were
scraped and flushed as never before.

The "household cleanser" used everywhere above decks
was urine! A collecting barrel is lashed to the bulwarks near
the fo'castle and twenty or thirty gallons of its contents have
been applied, along with elbow grease, from stem to stern of
the *Daisy*. As though the fluid was not already sufficiently potent, the mate added a good quantity of blubber ash from the
furnaces beneath the try-pots. This residue is rich in lye, so
altogether we have had a mixture fit to burn paint off wood,
not to mention skin off muscle and bone. The cleansing was
followed by a free-for-all water fight when the men rinsed and
showered the craft with innumerable wooden buckets of sea

water. Fearful and wonderful are the traditions of Yankee whaling!

APRIL 6.   Lat. 23° 00' S.; long. 30° 05' W.

Overcast, hot, and too calm during most of the day. What little breeze we enjoyed was fair, and it increased toward evening. An orgy of shaves, baths and haircuts has been taking place all over the *Daisy*'s deck. Johnny gave me a good trimming à la Sing Sing. Blankets are being discarded at night.

Roderick has undertaken some expert repairs to my clothes, and I give him credit for being able to sew even better than he sings. He bewails the fact that we have no doeskin or white duck, for he avers that his bespoke suits would make me the best dressed gentleman in the West Indies!

Roderick, who never went whaling before this voyage, seems to have learnt somewhere an unlimited store of songs and chanteys. I doubt whether he knows what they are all about, for some of the words and lines are quite unintelligible, even when he repeats them to me. This evening, in the second dogwatch, he was coaching Conrad, Feddy, Elise, John Paul, and other Dominican boys in a new one. The Portuguese sailors don't fall in with them, but stick rather to three or four well-known New Bedford songs. On most ships these are led by the "doctor" (meaning the cook), but on *Daisy* the cook, who is not even called doctor, is a silent bird. Mr. Almeida is our usual tenor hero during cutting-in and anchor-weigh.

Anyway, Roderick's new ditty begins,

> Ho! for Japan and wideawake!
> There's plenty of whales for us to take.

Presently the singers lower and go after one.

> And now the whale is on the run.
> The iron holds fast, but his flukes we shun.
> His flukes we shun for they'd break our bones
> And send us down to Davy Jones.

They finally bring their catch alongside, to find the cook prepared for the hungry crews.

> And now the doctor's made some duff,
> Likewise horse-pie, but not enough.
> So we'll fill our bellies with blubber and tar
> And sleep our watch on the capstan bar.

> And now the ship is bound for home,
> And in her teeth she carries a bone.
> When we get there we'll raise the hair,
> Get soused, and love the girls for fair.

I don't know what raising the hair means, except that St. Elmo recently raised mine.

The Old Man's conscience (or whatever he wears in lieu of one) may be beginning to prick him because of all the help he didn't give me at South Georgia. At any rate, he has told me that the jaw of our eighty-barrel sperm whale is to come, teeth and all, to the Museum. He's in a glozing-over mood.

During idle periods of the past few days, some of the men have been working on the pan bone and teeth of other whales, chiefly turning out walking sticks through their use of files and hand lathe. One sailor has also etched a whaleship on a polished tooth, but the work is crude and not to be compared either in craft or picturesqueness with the older scrimshaw, of which we saw so much in New Bedford last spring. The best of this art died with the Yankee whalemen, and I am now seeing the last flutter of something that has petered out.

Scrimshaw (nobody is sure how the name originated) is a very inclusive term. It comprises the wide range of trinkets, ornaments, and beautified objects of utility, some of them of notable artistic worth, which were fashioned by whalemen from sperm whale ivory, often in combination with bone, whalebone, wood, silver, and mother-of-pearl. Etched teeth, canes, jewel boxes, and pastry markers or "jaggin' wheels" are among the commonest of such productions, although the vari-

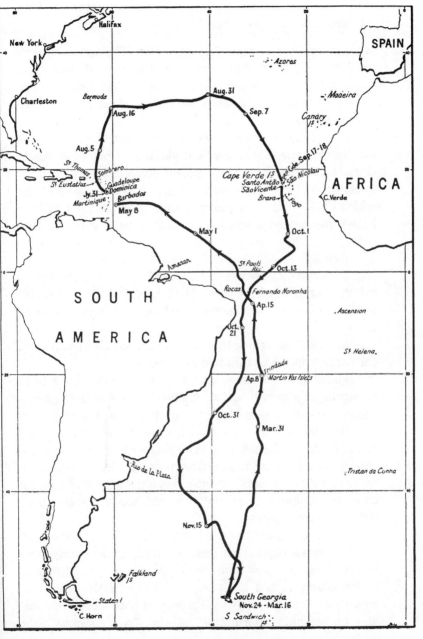

CRUISE OF THE *Daisy*, 1912-1913

ety is as limitless as sailors' imaginations. This art was developed by American whalemen, and disappeared with their passing. It is extraordinarily interesting in that it constitutes, perhaps, the only truly native handicraft of the people of the United States.

About sunset I went to the mainmasthead and swept the northward horizon with my field glass. Just before darkness closed in, I made out the faint purple peaks of South Trinidad Islet, about forty miles dead ahead. It was a moment for which I have long been waiting, and, although the Old Man hasn't vouchsafed a word, I hope that he is going to stop there.

APRIL 7.   Lat. 21° 30' S.; long. 30° 04' W.

This morning we could see Trindade, as the Brazilians call it, bearing north by west. The island was, however, still many miles away, and there was no breeze to carry us toward it.

About three o'clock this afternoon, a gentle breath from the south brought us rain and motion.

Many terns, boobies, and man-o'-war birds have been about the brig, as well as two kinds of petrels of the size of a pigeon. One of them is black, the other brown and white.

We fastened to a bit of driftwood from a wreck, and towed it, thus luring a host of fish along with us. Among those captured was a shark that had been practically concealed inside a cloud of very small, faintly-banded young pilot fish. An enormous dolphin flirted with us, but was too wary to be either hooked or ironed.

APRIL 8.   At daybreak this morning Trindade bore north by east, distant eight or nine miles. The brig was barely moving, so about half past nine the Old Man ordered us to stand by for lowering, and I made ready to go in Mr. Almeida's whaleboat. I was already well crammed with such historical and topographic information as the *South Atlantic Pilot* afforded. This proved sufficiently exciting, because it seems that even the critical eye of science and navigation has warmed up under the spell of Trindade. The island was discovered in the sixteenth century by Tristão da Cunha, and was later a haunt of pirates. In 1700 it was visited by the Astronomer Royal, Edmund Halley, he of comet fame. But it has never had a permanent settlement, and relatively little is yet known about its natural history.

The gray pile, its fantastic peaks overhung with pennons of torn cloud, now lay right in our path, and the rocks of Martin Vas were barely visible in the east. The order for lowering the boats was given; we left the *Daisy* in the offing, and pulled ahead, fired with enthusiasm, toward the white-lined coast. Three man-o'-war birds were winding in and out around the topmasts of the brig. An inquisitive booby flew between two of the oarsmen in our whaleboat, and the noddies were scarcely less familiar. The fairy terns and the native petrels were also very numerous, but they kept their distance, through indifference rather than fear.

During the pull toward shore the thunder of surf rang louder and louder in our ears, the sound rebounding from many rocky walls. The air was perfectly calm, but a southeasterly ground swell heaped up a tremendous surge of waters on the ironbound coast, which was formed either of the precipitous cliffs themselves, or of beaches about a yard wide completely strewn with sharp blocks of the mountain. The line of breaking water was, nevertheless, so narrow that at some places we could safely come within twenty feet of shore.

We approached the island at a southerly peninsula of columnar rock which suggests a bit of the Giants' Causeway. From here we skirted the western end, ultimately rounding North Point, but nowhere finding a landing place. Whenever the whaleboat's prow was pushed close to the rock in a sheltered angle, the whole craft rose and fell in such a dizzy and appalling manner that several of our seasoned whalemen became seasick.

From both the brig and the whaleboat I was able to enjoy a good view of the island's skyline and general structure through its length of four or five miles. At the southeastern end is a ridge-roofed promontory of brick-red volcanic tufa, terminating in the cliff of South Point, which is pierced by an archway. According to the *South Atlantic Pilot*, the surf sometimes breaks two hundred feet above its base. Overtowering this is the Sugarloaf (1,160 ft.), which resembles the conical mount of the same name at Rio de Janeiro. The volcanic rock is so worn and grottoed by pluvial action that its texture is like the cut surface of a Swiss cheese. Under this mount, says tradition, there was an immense treasure buried, consisting principally of the plunder of Peruvian churches! Northwest of the Sugarloaf lies a green valley containing many clumps of shrubs. Mr. da Lomba, who had once been ashore, told me that there is a cluster of stone-marked graves on the northern slope of this valley.

The highest point of Trindade, 2,020 feet on the Admiralty chart, but 3,000 according to the *South Atlantic Pilot*, is near the center of the island. The summits of the ridges are more than serrate, being a succession of needlelike pinnacles. At the western end stands a most remarkable rock structure, the Ninepin of Halley, known also as the Monument or the Priest. It is a cylindrical tower of dark gray stone, doubtless a volcanic dike, rising from the ocean to a height of nearly nine hundred feet. In common with all the bare steeps of this isle, the surface of the Ninepin is pitted and undercut into designs like arabesques. In outline and proportion the great column may be compared with the two distal phalanges of an index finger. Leaning slightly less than the Tower of Pisa, planned on the grandest scale of Nature's architecture, its utterly inaccessible wall furnishes nesting chambers for tens of thousands of feathered sprites, which sit within their niches like saints of a cathedral spire. No sight had ever seemed so impressive as I gazed from the small boat straight upward to the Ninepin's lofty summit, enveloped in a cloud of midge-like birds.

Since landing was out of the question, we began fishing with considerable success off the West Point, just outside the line of breaking sea. The bottom was very rocky, varying in depth from three to seven fathoms. Many of the captured bottom fishes were brilliantly colored. The largest species, excepting sharks, was a red-spotted garupa; some of our examples were over four feet long and weighed fifty or sixty pounds. Several kinds of triggerfish proved abundant. Here, as at Fernando Noronha, we lost many of our prizes because of sharks, the lines often coming inboard with nothing but fishes' heads on the hooks. Even one of our largest garupas was nipped in half. It gave me a rather awesome feeling to see a huge head come over the gunwale with its jaws still gasping but no tail behind the gills!

We succeeded in hooking and harpooning a number of cat sharks, or nurse sharks, the ugly mouths of which harbored curious, extensible leeches. Larger sharks were around the brig all day, and a booby which was shot from deck and wounded so that it fell into the water, first had its legs bitten off, and was then devoured as one morsel. At the surface of the sea near the cliffs were schools of halfbeaks or needlegars. The mandible in these small fishes is long, resembling the beak of a swordfish, but the upper jaw is very short. They have an especially comical appearance when they open their mouths widely to feed, the seemingly useless bill merely passing beneath a bit of food. Our sailors threw scraps of fat into the water alongside the whaleboat, and captured many of the needlegars with their hands. Altogether we caught approximately two hundred fishes, representing nine species.

While we were fishing, a number of flat, triangular feather flies, which live as parasites in the plumage of boobies and man-o'-war birds, flew into the boat. They scuttled sidewise like crabs, adroitly dodging capture, and seemed bent on getting on the under side of whatever they alighted upon, whether a gunstock, one's hand, or a thwart of the boat. These flies were the only insects we saw.

Birds were about in countless hosts, filling the air and covering the rocks. The noddies were incredibly confident and curious, hovering round our heads, even alighting upon them, and peering into our faces so closely that one had to look at them cross-eyed. It was the simplest matter to catch them in the hand as they fluttered among us. Four of them I banded with aluminum rings of the American Bird Banding Association—numbers 7941, 7943, 7945, 7947; may their wearers once again entrust themselves within the clutches of a naturalist! But the noddies were not one whit more abundant than the exquisite fairy terns or lovebirds. At Trindade there are more of these terns than anywhere else in the South Atlantic. They were flying mostly in pairs, as at Fernando Noronha, and pairs also were sitting together in many rocky niches. Most delicate and wraithlike of birds are these white terns; when they fly against the glare transmitted from a bright sky, the dark line of their wing bones is projected like an X-ray shadow through the feathers.

Boobies soared among the pinnacles a thousand feet above us. Man-o'-war birds, flying overhead, seemed all head, wings, and tail. There are two species at Trindade, and both were more interested in the brig offshore than in our tiny whaleboats. The man-o'-war birds are notorious pirates in their feeding habits, but I saw a troop of the smaller kind fishing for themselves. Half a dozen of them hovered in a row over a school of surface fish, and faced in a direction opposite to that in which the fish were moving. While the birds poised close over the water, they beat their big wings slowly. Then at the right moment they struck downward, swinging their long bills like scimitars back under their bodies, the hooked tip seizing a fish from the rear. They seemed to catch three or four a minute, and yet made no commotion among the moving school of their victims. One man-o'-war bird was caught on a fishhook from the *Daisy*.

The rare petrels, which are peculiar to Trindade, were as numberless as the noddies. Some were brooding, or perhaps only resting, in water-worn cells of the rock. Others quarreled in the air, chattering like terns. It was aggravating to be unable to land among them, but at least I could collect samples of both the black and the bicolored forms, which will be the first specimens for any museum in the United States. Shortly before noon I had shot one of the dark birds with the right barrel of my gun, in the vicinity of two small rocks off the Ninepin, when a very white petrel flew swiftly toward us from the sea. Intuitively, in that momentary glimpse, I recognized a bird with which I was not familiar. A fortunate, long shot, straight up from the shoulder, brought it spinning to the water, and we reached it sooner than the sharks. It proved to be a form or phase new to science, more beautiful than its congeners, clad in a snowy, black-flecked cloak, like the ermine of royalty.

All the birds that we saw were, of course, sea birds—none others have been found at Trindade. But through the whole day, while our little boat skirted the seething edge of ocean, I gazed longingly at the tree ferns far above, and could not help thinking that there may possibly have been unknown land birds there, among the spires of the fascinating unattainable mountains.

Historically, Trindade has been sought as a check on the

nautical reckoning by vessels making the Cape Horn passage. It is therefore not surprising that we sighted two merchant craft during the day. One was a four-masted ship of unknown nationality, headed for the Horn; the other a German bark, with skysails set, bound north.

9 Death, Doldrums and Deliverance

APRIL 9.   Lat. 18° 57' S.; long. 30° 03' W.

The memory of our brief stay at Trindade will always remain green, despite the tantalization of being unable to get ashore.

Today has been squally, interspersed with spells of dead calm. The Old Man believes that we are passing out of the horse latitudes, or from the zone of uncertain winds to that of the southeast trades.

Although we are only a short distance north of Trindade, we have seen not a single one of the petrels that nest there. This is curious because I noted these birds every day for several hundred miles to the south. The only living souvenir of the island has been one of the feather flies, which alighted on my wrist at the mainmasthead at five o'clock this afternoon. It made a tactical error in transferring from a booby to a naturalist, because I promptly clapped it into a cyanide bottle.

APRIL 10.   Lat. 16° 42' S.; long. 30° 43' W.

Brisk and welcome trade winds, blowing from nearly east all day. Most of the time since leaving Trindade I have been preparing the spoils and have had very little time to write. My beautiful, ermine-caped petrel has been made up with special care, because it may prove to be the type specimen of a hitherto unknown species.

Today we have had our first death. The Dominican boy, William Elwin, was a member of a boat's crew that had to swim ashore at the Bay of Isles in the terrible storm of February first, a hardship from which he never recovered. For a time he was able to get about occasionally, and even to do a little work, but since a month before we departed from South Georgia, he has been nearly helpless with what the Old Man calls rheumatism, and has not been able to stand.

At South Georgia I did not even know about his condition, because he had simply disappeared into the black hole of the forecastle. Neither the Old Man nor the officers ever mentioned him, and I didn't miss his presence until he was recently brought on deck to lie on his blanket, after the weather began to grow warm. It is possible that Dr. Leach at Prince Olaf Harbor might have been able to do something for him if any effort had been made.

This noon Elwin asked to be carried up to the sunlight, but as soon as his shipmates had laid him down, he gasped three or four times and died. The Old Man was called up just before the end, and he hurried with a stimulant from his medicine chest, cursing the steward anew for having filched all his rum. It was too late; I found that pulse and respiration had stopped at half past one.

At four o'clock, while he lay wrapped in his blanket on the carpenter's bench, Mr. da Lomba and the boatsteerers sewed him up in sailcloth, and his body is to lie through the night on his final watch, covered with a blue flag.

APRIL 11.   Lat. 13° 42' S.; long. 31° 12' W.

At eight o'clock this morning the sails were hauled aback, and Old Glory was run up to half-mast. The section of bulwarks abreast the cutting stage was removed, and the body of our sailor was laid on a hatch in the waist, with a bag of sand attached to the foot of the winding sheet.

The captain then read the order of the burial of the dead from an Anglican Book of Common Prayer.

"I am the resurrection and the life, saith the Lord . . ."

The members of the crew crowded around, solemnly, curiously. Only a few of the West Indians, at most, had any familiarity with the wording. They regarded it, however, as appropriate, as something due a man when he was dead, and the strange incongruities passed unnoticed.

"For a man walketh in a vain shadow, and disquieteth himself in vain: he heapeth up riches, and cannot tell who shall gather them."

(If the riches of this corpse, thought I, yield a hundred dollars to the heirs or assigns at the final division next summer, someone will have failed to enter sufficient costs against his account.)

"For as much as it hath pleased Almighty God of his great mercy to take unto himself the soul of our dear brother here departed, we therefore commit his body to the deep, to be turned into corruption, looking for the resurrection of the body (when the Sea shall give up her dead), and the life of the world to come, through our Lord Jesus Christ; who . . ."

Here Mr. da Lomba gave a sign. Six of the Dominican sailors raised the inner end of the hatch and the remains of William Elwin plunged, feet first, into the depths.

Snapping the prayer book shut with a bang, the Old Man bellowed: "Haul down the clews of the foresail! Raise up your wheel!"

The end of the Commitment, the Lord's Prayer, the Collect, and the Benediction were forgotten. The *Daisy* resumed her course in the trade wind.

Later the Old Man asked my opinion as to what should

be entered in the log as the cause of the sailor's death. The
words in my mind were "neglect" and "abuse," but all I would
allow myself to say was "exposure." That didn't go very well,
either, and we finally compromised on rheumatic fever. Elwin
was the chubbiest man on the ship when we left Dominica,
but he had wasted away to a shadow. He is said to have
prophesied to his shipmates the very date of his death, and
even to have disposed in a written will of his few effects and
the lay that was to be coming to him at the end of the voyage.
I learned none of these things until after he had died, and I
have not seen the paper, which one of the Dominican boys is
said to have in his chest.

Yesterday I had been thinking of Omar Khayyám's pots
and potter, and my mind had been running on whimsical in-
terdependences of human lives and inanimate objects, such as
Meleager's brand. At the end of our midday meal today, I
accidentally overturned and broke a primitive type of pot, my
red clay Dominican water cooler which has been used
throughout the voyage. It was at that moment that Johnny
came in to tell us that a sailor was dying.

This evening, when it is all too late, Mr. Almeida has
given me an idea of the hell that poor Elwin had gone through
in the dark, evil-smelling, and often wet forecastle. I am learning at least that there were some on board who cared, and did
their poor and ignorant best for a fellow voyager. It is pitiful
to die so far in space and time and comfort from all that is
dear to one.

As a result of Elwin's death, I now learn that there is another sick man in that black hole, the Cape Verder named
Antão Dias but whom everybody calls Ferleão. I had
just begun to miss his presence on deck because he was always a good worker and a good oarsman, besides being the
most ebony-black individual on the ship, even though his features are more Latin than Negro. They now tell me that he

has been gradually wasting away for a month or more with some malignant illness marked by internal hemorrhages. I have been to see him and find that he suffers very little pain. All I could give him was my last jar of beef tea, which seems to be the first food that he has been able to swallow and keep down for many days. I judge that he has not one chance in a thousand of ever reaching a hospital or seeing land.

It will shock you, no doubt, to learn that such things can take place on a whaleship without the knowledge of one who has been living self-centeredly, and relatively comfortably, within 125 feet of the dead and the dying. It has rather bowled me over also.

We have had brisk trade winds and have covered three degrees of latitude during the twenty-four hours between five bells yesterday afternoon and the same time today. It is the best run since we left South Georgia. We are now only about as far south of the equator as Barbados is north of it, and I am praying for still stronger trades.

APRIL 12.   Lat. 10° 52' S.; long. 31° 12' W.

The trade wind still holds, though it is so far in the east that it keeps us too sharply up to the wind. I have grown so impatient that it is hard for me to turn my mind composedly to any task. The watches are working on our whaling gear.

It is spring, or it will be as soon as we cross the equator. We have all heard how the "young man's fancy lightly turns" at that season. Our officers and boatsteerers are thinking and talking about something they haven't seen for a long while— women. If stud bulls, whose interests are presumably limited, could use human speech, their conversation at the Riverhead Fair would no doubt resemble what I now overhear along the break of the poop. The men speak English, partly from habit but more because it is the common medium of Mr. Vincent and the Portuguese.

One of our officers has roamed the African coast, liberally sampling the wares it offers. He now enjoys gloating—and whetting the appetites of the others—over detailed reminiscences of his prowess among fat-buttocked Hottentots and the Angola women whose labia reach halfway to their knees.

Today, just as the aristate moonface of Mr. Almeida appeared above the forward companionway, the aforementioned officer asked, "Do you like a fat woman or a thin one?"

"Any goddam thing!" shouted Almeida, angry at being reminded, and ducking below again.

APRIL 13.   Lat. 8° 09' S.; long. 31° 08' W.

Sunday and the latitude of Pernambuco!

The wind is moderating, but anyway we have almost rounded Cape São Roque, the easternmost projection of South America. I am now counting on port within a month.

This afternoon we lowered for the first sperm whales of our homeward voyage, but the whole school disappeared as if by magic in the dazzling path of the late sun.

I finished the day by reading *The Taming of the Shrew.*

APRIL 14.   Lat. 6° 55' S.; long. 31° 44' W.

Perfectly calm. Nothing to report all day except that I saw one Wilson's petrel and naught else. I walked miles in twenty-foot laps on the quarterdeck, whistling for a wind.

Ferleão, whom I now see daily, is going out like the last flickers from the wick of a whale-oil lamp. He seems completely listless and at peace. The tenderness and consideration of his shipmates is a revelation of man's innate mercy. They know that he has only days to live. Their role and responsibility are something quite apart from the quarterdeck and cabin. They vie with one another, like nuns, to give comfort. They feed him, wash him with warm water from the galley, keep him clad in clean shirt and cotton trousers, and neither balk nor gag because of vomit, blood, or excrement.

It is easy to call men black, lazy, dissolute, or any other name to which you choose to attach opprobrium. But saintliness is, nevertheless, where you find it, and charity shines in the peak between *Daisy's* bluff bows.

APRIL 15.   Lat. 6° 03' S.; no sight for the meridian.

Very light winds, and we took no advantage of them because we were hauled aback.

Soon after breakfast all four boats were lowered for whales. There must be many calves in the school because some of the animals and their spouts were so small that at times we mistook them for blackfish. They led the boats a merry chase, and at present two of our crews are out of sight from deck, although the mastheads report that they can still be seen, miles away. I wish that the miserable whales would stay out of sight, particularly if they have no intention of being caught.

In afternoon I regretted that I had not gone off with one of the boats, because any excitement being experienced was far from this stationary brig.

Not holding even a bleacher seat, I spent part of the afternoon reading *Titus Andronicus*. I though *Pericles* was stupidly horrible, but *Titus* is worse, if possible—quite the most dismal and insane thing I ever read. Bill must have been in a perverse and slaughtering mood when he wrote it. I wonder how the creator of *Macbeth* and *A Midsummer Night's Dream* could have tumbled so far from his eminence.

Evening. Our whalemen have had a work-out today not previously equaled on the entire voyage. From the edge of the horizon the forspent crews have all come slowly and painfully home towing whales. One boat brought one, two brought two, and Mr. da Lomba's three. Trust Long John to do a little better than anybody else! The eight carcasses, all small, are now chained alongside. Because of the back-breaking labor already undergone, the skipper has deferred cutting-in until morning. This means further delay, to my sorrow, but who am I to cavil at a generous impulse if the Old Man happens to have one?

It is just a month this evening since we left the ice of Possession Bay. I reckoned then on crossing the line about April 19, and we might have done it but for this unexpected catch.

The Old Man has many quaint traits and odd tastes, as you have long since learned. One of the strangest is his fondness for eating raw and rotten fish. By this I do not refer to kippered herring or to the various dried, smoked, or pickled sea products that I have facetiously called "putrefied fish" even while smacking my lips over them.

No, the Old Man is much more forthright. After our big haul of fish at Trindade, he selected for himself a good-sized sarugo, which is a kind of grunt, and also a garupa about two feet long. These were gutted and washed, after which the skipper tied them firmly with cod line to the main shrouds, where they have hung in the sun this past week. They soon began to smell somewhat like strong cheese, and then considerably worse. I don't like to go near enough to learn anything more about them, but they have obviously cured to a point at which the flakes of muscle come off at the slightest touch. In other words, the carcasses would fall apart of their own weight but for the fact that they have begun to dry out and shrink.

This is the stage for which the Old Man has been avidly waiting. He now walks past fifteen or twenty times a day, pulls a small chunk out of one fish or the other and eats it with the greatest gusto.

APRIL 16. Lat. 5° 40' S.; long. 32° 50' W.

I have loafed today while everybody else has labored very, very hard. After revising some South Georgian notes, I read *Coriolanus*. Only the *Henrys* remain to complete my reading on this voyage of everything that Shakespeare wrote. Once is enough for some of the plays, and in future I can confine my rereading to those I like.

I have also taken out of Captain Cleveland's records,

many of which I have kept for him, a sample of the costs to be deducted from a whaleman's lay at the time he receives his share of the net proceeds of the voyage. Following is the slop chest account of Attenaze Jean-Baptiste, the Martinican.

July 25, 1912	1 box cigarettes	.35
Aug. 3	1 pair blankets	2.45
	1 jacket	3.25
	1 denim jumper	.75
	2 pairs denim pants	2.50
	2 cotton shirts	1.50
	1 cap	.95
	1 oil hat	.85
	1 sheath and belt	.30
	1 knife	.40
	thread and needle	.15
Aug. 6	1 oil suit	4.00
Sept. 6	1 pair brogans	2.50
Sept. 10	1 tin cup	.15
Sept. 12	1 lb. tobacco	.60
Sept. 28	pot and pan	.30
Oct. 13	2 pairs wool pants	5.50
	2 wool shirts	3.50
	2 wool undershirts	2.00
	2 pairs drawers	2.00
	2 denim frocks	2.00
Oct. 31	1 pair mittens	.60
	2 pairs woolen stockings	1.50
Nov. 17	1 pair leather boots	5.00
Jan. 28, 1913	1 oil suit	4.50
Feb. 3	1 pair mittens	.60
Apr. 1	1 cap	.75

I do not mean to imply that there is anything extortionate in these charges. There are, however, certain inconsistencies in the cost of the same kind of item, and I have had occasion to conclude that the charge against a sailor depends not altogether on the original wholesale cost of the article, but also somewhat upon the Old Man's mood when the entry is made. He has told me that the law allows the owners to make 12 per cent profit on the slop chest, and I am confident that they try not to cheat themselves. There is this saving grace, however, that slop chest profits are supposed to enter into the lay of every member of the crew.

Before the largest bull whale carcass was cut adrift, its pizzle was severed at the base and hoisted to the deck, where it became the object of much noisy and ribald admiration. The purpose was quite serious, however, for Victor skinned it and immediately frapped and laced strips of the black, shiny hide onto several oarlocks. Whaleboat oarlocks always need muffling. The usual method is to braid thole mats from cordage, but black rawhide of the sort mentioned shrinks on the steel as it dries, making a smooth and long-enduring silencer for the loom of an oar.

All eight whales were cut-in—a good day's job. The air has been odoriferous. The tryworks are belching fire and smoke this evening. The ship is full of sick men, Frank the harponeer being near the nadir of his long incapacity. We are still five degrees south of the equator and are in the doldrums at a season when the trade wind should be blowing strongly.

This morning, during the cutting-in, I saw a shark along-side with its gullet and stomach everted and trailing like a stocking from its mouth. The phenomenon was "impossible," but I then remembered something I had read months ago in the *Journal of Sir Joseph Banks*. I have just looked it up in the index of his volume, and quote the following, which was written here in the South Atlantic in the year 1768.

"*8th December.*   Soon after daybreak a shark appeared, which took the bait very readily. While we were playing him under the cabin window he cast something out of his mouth which either was, or appeared very like, his stomach; this it threw out and drew in again many times. I have often heard from seamen that they can do it, but never saw anything like it.

"*11th.* This morning we took a shark, which cast up its stomach when hooked, or at least appeared to do so."

I have never heard of this before, but now I know it!

APRIL 17.   Lat. 4° 40' S.; long. 33° 20' W.

Light easterly winds while we were still trying out blubber, but a dead calm as soon as we were ready to get under way. It is now a glorious moonlit night, but here we sit.

Once again we are near Fernando Noronha, and possibly we shall call there. If we have this nearly breezeless weather for the next nine hundred miles, I don't know when we'll ever see the blessed Indies.

The lady in the moon has almost righted herself, and the Southern Cross begins to look as it did from Dominica. I try to be cheerful in such thoughts, but why, oh why, did your letters never come? It is discouraging to be penned in an old hulk that must rely entirely upon the gift of heaven. I'm going to name the day of our arrival, anyway. I'll call it May 20, and hold on to my patience with that date in view.

APRIL 18.   Lat. 3° 40' S.; long. 33° 35' W.

We have passed Rocas Reef. I went to the masthead twice while we were within sight of the atoll, and had a long look through my glass. The *Pilot Book* states that it is a desert island containing nothing but coral rock, sand, sea birds, and a few introduced coconut palms, but, although it was a long way off, I could make out a little house, another building, and a water tank, and could see the breakers crashing on the southern shore.

Fernando Noronha is about sixty miles to the east of us. We have rounded Cape São Roque and have now set our course for the Lesser Antilles. I estimate our present distance from Barbados to be 1,700 miles. That wouldn't take long to cover at two degrees a day, but at the present rate it might require five or six weeks, to which a week or two would need to be added for sperm whaling delays.

This evening I felt a strong longing to be alone, so I climbed into the foretop and stretched myself out flat in the belly of the lower foretopsail. It was a comfortable hammock, infinitely remote from the dark deck. It rocked and swayed gently but, running as we were before a favorable breeze, there was no chance of the sail coming aback and shaking me out through the roach.

It is always strange how any rhythmic sound, such as the lapping of water along the ship's sides, and the regular tautening and easing of rigging, can be made to fall into almost any musical time. If you have ever hummed through a dull hour in a Pullman berth, to the pounding of the wheels below, you will know exactly what I mean.

While I lay there in the sail, with the stars dancing overhead, I could whistle or sing whatever tune I chose, and at once the waves, the whining of sheaves in the blocks, and the fluttering of canvas would chime with the beat of my melody. Dreamily playing with this idea, I heard a chorus of other and quite absurd sounds begin to well up all about me. I imagined that I could distinguish the singing of the wind among leaves, the tumbling of a brook over rocks, and even the distant calling of whippoorwills and the night song of an ovenbird. Then I began to think about our cargo, and of cargoes in general, and of John Masefield's "Cargoes," and of the rhythmical resemblance between "dirty British coaster" and "greasy Yankee whaler."

Next, the poem began to sing itself to me in a new tune. "If this is the way a composer does his job," thought I, "what a lazy life he leads!"

Here it is:

Quin - qui - reme of Nin - e - veh from dis - tant O - phir, Row - ing home to hav - en in sun - ny Pal - es - tine, With a car - go of iv - o - ry, And apes and pea - cocks, San - dal - wood, ce - dar - wood, and sweet white wine.

From such ridiculous yet convincing fantasies I was suddenly aroused by the brassy ring of four bells—ten o'clock. So I came down to deck, cautiously feeling with my foot for each ratline in the darkness. Nobody knew I had been up there.

APRIL 19.   Lat. 3° 15' S.; long. 33° 40' W.

Do you know that the smell of dew, drying from the deck after sunrise, is as sweet in one's nostrils as in a forest glade? Sweeter, perhaps, because the ocean is, in a way, drier than any woodland.

Dead calm all day. Schools of albacore played about the ship. Large flocks of noddies, sooty terns, and boobies, indicating the close proximity of islands, hovered over the fish and plunged or stooped to profit by the round-up of small fry.

I lowered the *Grace Emeline* and shot nine Wilson's petrels, which come from the far south, and three Leach's petrels, which come from the northern part of the northern hemisphere. This, then, is the common mingling ground of two familiar Mother Carey's chickens from opposite ends of the earth.

About the middle of the day, when the Old Man and I were standing together on the quarterdeck, resting our elbows on either side of the companionway, Johnny came aft and announced quietly, "Ferleão, he say he going die today."

The Old Man spit out an oath, banged the painted canvas

with his fist, and told Johnny to get below and bring no more
foolish messages from the forecastle. His show of temper was,
however, nothing other than an attempt to rustle up a confidence which he could not feel, because as soon as the cabin
boy was out of sight, the captain turned to me and whispered
weakly, "When they say they are going to die, they always
do."

A little later, he and Mr. da Lomba went forward to see
the sick man, and they later reported that he was "about the
same."

The evening has been a continuation of the day, and the
ocean lies like a polished silver tray under the round moon. I
believe that we have not moved three miles since dewy sunrise. On the outward voyage, I could have reveled in the sub-
limity of such a night, but not now when it has held up my
course toward you.

Just before the ship's bell struck the hour for seven
o'clock this evening, the steward approached the captain and
me in the moonlight to announce that Ferleão had been
found dead and already cold. His light had gone out calmly
and silently, without even the knowledge of two men who had
been sitting below his bunk. His mind had been clearer today
than for the past week or longer, and he had eaten a little for
the first time in several days. His Cape Verde shipmates had
given him a sponge bath this morning and had once more
dressed him in two clean garments.

"Swellings," which seem to me to be a form of beriberi,
have affected eight or ten of the men in the forecastle, and
two of the boatsteerers. Captain Cleveland states, nevertheless, that he is headed for the Twelve-Forty Grounds, a traditional sperm whaling area east of the Antilles and centering
around latitude 12° N., longitude 40° W. He plans to stop
and cruise there, and to fill the ullage of our casks, if we ever
get a wind to carry us. Deaths in the forecastle doubtless

annoy him, but I doubt whether he realizes the likelihood of more funerals to follow unless he gets his men back to sources of fresh food. Some of the crew have told the cooper that their agreed term of service will be up on April 30, and that they are going to refuse whaling after that, if they go in irons for it. They even hint darkly of an intent to ratten the whaling equipment, which is only one step below mutiny.

APRIL 20.   Lat. 2° 47' S.; long. 34° 15' W.

We sank Ferleão about nine o'clock this morning. The Cape Verders have a Portuguese ceremoniousness lacking among the West Indians. They clad their shipmate in his "long togs" (meaning a store suit as opposed to dungarees) and bound his head in a spotless white scarf—obtained I don't know where—before he was stitched into sailcloth. The funeral service terminated as abruptly as the last one, and the Old Man began to shout a string of orders that had everybody hopping.

Many necks craned over the bulwarks as the body plummeted. Afterwards I heard numerous soft discussions as to when Ferleão would reach the bottom, or whether he would ever reach the bottom at all.

Three blue sharks about seven feet long, and a smaller shark of a different kind, had been hanging under the counter since dark of the morning. The old conviction that these hated brutes had come expressly for the corpse was breathed about the ship. I noted particularly that the sharks paid no attention when the shroud went overboard, and that all four of them have been following us uninterruptedly since we resumed our course. As a matter of fact, we are barely moving, but at least the sharks have stayed right here at the surface. One of them is very symmetrically decorated, for it has a remora attached upside down on the upper surface of each pectoral fin.

I took the *Notes of a Naturalist* during the voyage of the

Beagle to my chair atop the cabin, and for several hours have wandered again with Darwin over the pampas of Patagonia, through the Galápagos Isles, across the Pacific to Tahiti, and then on to Keeling in the Indian Ocean. How I long to see with the eyes of that matchless man of science, and to write with his pen! When I come home, I must study more geology. I want to be able to grasp something of the whole scope of nature in the lands and seas I visit; to be broad, not narrow; to be both a naturalist and a humanist, not a mere specialist. In technical work a man of this age must specialize, but in a reconnaissance of a part of earth's face, whether soil or sea, I want my comprehension, like that of Charles Darwin, to be able to interpret the underlying significance of clouds, hailstones, argillaceous rock, hot springs, cacti, land planarians, ice-borne boulders, carrion beetles, wingless flies, graminivorous birds, nest-building fish, viviparous reptiles, dodders, omnivorous rodents, sessile-eyed crustaceans, insect-eating plants, and foraminiferous protozoans! Nature is a chain, a million-knotted web or fishnet of life. Nothing exists of or for itself, but only in relation to other organisms, as Darwin seemed to know more thoroughly than anyone else.

I hope that I have approached near enough to my ideal so that you will, in a measure, see South Georgia as I saw it.

At evening a rainstorm came before a southwesterly breeze, whisking us a mile or two forward, but wind and rain stopped together before ten o'clock.

APRIL 21.   Lat. 2° 45' S.; long. 34° 30' W.

Still dead calm. In such weather we merely exist. I can endure the poor food and discomforts with equanimity just so long as we are moving toward better days.

The good little rat-catching cat, which we took aboard at São Vicente last September, died this morning, apparently from the heat. I don't know what Cadella will do without her because she and the cat played endlessly, more so than any dog and cat I have ever seen together.

The first cases of undoubted scurvy, with all the mouth symptoms, have just been noted, the victims being two Dominicans, Stephen Ismael and Joe Jimmot. I suspect that one of the best of their compatriots, Ed Evelyn, is about to reach the same state. Half a dozen of the Cape Verde men are likewise looking rheumy-eyed and puffy in the jowls! God help them!

I shampooed today in rain water, of which we caught several tubfuls yesterday by attaching a big piece of sailcloth to the boom and making a funnel. No other water makes such wonderful suds. Later I read *Timon of Athens*, *The Tempest*, *The Merry Wives of Windsor*, and some of the sonnets.

> From you have I been absent in the spring,
> When proud-pied April, dress'd in all his trim,
> Hath put a spirit of youth in everything,
> That heavy Saturn laugh'd and leap'd with him.

Evening. Yesterday the latitude was 2° 47' S.; today it is 2° 45' S. The moral is that I am now two miles nearer to you than I was then, for which I am humbly thankful.

APRIL 22. Lat. 1° 54' S.; long. 34° 18' W.

A beautiful calm day—so that we haven't needed an anchor to keep us where we were yesterday, and the day before, and the day before that. There have been showers now and then, and between times. For excitement I cleaned my guns, shot rats in the water after they had been tossed overboard from the cage trap (very unsporting), donned clean clothes, fiddled with an albatross skeleton, had the captain take my picture, and read *The Merchant of Venice* again. For the last half hour I've been lying on my couch, waiting for the supper bell to ring so that I can quit work!

Will us "fair winds, auspicious gales, and sail so expeditious." I want to come home. We have a straight road to Barbados; nothing in the way, and not a single twist. Oh if Aeolus would give me all winds but the east in a leathern bag!

Evening. We lie on the silver tray under a pile of gray and lavender clouds, with a few stars peeping over their edges. Our bow is pointing southeast, because there is no moving air to make it point another direction.

It seems to me that I have enjoyed more wonderful sunsets than any other mortal, but this evening's was so still different, with its dark blues and purples, and pure gold, that I wished especially you had watched it with me.

APRIL 23.   Lat. 1° 34' S.; long. 34° 10' W.

During the night a steady rain was added to steady calm, and now many little rills are running and dripping from the ceiling of this miserable mousetrap of a cabin. Tin cans swing gracefully under some of them, and when they overflow, Johnny empties and rehangs them, but our supply of tins is not large enough to catch all the leaks. Some of my clothes were well soaked before I awoke. I have decided that a dry calm is a lesser evil than a wet calm. When the sun shines, I can at least see my hand before my face in the cabin, but on a morning like this, the place is a Stygian cave forlorn.

In the course of the day I reread *Troilus and Cressida* and *Julius Caesar*, and I am now deep in the *Henry Fourths*.

At dusk a brown booby flew around the *Daisy* and finally alighted on the gunwale of the spare whaleboat across the stern, where it seems to have snuggled down for the night. I walked up close, but it eyed me without suspicion and tucked its head into the groove of the back, where the scapular feathers cover its bill. Even the shouting and barking of a late rat hunt on deck did not disturb the fowl. The rat, by the way, leaped down the twelve-foot steerage companionway, without touching a step, and escaped.

APRIL 24.   Lat. 0° 36' S.; long. 33° 57' W.

The booby slumbered until 5:30 this morning, and then somebody scared it off by going into the stern boat for a bucket. Anyone could sleep very comfortably last night, even a booby standing on one foot, because the weather was so still and calm. The brig lay innocent-like upon the placid ocean, and a piece of cork alongside in the evening was still there this morning—although it was nearer the stern, proving that we had progressed somewhat. But sh! a breath of air, which almost deserves the name of zephyr, is coming out of the northwest. I am below, where it can't see me write this, and I'll pretend not to notice, and talk very quietly, and maybe it will increase.

Evening. But it didn't continue long, and now we lie on a glassy sea, our bow swung helplessly toward the southwest, and under the maddening beauty of a pink and heliotrope sunset. We are half a degree south of the equator, and if we can only cross I'll not despair. If we can once pull into the other hemisphere, I hope and believe that we'll get home again.

APRIL 25.   Lat. 0° 03' S.; long. 34° 00' W.

A calm morning, following a calm night. At breakfast time a miniature squall popped out of the east, carried us forward about a mile, and then died in its tracks. Thereafter, between 7:30 and 7:45 A.M. came a display of the most wonderful double rainbow that I have ever seen. It should not be called a bow, because its inner arc made a circle, except for a very narrow gap at the bottom. The refraction all took place on a falling mist, and the lower ends of the primary bow had the appearance of curving forward on the water and of almost meeting in the shadow of the hull, just below the level of my feet on the quarterdeck. In the primary bow the red, orange, and yellow bands, which were outermost, were extended only a short distance below the horizon, but the inner green and blue bands continued so as to form the all-but-complete circle.

The outer or secondary bow, no part of which carried below the horizon, had the order of the spectral colors reversed.

In midforenoon, just as I thought we were in for another twenty-four hours of motionlessness, a light north-northeast breeze sprang up, and we presently began to move almost imperceptibly forward. I found myself obsessed by the crossing of imaginary lines, about five yards apart, and my fancy carried me back to football games that you and I have watched together during the past three years. Can we cross the goal in today's game?, I kept asking myself over and over again, finally drifting off into reverie.

Sprackling has sent the ball down the field on two forward passes to the seven-yard line. Two rushes through left guard have gained five yards, and now it is second down, with forty-five seconds of the game left to play, and the score 0-0. The thrilling numbers are called; the Podunk forward wall stands firm as a rock to stave off defeat. Charlie Sisson snaps the pigskin, and Sprack slams it into the pit of Russ McKay's stomach, who plunges forward like a battering ram into the hole my brother Ed is making. The teams fight and sway; the very last cubic inch of breath is squeezed out of the players in the center of that struggling crest, and stalwart legs strain until they almost snap their semi-tendinosi! The Podunk line will not give, it seems, but finally the shrill whistle blows and the trembling, silent multitude waits feverishly for the arms and heads and legs to extricate themselves from the heap under Podunk's goal posts. There lies Russ on the ball, which he seems loath to leave. The officials gather round, and, after several seconds, the field judge's decision "Touchdown!" is lost in a mighty, stentorian chorus from the Brown stands. For the ball is over the line,

AND SO ARE WE!

Yea, verily! You need a pair of dividers to tell it, but it's a sure touchdown, nonetheless.

It was four o'clock when the Old Man figured we had crossed over, and at that time we were making the breakneck speed of nearly three knots. I hardly dare to speak of the little catspaw from the northeast, fearing its inconstancy. But anyway we are moving, and this evening the beloved Great Bear is upside down in the heavens to starboard. We can follow the pointers toward the spot at which Polaris lies just under the horizon, ready to pop up and welcome us back. I shall hope to look him in the eye day after tomorrow, if this breath of wind continues to blow us northward.

APRIL 26.   Lat. 1° 06' N.; long. 35° 28' W.

The night was one of perfect clarity and wonderful stars. The Milky Way was sharper and more brilliant than ever I remember it, and, standing almost astride the equator, we could see and name a rare panoply of constellations belonging to each hemisphere. Moreover, I saw the first shooting stars that I can recall for many months.

Following a squall in early evening, we had only about one hour's calm throughout the whole night. A gentle north-easterly wind has been helping us slowly along. If it will only hold, we shall be carried into the steady northeast trades within two or three days and our uncertainty will be over. The trade wind extends at this season southward to about 3° N., and we are already a full degree north of the equator. When once we enter the sweep of the "steadies," twelve days' sailing should bring us into port, not allowing for whales. Every time a sperm whale is sighted, it means a delay of several hours, and every time a cut is captured, it means the loss of a day or two. However, since we are now no more than 1,200 miles from Barbados, I am moving forward the date of our arrival to May 17.

I have overhauled and packed my equipment, stored all my winter clothes, blankets, heavy specimens, guns, ammunition, traps, etc. in containers that are not to be disturbed until the *Daisy* reaches New Bedford. My personal luggage is stripped down to necessities, so that I shall be ready when the great day comes.

APRIL 27.   No astronomical observations. The night was calm, but I now believe that the trade wind has picked us up. Since three o'clock this morning, it has been blowing briskly from the northeast. A heavy rain is falling, but the wind seems to hold through it.

Afternoon. It is surely the trade wind; we have passed the doldrums; we are ploughing along as rapidly as we can, close-hauled. Farther north we shall head more to westward, run free, and make better time. The sun has not shone for two days, but who cares, because the ocean is alive. It is a treat to see it dance, and to whisk over it after the long, long days and nights of calm.

APRIL 28.   Lat. 2° 36' N.; long. 36° 24' W.

The wind blew steadily all night. We are scurrying north-westward before a breeze as brisk and happy as anyone could wish. It promises to push us to port so fast that I can now move forward the date of our arrival to May 15.

APRIL 29.   Lat. 3° 57' N.; long. 38° 18' W.

My appreciation to you and everybody for all your birthday wishes. I am very well and happy at twenty-six, thank you! Just as you write this morning, I am already beginning to talk in a casual and offhand manner about events that took place "a little over a quarter century ago!" It's quite an old-ster I am. I agree with you also that our separation has been only a night between two summer days, and a night full of the stars of memory and hope. What a letter bag! What a bride!

A beautiful albacore was caught early this morning on one of the lines that we constantly troll. It is large enough to feed all hands, and fresh fish is a blessing for men in the precarious condition of most of our crew. The ship's fare has not affected me unfavorably, but I admit that the craving for fresh food, whether plant or animal, is like a constant gnawing. Perhaps my present low-protein diet is even beneficial, but when I get ashore, I shall surely guzzle fruits, vegetables, eggs, and meat. Not long since, a keg of West Indian limes, preserved in brine, was discovered in the ship's run. The rinds have discolored, but the pulp is sound, and I have been eating one or two of them every day, even though they set my teeth on edge.

This afternoon I saw a skua. It flew right between our masts, so there is no possible doubt about the identification. So far as I know, there is no previous record for a bird of this species within 1,500 miles of our present latitude.

Evening. We have caught another albacore. The trade wind is glorious tonight. After measuring our course to Barbados, I may now make another move in my little game, and date our arrival as May 14.

APRIL 30. Lat. 6° 00' N.; long. 40° 30' W.

Strong trade winds. At noon another skua passed across the deck between the masts, hovering for a moment above the foreyard. It then flew off to leeward and disappeared in the northwest.

I have finished the first part of *Pilgrim's Progress* and, after leaving Christian and Hopeful safe in the Coelestial City, I am now accompanying Christiana, Mercy, and the "sweet babes" on their journey. I find it rather odd that Mercy puts the babes to bed one night, and yet a few days later she marries off one of them!

Evening. Tonight I can see the first faint twinklings of the North Star, proof that we are in the northern oceans again. We have made a run of 180 miles during the past twenty-four hours. A prolongation of that will land us at Barbados in short order.

The process of cleaning ship has been continuing for weeks. Now we are scraping spars. The foremast was finished today and rubbed down with sperm oil, so that it appears like a brand new stick.

I wish that I could go to sleep for four or five days.

MAY 1.   Lat. 7° 36' N.; long. 43° 20' W.

A bright and sunny morning with a strong and reliable northeast trade, the very best wind we have thus far had on the homeward voyage. Nine days more may do it.

April is gone and the warblers at home are now flooding Neutaconkanet Hill in the early morning. Do you remember the spray of apple blossoms that I picked for you there, two years ago at sunrise of May Day?

The third mate, Mr. Almeida, is added to our sick list and has a disturbingly corpselike appearance. His fatness, the shape of his beard, and the way that his dark skin has turned pale, make him look like King Henry VIII in his coffin.

We have seen all day an extraordinary number of flying fish and Portuguese men-o'-war, more of the latter than ever before. At one time I counted fifty of these oceanic jewels bobbing on what I estimated to be an acre of the surface. The Old Man says that's nothing; he has seen one to each square yard, which would be nearly 5,000 to the acre! I haven't dared asked Johnny what *his* maximum was.

Several of our Cape Verders, and more of our West Indians, have fallen afoul of a Portuguese man-o'-war, mostly in childhood, and they hold the creature in great respect. It is what zoologists call a float-bearing siphonophore, and it trails beneath the surface a great number of tentacles armed with stinging cells. The latter are tiny capsules, each of which contains a barbed thread which is a sort of flexible harpoon. The cells also have external trigger hairs, and, when these are touched off, they cause the muscles of the capsules to contract violently and to shoot out the barbed threads, which carry a nerve poison into the blood stream of any animal they may pierce. For an hour, more or less, after such an encounter, the resulting pain is extremely severe, as one of my museum colleagues has told me, following an unhappy experience of his own.

The Portuguese man-o'-war has an odd status among animals, because it is not an individual but is a colony of organisms. It has no power of propulsion, and, as it floats and drifts, it merely waits for some other creature to collide with it. Certain kinds of small fish live unharmed in the jungle of its weapons, but others, upon stimulating it, are stung by the nettle cells and entangled in the long tentacles. The latter draw the victims up into contact with the mouths of the siphons, which spread over them and enclose them in the deathtrap of their mantles.

To me, safe on the deck of *Daisy*, the creature is more renowned for its indescribable beauty than notorious for its lethal stings. Its float, or bladder, which has a crimped upper ridge, gleams in the sunlight with various delicate tints of blue, purple, pink, and yellow, the general effect being like the opalescence of ancient Roman glass. The fleets today make me think that large opals are afloat in this latitude or that fragments of a rainbow are scattered over the sea.

This evening the North Star is well above the horizon, twinkling clearly and invitingly. The trade wind sounds like the singing of a deep-caved sea shell, and darts of light form in the water where the flying fish leap before our stem. It is gleeful to feel a good ship in a living breeze, and if I were a poet, I would sing tonight of the northeast trades. I have just been again to the foretop in the dark, where I lay awhile in the cradle of the bellying sail.

MAY 2.   Lat. 9° 14' N.; long. 46° 13' W.

We are still tearing northward, and I suspect that many
hearts besides mine are riding high. Mr. Almeida's condition
proved an undue alarm. He is up and about, though looking
flabby and unwholesome, and I judge that the ravages of
scurvy are on him.

The last of my bird skins have dried sufficiently to be
packed snugly away for shipment from Barbados. I am going
to leave only the heavy and relatively imperishable specimens, such as skeletons, rocks, and pickled material, aboard
the *Daisy* until she docks at New Bedford.

I have finished *Pilgrim's Progress* and have enjoyed the
whole book enormously. What a pity so few readers realize
that the second part of this work stands foremost among the
unconsciously comical pearls of literature, besides having
other virtues!

MAY 3. See where we have arrived—lat. 11° 18' N.;
long. 48° 58' W.

My latest estimate for Barbados was May 10, but now,
barring a setback, we may even make it by the ninth. Tomorrow may possibly be my last Sunday away from you. I wonder
where you are now, whether in Providence, New York, or the
West Indies. Have you pictured me as flying toward you in the
trade wind? Only now and then a faint cloud passes over the
sun in my heart, which is when I ask, in spite of myself, why
your November letter never reached me at South Georgia.

The Old Man has been tasting the ocean water, and vows
that it is nearly fresh at the surface from the outpourings
of the mighty Amazon. I would call it rather strongly brack-
ish. However, at the beginning of the sixteenth century,
Vicente Yañez Pinzón filled his casks somewhere in this wide
ocean, far out of sight of the continent, and then went back
to Spain to report that the tropical Atlantic was composed of
fresh water!

Breakfast and dinner today reached an all-time low in hog-trough meals. This afternoon, however, we hooked a fine dolphin, weighing all of sixty pounds, so for supper we gorged on prime fish and really excellent baked beans.

MAY 4.   Lat. 13° 16' N; long. 51° 34' W.

The trade wind has moderated and is swinging around into the north, which does not affect us unfavorably because of the high latitude we have already attained. The remainder of our course to Barbados is across the meridians. We are now heading almost west.

Personal difficulties on the *Daisy* have not hitherto transgressed across what one might call the social strata, except in so far as the captain, who is immune to retaliation, bawls out anybody he pleases. This morning, however, a Portuguese boatsteerer and a West Indian sailor got into a first-class fight, and the sailor drew his sheath knife and stuck the boatsteerer between the ribs. It not only broke the skin, but pushed some of the textile of the man's shirt into the wound. The knife had, fortunately, had its point ground both square and dull, for otherwise it would have gone in all the way to the haft. The boatsteerer, more enraged than injured, lost no time in yanking an ax out of a chopping block on deck and heading back into the fray. Ten or more men rushed between the combatants just in time to prevent us from having brains, as well as gore, on the deck.

The boy who was so handy with his knife is now in irons in the lazaret, but the Old Man has made surprisingly little fuss about the matter. On the contrary, he has recently become softspoken, peacemaking, and as genial as a bishop at a tea party, even paying a compliment now and then to a sailor doing a job. All of this signifies to me that he has made up his mind to get into port as rapidly as we can, and, of course, he wants everybody to arrive with a heart full of contentment, brotherly love, and the kindest memories of our happy voyage.

This afternoon we caught another dolphin, but to my disgust, the transverse slabs of the fish were cooked in sea elephant oil, which did not add to their palatability. The steward says that he now has no other fat left.

Evening. We are gliding smoothly westward before a light wind from the starboard quarter. We are not making speed, but the circumstances are very different from a calm, and I can fall asleep with the happy assurance of being sixty or seventy miles nearer my heart's desire when I wake up in the morning. It is not now unreasonable to hope that we shall drop anchor in the roadstead of Barbados by Thursday, May 8.

MAY 5.   Lat. 13° 47' N.; long. 53° 44' W.

The wind is a little fresher. Day after tomorrow, or the next, should make it.

This is the season of molting plumage. For several days I have been giving away a great variety of worn and unwanted clothing. You will remember that I brought with me every old garment in my possession, and most of them I have had no opportunity to wear. The steward, the cabin boy, and many members of the crew will disport in Barbados in the former hosiery and shirts of your husband.

I have also become outrageously clean, in contrast with my normal, healthy, and natural life at South Georgia. For two or three weeks I have indulged in a complete bath almost every evening. Now I have even shaved off my aristocratic moustache, to the regretful disapproval of Johnny. He would give years of his life to be able to cultivate a similar adornment, and he makes it clear that I have ruthlessly wasted a major gift of the Creator.

MAY 6.   Lat. 13° 46' N.; long. 56° 00' W.

The wind has gone around to east or southeast and is so light that we are hardly more than drifting before it. I am spending a good deal of time at the masthead, and I am almost ill with eagerness. My present prospect is for only two nights more on the *Daisy*, for I estimate that we shall drop anchor during the forenoon of Thursday—day after tomorrow.

MAY 7. Lat. 13° 45' N.; long. 57° 54' W.

The last full day, I hope! Everything bodes fair, although the wind remains light. Flocks of boobies, noddies, and an occasional tropic-bird are once more within range, telling of the proximity of islands. Just think, we are no farther from port than Montauk Point is from New York Harbor. We have only the length of Long Island Sound to sail!

I can't work, and I find it very hard to keep my mind occupied cheerfully. The Old Man and I have just figured out the longitude together, arriving at the same position of 57° 54' W. We have been running under square sails alone, but enough wind has now arisen so that the mainsail has been set. This will mean better speed during the next twelve hours, and I expect to sight Barbados early tomorrow.

I spent a long while at the masthead this afternoon, where my overheated senses played me an awesome trick. It seemed from time to time that I was not perched high above sea level, but rather as though I and the mast, and the infinitely tiny ship, were in the bottom of a vast funnel in the ocean, with all the slope roundabout running upward to the ring of lofty horizon.

Just as the last fragment of the sun disappeared beyond the clear circle, there was a green flash, as rapid as lightning, shooting up into the western sky. This is a rare phenomenon of light refraction, about which I have read but which I have never before seen.

This evening I heard, let us hope for the last time, the

day's end cry, "Alow from aloft!" that calls the mastheads down to deck.

MAY 8.   This is the Great Day!

I am at the mainmasthead, and the morning is still as black as Tophet. I can barely see the white page of my notebook, and not a word of what my pencil is inscribing. I have never before written to you from my pinnacle of Simon Stylites in the masthead hoops.

Now the tall, gray, and ghostly tent of the zodiacal light —the "phantom of false morning" of Omar—is stalking up our wake from the eastern horizon. There is not yet a glimmer of approaching sunrise, but red Mars, well up, is plotting its course.

Now I can detect a hint of day-blue in the eastern sky, where glowing Lucifer, just lifted into the clear above the ring of haze, makes the morning star promise of a flawless dawn.

A faint and repetitive flash in the dark west must come from a revolving light, still below the rim of ocean. I think now, despite myself, of certain lines from the *Paradiso* that I have read many times on this voyage:

> e legno vidi già dritto e veloce
>   correr lo mar per tutto suo cammino,
>   perire al fine a l'intrar de la foce.

—ere now I have seen a ship fare straight and swift through all her course, to perish in the end at the harbor's mouth.

Beneath my shirt I feel the oilskin folder containing your one unread letter, the message to which I was to turn only if it seemed certain that I could never come back to you. It is still unopened, but it has never been off my person, day or night, throughout the months since our parting. Have you realized that for 293 successive nights, or since July 18, 1912, I have slept aboard this craft? What a yarn to tell the grandchildren! But forgive me for leap-frogging a whole generation before I even know that you are as safe and well and potentially joyful as I.

It *is* the lighthouse; its intermittent beams are now saluting the first segment of the rising sun. During the night the breeze improved, and we have bettered our allotted time.

I can now see the skyline of Barbados and the whole white length of the lighthouse. Through my glasses I can distinguish the squares of the sugar cane fields. A few flaky pink clouds hang over the island, and the sun has just climbed up behind us. Now I can make out the long, low southwestward point, around which we must sail to reach Bridgetown.

Forenoon. Before breakfast time I grew hungry at the masthead. Then, on my way down to deck, I felt almost seasick, though not from any motion of the sea. I had to lie down with closed eyes and wait awhile before I could eat.

The southern coast and slopes of Barbados now stretch out before us like a map, although we are still many miles offshore.

Evening. We dropped anchor at noon. Mr. Lewis, of the *Daisy*'s agents, inquired for you from his launch while the medical inspection was under way, so I knew that you had not come here. Neither had I expected you, because the only messages you could have received from me were equally vague about the date and the place of our landfall. For this we may thank the clamlike eagerness with which the Old Man shares his intentions!

The port physician told me that I am fit as a fiddle. The authorities were cordially expeditious, and within half an hour the skipper and I were racing ashore in Lewis's launch. He telephoned the American Consul and learned that my mail was on his desk. So I hailed a brougham and drove for it. Mr. Martin awaited me with your letter in his hand, and I saw the postmark, "April 8, 1913."

O isplendor di viva luce eterna!

The mere envelope shone upon my eyes like the sancti-fied face of Beatrice, and who am I to seek words which even Dante failed to find?

I sat, completely lost to the world, and read and smiled and laughed, and wept from relief. One letter, of all those you have scattered far and wide, has come through to me during nine months and eight days. I judge from your references that all my communications from glacier land reached you. While those from the Cape Verdes and Fernando Noronha are not mentioned, I suppose that they were answered in the letters to South Georgia which are still adrift. Your statement that they were all sent by registered post, as requested, undoubt-edly explains everything. They were presumably delayed for "safety's sake," whereas Captain Cleveland's ordinary mail took the first means of transportation at every step of the journey.

I had kept my cabby waiting, so we drove to the cable office, where they told me, alas!, that I can hardly expect an answer before tomorrow morning.

Then I had luncheon, guess what—pâté de foie gras, the most foam-like of omelets, soft rolls, fresh butter, and a whiskey and soda. Then I looked over about a month's supply of American, British, and French newspapers. But why bother! How could so many things take place in the world during my absence?

I have quarters in the Hotel Balmoral and have had our consul, Mr. Chester W. Martin, to dinner with me. He had heard of you several times from different sources since you last saw him, nearly a year ago.

After reading your letter, I no longer have any doubt that the long months we have given up were for the best, and that we can build on them for the rest of our days.

(Form No. 15—Consular.)

CERTIFICATE OF DISCHARGE OF SEAMAN.

American Consular Service,

Barbados. W. I. May 9th. 1913. ___, 19

Name of ship, __Brig "DAISY".__

Official number, __6752.__

Port of registry, __New Bedford.__

Tonnage, __316 net.__

Description of voyage or employment, __Whaling cruise.__

Name of seaman, __R. C. Murphy.__

Place of birth, __New York.__

Age, __26.__ ___ years

Character, __Good.__

Ability, __Good.__

Capacity, __Assistant Navigator__

Date of entry, __June 10th.__, 19 __12.__ Date of discharge, __May 9th.__, 19 __13.__

Place of discharge, __Barbados. W. I.__

Cause of discharge, __Mutual consent.__

I CERTIFY that the above particulars are correct, and that the above-named seaman was discharged accordingly.

Robert Cushman Murphy _Benjamin D. Cleave Caroso_
Seaman. Master.

Given to the above-named seaman in my presence this __9th.__ day of __May__, A. D. 19 __13.__

Chester W. Martin

American __Consul.__

MAY 9.   This morning before many members of the crowded population of Barbados were stirring, I received your cable, and I am now completely happy.

The first steamer upon which I can obtain passage is the *Vestris*, at present en route between Rio de Janeiro and Trinidad, but expected here on May 13. She is a fast vessel, scheduled to make a direct six-day voyage to New York. A consignment of my specimens is going on the old *Guayana*, which leaves sooner but arrives later.

I have cabled you to meet me at the pier ten days hence. The enforced delay will at least permit me to obtain a small supply of civilized clothing, because I find that among my old summer shirts there is now only one that I can button around my neck. That should convince you that I have not wasted away during nearly eleven months on the *Daisy*.

I am going aboard this afternoon to say farewell to the crew. Some of the men I hope to greet again in New Bedford by the end of summer, but many of the West Indians will be discharged at Dominica before this month is up. Most of them are my friends. We stand as close to a relationship of warm esteem as is possible for comrades whose paths are not likely to cross again. It touches me to realize that I have never had so much as an irritable glance from one of them through all their trials. They were always willing to help me far beyond the limits of the Old Man's sanction, and never with anticipation of favor or reward. They have shown no envy of my relative comfort, as contrasted with their own plight. They have accepted me, man to man, even at the oar of a whaleboat. In carrying out their duties by fair weather and foul; in mortal combat—"wood to blackskin"—with mighty adversaries; and, for the most part, in dealings one with another, they have proved their possession of no mean stock of the cardinal virtues, and even of as goodly a share of the beatitudes as more fortunate human beings would dare to claim.

The Old Man and I have appeared before the consul to obtain my discharge. Mr. Vincent and Mr. Almeida, now aged thirty-two and twenty-nine respectively, received theirs at the same time. They shipped on October 9, 1911, which means that they have been nineteen months with the *Daisy*. Both expect to sign on another whaler from Barbados. Mr. Almeida's lay with us has been one thirty-third. Both officers seem entirely satisfied with a small advance from Captain Cleveland. Their final settlement will probably be made after the *Daisy*'s oil has been sold. Mr. da Lomba and "Mr. Robinson" (Victor) will be top officers on the voyage to New Bedford through the sperm whaling waters of the Hatteras Grounds.

And now, beloved, my logbook closes, or, as the skipper indites each day in his own entry, "So ends."

In your letter bag, which has been a never-ending solace throughout our absence, I found close to the termination of the voyage an anonymous bit of verse enclosed within a note from my brother Ed. He wrote that while looking for a gem to send me, he had discovered this emerald:

THE SEEKERS

Says she:

> " 'Tis a long way ye've traveled, mavourneen,
> 'Tis a long trip ye've made on the sea
> For the sake of a slip of a girl like me,
> To be gettin' a kiss no better than this,
> 'Tis a long road ye've traveled, machree."

Says he:

> " 'Twas a long way and lone way, me true love,
> But 'tis millions of miles, as He knows,
> That a hungerin', wanderin' sunbeam goes
> To be gettin' a kiss no better than this
> From the lips of no sweeter a rose."

**a note about the production
of this book**

The typeface for this special edition of *Logbook for Grace* is Century Expanded. It was photocomposed at Time Inc. under the direction of Albert J. Dunn and Arthur J. Dunn, and printed and bound by J. W. Clement Co., Buffalo, New York. The cover was printed by Livermore and Knight Co., a division of Printing Corporation of America, in Providence, Rhode Island.

x

The paper, TIME Reading Text, is from The Mead Corporation, Dayton, Ohio. The cover stock is from The Plastic Coating Corporation, Holyoke, Massachusetts.